Economics Transformed

Economics Transformed

Discovering the Brilliance of Marx

ROBERT ALBRITTON

Pluto Press

LONDON • ANN ARBOR, MI

First published 2007 by Pluto Press
345 Archway Road, London N6 5AA
and 839 Greene Street, Ann Arbor, MI 48106

www.plutobooks.com
British Library Cataloguing in Publication Data
A catalogue record for this book is available from the British Library

Hardback
ISBN-13   978 0 7453 2658 0
ISBN-10   0 7453 2658 7

Paperback
ISBN-13   978 0 7453 2657 3
ISBN-10   0 7453 2657 9

Library of Congress Cataloging in Publication Data applied for

This book in printed on paper suitable for recycling and made from fully managed
and sustained forest sources. Logging, pulping and manufacturing processes are
expected to conform to the environmental regulations of the country of origin.

10 9 8 7 6 5 4 3 2 1

Designed and produced for Pluto Press by
Chase Publishing Services Ltd, Fortescue, Sidmouth, EX10 9QG, England
Typeset from disk by Stanford DTP Services, Northampton
Printed and bound in the European Union by
CPI Antony Rowe Ltd, Chippenham and Eastbourne

Contents

Acknowledgements

This book is made possible by a 36-year career of teaching Marx's *Capital* at York University in Toronto, and by my close collaboration with Tom Sekine over most of those years. It was from him that I learned of the latent dialectical rigour resting within the commodity-economic logic of Marx's *Capital*. Sekine, in turn, was influenced by the work of Japanese political economist Kozo Uno, whose work would have been inaccessible to me but for the translation of Sekine and others. I have also been blessed by teaching at a University where many graduate students have been keen to study such a demanding work as *Capital*. Besides receiving feedback from Sekine, professors Westra and Bell have also given me feedback. Over the years my thought has been continually challenged, and, as a result, sharpened by my students. In particular I want to thank Stefanos Kourkoulakos, Michael Marder, John Simoulidis, and Nchamah Miller for their feedback on this manuscript. Finally my wife, Jennifer Welsh, has not only been patient with my authorial preoccupations, but also has read and commented upon the entire manuscript. Any remaining unclarities or errors of judgement, however, remain my own.

1
Introduction

The label of a system of ideas is distinguished from that of other articles, among other things, by the fact that it deceives not only the buyer, but often the seller as well. (Marx, Capital vol. I, 435–6)

The intimate connection between the pangs of hunger suffered by the most industrious layers of the working class, and the extravagant consumption, coarse or refined, of the rich, for which capitalist accumulation is the basis, is only uncovered when the economic laws are known. (Marx, Capital vol. II, 811)

The good Price was simply dazzled by the enormous quantities resulting from geometrical progression of numbers. Since he regards capital as a self-acting thing, without any regard to the conditions of reproduction of labour, as a mere self-increasing number, he was able to believe that he had found the laws of its growth... (Marx, Grundrisse, 842–3)

The prestige that has generally been accorded the "science" of economics is a great academic scandal, and in this book I shall argue that as a system of ideas it has generally deceived both buyer and seller. When so-called "economic science" utilizes quantitative, formal and abstract categories without clearly situating them in relation to qualitative, substantive and concrete categories, the effect is to promote in theory the reification or objectification that capitalism promotes in practice. It is to promote the rule of the commodity form (operating through capitalist markets) as though such rule were natural and beyond questioning to the benefit of all. Since the commodity form itself is never questioned, neither are the quantifications attached to it in markets. According to many a Nobel Prize winning economist, in principle, total commodification means that capital can single-mindedly maximize short-term profits and in so doing promote an equilibrium that maximally benefits all.[1] The naked truth is that such an economic orientation ignores the structuring of social demand by class such that even in a state of equilibrium in the most ideal capitalist market system, that which is optimal is so only relative to a social demand already structured by class. And when idealized

1. So-called "Pareto Optimality".

conceptions of the market that ignore class are applied directly to policy formation in particular historical contexts, the potentials for social injustice loom large. Indeed, a great deal of capitalist history is the history of damage-control operations aimed at containing or covering up the destructive spin-offs of capital accumulation.

By universalizing abstract economic theory and by formalizing it far beyond any contact with reality, mainstream economic theorists fail both to understand the deep economic structures specific to capitalism and to develop the theoretical mediations that might successfully connect abstract theory to historical specificity.[2] In short, their failure is both theoretical and empirical. By assuming the commodity form to be more or less universal and natural, they fail in the all important task of problematizing it. The commodification that they correctly assume to be complete at the level of abstract theory is never complete at the level of history, being always supported politically or ideologically. In moving from the abstract to the concrete, then, it is necessary to theorize different degrees of commodification and different types of supports.[3] Failure to do this will either produce a formalistic economic theory that revolves in outer space, or one that turns history into a function of the economic by failing to develop mediations that would bring in relatively autonomous practices and human agency as they interact with the economic and help shape historical outcomes.[4]

And despite the pronounced "chill" on critical thought that has developed in the United States in the early twenty-first century, there is a growing awareness, both in the US and abroad, of the severe deficiencies of orthodox economics.[5] For example, in June 2000 a

2. Hodgson (2001) presents a very thorough and interesting analysis of the failure to successfully address the problem of historical specificity throughout the history of economic theory. I agree with his concern for the problem of historical specificity when he writes: "I have believed for over thirty years that the problem of historical specificity was one of the key questions in the social sciences" (2001, xiii).

3. Commodification is complete when the capitalistic commodity form is regulated entirely by fully competitive markets not distorted by extra-economic force from within or without.

4. Lawson (1997) offers particularly strong arguments against neo-classical economics for failing to meaningfully address human agency.

5. On top of the chill, "American social science bears the distinctive mark of its national origin.... Its liberal values, practical bent, shallow historical vision, and technocratic confidence are recognizable features of twentieth century America.... these characteristics make American social science ahistorical and scientistic..." (Ross 1991, cited in Hodgson 2001, 152).

group of France's leading students of economics posted a petition on the web protesting against the extreme mathematical formalism of academic economics that turns it into an "autistic science" out of touch with reality, and against the domination of a neo-classical orthodoxy that leaves no room for critical thought (Fullbrook 2003, 1). The *Post-autistic Economics Review* that grew out of this movement had 5,500 subscribers after only its first two years of publication (ibid., 4). This book can be considered a particularly radical contribution to this movement, for in it I shall argue that almost everyone who has been indoctrinated by academic economics has utterly failed to grasp the potentially unparalleled contributions to economic science made by Marx's economic writings, particularly *Capital*.[6] And even the famous French Marxist philosopher, Louis Althusser (1970, 15), who in *Reading Capital*, referred to Marx's *Capital* as "the founding moment of a science", in his last work (1992, 211), does an about face and refers to "the woolly and literally untenable labour theory of value".

RECOGNIZING THE BRILLIANCE OF MARX'S ECONOMIC THOUGHT

Lest the reader conclude from this blast aimed at mainstream economics that this book will primarily be a debunking project, let me immediately state my main focus. The book is primarily an appreciation of Marx's great achievements in economic theory, achievements that have never been fully recognized even by Marxists. My aim is to bring these achievements out of the shadows of ideological squabbling into the light of day for all to see. This will include not only his explicit theory, but also lines of thought or openings for thought that Marx may only have been dimly aware of if at all. Running through the book as a kind of sub-text will be frequent considerations of why it is that mainstream academic economics has been so blind to the contributions that Marx's economic thought can make to the advancement of economic science today. But instead of presenting yet another interpretation of Marx's economic theory as a whole or responding to all the various and sundry criticisms of his theory, my aim will be to emphasize Marx's most fundamental and lasting contributions and the undeveloped possibilities of his theories. And I shall explore why it is that orthodox economists

6. Unfortunately most Marxists have also failed to fully grasp the particular strengths of Marx's *Capital* that I am drawing out and emphasizing in this book.

and even unorthodox economists (including Marxists) have failed to grasp some of Marx's most brilliant achievements. In the process of arguing for a new economics based on Marx's work, I shall at least touch on some issues of ontology and epistemology, or, in other words, on issues concerning the basic nature of economics as an object of knowledge and the sorts of knowledge appropriate to such an object.[7]

It is not the case that Marx's economic writings by themselves offer some kind of total solution to the problems of theorizing the economic, but I shall argue that they do offer a strong basis from which to seek solutions. In some areas of theorizing the economic, Marx makes significant advances, in some areas confusions and contradictions need to be sorted out, and in other areas there are simply openings that, though promising, may be only slightly developed or even just hinted at. It is my aim to draw out Marxian economics in directions that demonstrate its vast superiority over competing approaches. This will include Marx's particular way of theorizing the economic in terms of a commodity form that absorbs and hides power relations, of a theory of surplus-value that both places profit-making at the centre and understands this profit-making in class terms, of an understanding of dialectical reason that moves his theorizing in the direction of a necessary unfolding of the commodity form, of recognizing the need for mediations that enable abstract theory to have at least the potentiality to address historical specificity, of connecting class to the quantitative variables of abstract economic theory, of connecting the economic and the ethical so that economics can be a form of critical theory, and finally of recognizing its necessary multiple-disciplinarity (or perhaps more accurately transdisciplinarity) that is cognizant of the importance of the relations between the economic and other relatively autonomous social practices.[8] And in opposition to the strongly held views of many, I shall argue that the labour theory of value, far from being an incubus on this renewal of economic theory, should be central to it.

7. My interpretation of Marx is strongly influenced by the work of Japanese Political Economists Kozo Uno (1980) and Tom Sekine (1986; 1997). It is primarily their work that has aided my thought about the unique ontology of capital, and it is the work of Bhaskar (1989) that has made it clear how important it is to consider ontological issues.
8. In my usage "relative autonomy" does not preclude interpenetration, in which, for example, the economic may become politicized.

SOME SHORTCOMINGS OF ECONOMIC THEORY

Arguably, developing adequate connections between theory and history is *the* central problem of the social sciences, but because of the way in which economic science is constituted, far from contributing solutions, it has tended to exacerbate the problem. For example, the influential academic economist Joan Robinson, who is sympathetic to Marx, seems to think that Marx is an empiricist offering a model that should be evaluated by positivist criteria. According to Robinson (1966, xi): "The concept of *value* seems to me to be a remarkable example of how a metaphysical notion can inspire original thought, though in itself is quite devoid of operational meaning." She is breaking with positivism here insofar as she considers that metaphysical notions may not be completely empty, yet she is still operating with the metaphysical/operational binary. If we take "operational" to mean convertible into verifiable propositions, then Marx's theory of value may ultimately be "operational". For example, take the proposition: "In history the capitalist state continually seeks ways to maintain the commodification of labour-power." While this proposition cannot be derived directly from Marx's theory of value, it can be derived from mid-range theory that is informed by Marx's theory of value. And while it may be argued that generating verifiable propositions is of central importance in the natural sciences and strictly empirical social sciences, it is not the central concern in the theory of capital's deep structures.[9] For here we are first of all theorizing how the commodity form by itself can reproduce and expand the basic socio-economic relations of a society. That is, the aim is to lay out the necessary inner connections amongst all basic capitalist economic categories when they are completely subsumed to the commodity form. It is only then that we can begin to think how the theory of capital's deep structures might be utilized as an aid to more concrete levels of analysis. Ultimately, we may want to generate testable propositions, but presumably this would occur primarily at the level of historical analysis where the central concern is with historical causality.

Generating verifiable propositions is not, however, what is most important about the theory of value, and it is certainly not the *sine qua non* that makes it meaningful. Rather it takes basic economic categories that are meaningful because they are deeply embedded in

9. I use "theory of capital's inner logic", "theory of capital's deep structures", "dialectic of capital" and "theory of a purely capitalist society" interchangeably to emphasize different aspects of the most abstract level of theory.

the everyday life and history of capitalism (for example, commodity, money, capital, wage, price, profit, rent, interest, accumulation) and theorizes how they must interrelate insofar as they are completely commodified and as a result can be thought quantitatively. In other words, economic theory essentially sharpens meanings that are already deeply embedded in history by following the self-reifying logic of capital.[10] It does not proceed through the method of stipulative definitions that is common in empirical sciences where precise boundaries are required for data collecting.

The binary metaphysical/operational, which stems from positivist philosophers like A.J. Ayer (1952), often takes the position that only verifiable propositions are meaningful and that all other propositions are empty, or, what is the same thing, "metaphysical". But this binary, so central to positivist philosophy, not only fails to capture what is going on in Marx's theory, but is also meaningless in its own terms because it cannot be verified. Robinson avoids this by arguing for two kinds of metaphysical propositions: on the one hand those that are meaningless, and on the other, analytic propositions, that though not themselves verifiable, are the basis of an analytic framework that can generate verifiable propositions. Without pursuing this issue in the depth that it deserves, at least one can say that up to this point it is unclear just how we are to assess analytic propositions as opposed to the hot air types of metaphysical propositions.[11] It is also unclear how Robinson would utilize abstract economic theory to understand historical specificity without engaging in extreme forms of economic reductionism.[12]

Another example of a theoretical perspective that is inadequate when it comes to developing theoretical mediations that would connect abstract theory and history is the work of Ian Steedman (1977). For example, he is so taken in by the mathematical "correctness" of his Sraffa-based formalistic model of price determination that he totally rejects the incredibly rich potentials of Marx's value theory as a basis for both understanding capital's inner logic and developing the sort of theoretical mediations (levels of analysis) required for connecting abstract theory with concrete history.[13] Instead he presents a

---

10. In Chapter 4 I shall make the case that capital is self-reifying and hence self-defining.
11. See Hollis and Nell (1975) for an extensive critique of the positivist assumptions of mainstream economic theory.
12. See Chapter 8 for more on Robinson.
13. See Sraffa (1960). Sekine (1997) demonstrates the incorrectness of Steedman's theory of price determination. See Chapter 8.

formalistic theory of price determination, that in its universality is not connected to any historically specific mode of production, and then seems more or less lost when it comes to seeking paths that might connect his theory to historical specificity. Indeed, one of my most important arguments is that epistemological projects connected with economic theory that tend to make history a simple function of abstract theory or abstract theory a simple abstraction from empirical history are deeply problematic.[14]

The solution offered here involves the hard work of developing theoretical mediations or distinct levels of theory that can connect theory and history while avoiding all simplistic deductivism and inductivism. In the case of the theory of capitalism, I shall argue that at least three levels of analysis are necessary.[15] Many theorists have advocated some sort of levels of analysis, but few have done much of the hard work required to theorize them and their interconnections.[16] In part this is because modern academia is not organized to provide much support for the interdisciplinary theorizing and collective research that would be necessary. For example, how many trained economists can venture to write at the level of historical analysis where economic causality is mixed with political and ideological causality in the form of relatively autonomous and interpenetrating practices?

There is a tendency for economics to be a hermetically sealed academic discipline, and this coupled with the worship of mathematics means that prices tend not to be seen in their connection with power relations whether economic, political or ideological.[17] In other words, there tends to be little consideration of how, through reification and commodification, power relations have been "disappeared" into quantitative market signals that we submit ourselves to. At the level

14. Althusser (1970) would argue against such "reflection" theories, which he would classify generally as empiricist. See also Hollis and Nell (1975).
15. Both Uno and Sekine argue for three levels of analysis. For my particular version of mid-range theory see Albritton (1991).
16. See Mandel (1975), Aglietta (1979), Althusser (1970), Hodgson (2001), Sayer (1995), Postone (1996), Saad-Filho (2002), Jameson (1990), Bhaskar (1989) and many more.
17. "The disciplinary demarcation criteria, and the narrowing view of the scope of economics, had major and global consequences for the erection of virtually impenetrable disciplinary boundaries after the Second World War" (Hodgson 2001, 121). "We are also wary of the electrified wire dividing some academic disciplines" (Hollis and Nell 1975, 1).

of abstract economic theory where commodification is assumed to be complete, power relations disappear into seemingly impersonal and neutral numbers that are seen to epitomize economic reason, which, in turn, is thought to epitomize human reason.[18] But in sharp contrast, at more concrete levels of analysis where power relations are not fully commodified, numbers only tell a part of the story. Marx makes it clear that even in pure capitalism where capitalistic rationality is totally in charge, the inequities associated with class exploitation are systematically reproduced.[19]

It is my contention that the quantification of social relations into mathematical equations only makes sense to the degree that we assume that the commodity form by itself rules economic life, or in other words, that all inputs and outputs of capitalistic production are fully and securely commodified.[20] For otherwise power relations that may have qualitative dimensions or may be structural enter the picture and disrupt any quantitative conclusions. But the commodity form is simply the form that private property takes in capitalism, and private property is fundamentally a power relation of exclusion. As Marx (C I, Chs. 6 and 7) has so powerfully demonstrated, pure capitalism rests first of all upon the full commodification of the means of production, which, as a result becomes exclusively owned by the capitalist class, and secondly upon labour power's full commodification that requires that each worker be excluded from ownership of any means of production. When commodification is complete the class relation becomes a relation of structural power (i.e. class struggle is absorbed into this structural relation) that makes it subsumable to mathematical formulations. But at more concrete levels of analysis, where commodification is incomplete, power relations including class struggle will always play a role in determining quantitative outcomes. In other words, at these more concrete levels of analysis, mathematical equations cannot stand on their own as explanations. And in turn, since it is unlikely that in most cases the power relations can be adequately understood in purely quantitative terms, qualitative analysis will need to play a role.

18. This formalist revolution eventually converted "the whole of economics into a branch of applied mathematics" (Blaug 1999, 276; cited in Hodgson 2001, 232).
19. See the reproduction schema at the end of *Capital* Volume Two for a schematic account of how the class relations can be reproduced entirely through the commodity form.
20. Criticizing "the marvelous inventions of Dr Price" Marx (G, 842–3) writes: "...he regards capital ... as a mere self-increasing number".

It is only in the context of a theory of a purely capitalist society where power relations get fully absorbed into socio-economic structures subsumed completely to the commodity form, that mathematical formulae can be employed. Clarity on this point is essential to the effective use of mathematics in economic theory.

In the case of capital, commodification represents a self-objectification of social relations, such that socio-economic life is directed by price signals emerging from the interrelations of commodities, money and capital in markets. Self-objectification per se is not necessarily a bad thing. Take, for example, the self-objectification represented by the deep structures of our grammar that permit communication to take place. Capital, however, is not so benign, as its deep structures are tied to power relations that are exploitative and often oppressive. It is therefore important for economics to always be aware of the power relations behind the numbers, so that these relations can emerge as it moves from abstract to more concrete levels of analysis. And for social science in general to orient towards degrees and types of self-objectification strikes me as an extremely positive research programme, because the very concept "self-objectification" invites consideration of whether or not the flourishing of the "self", considered as a set of social relations, is advanced or retarded by particular objectifications or degrees of objectification.[21]

A theory of the commodity form is a particularly important theory of social self-objectification, because it is so central to understanding the basic characteristics of the modern world. Marx clearly understood the radical difference between all pre-capitalist societies where the commodity form was peripheral and undeveloped, and capitalist societies where it becomes central and developed. And since all mainstream economic theory fails to recognize the central importance of this distinction, it may ideologically reflect aspects of capitalism, but it can never understand its specific historical uniqueness. It may be no exaggeration to claim that the most radical change in all of history was the subsumption of production to the commodity form, for it is this change that ultimately placed the earth and its people at the service of short-term profits no matter what the long-term consequences.[22]

21. See Albritton (forthcoming [a]) for a fuller discussion of this.
22. While economists generally remain oblivious to this, I am aware of two important anthropologists who have understood the centrality of the commodity form and profit-oriented production for understanding the modern world (Sahlins 1972; Polanyi 1944).

WHAT IS THE ECONOMIC?

In order to work our way out of the ideological constraints of economic orthodoxy, it is useful to start by considering what sorts of economic questions or problems that we, as humans living in the early twenty-first century, might most want to pose. To begin with, it is important to distinguish between the economic from the point of view of capital and the economic from the point of view of humans as historical beings who may want to alter capitalism. In the context of a purely capitalist society, capital defines itself as self-expanding value, and while such a definition of the economic is a necessary starting point, from our point of view as historical beings, we need a broader definition. I believe that it is consistent with Marx's theory of capital's deep structures to state that most fundamentally economics is about *how we spend our time and energy providing for ourselves and how the organizational forms and power relations resulting from this provisioning advance or retard human flourishing considered as deeply embedded in the natural environment.* I will argue that *capitalist* economics consists most fundamentally in provisioning activities organized by the private ownership of the means of production, which in turn is organized to compete through the commodity form in order to maximize profits. In other words, with capitalism, our life energy – insofar as it is devoted to economic activity – seems at first to be organized by capitalists who control the means of production. But it is important to realize that in the theory of capital's deep structures, ultimately capitalists are, in Marx's words, "the personifications of economic categories", such that their behaviour is determined by price signals generated by the commodity form.[23] In other words, the seeming agency of capitalists is subsumed to the self-expanding value of capital itself. And while societies can be more capitalist or less capitalist, they are the most capitalist when all inputs (including labour-power) and outputs of the production process are completely commodified.

I am suggesting, then, that instead of defining the economic in terms of the usual supply, demand and scarcity (an extremely one-sided and limited definition even at the level of pure capitalism), we consider focusing on how our life energies are channelled into provisioning activities, and how the results of these activities are

---

23. Marx frequently uses the metaphor "personification" to express the reifying force of capital (S I, 282; S III 476, 514–15; C I, 179, 254; C III, 953, 958, 963, 968–9).

distributed. Further, I shall argue later on that in the theory of capital's deep structures, it is the capitalist commodity form that subsumes and coordinates the substance of economic life, and Marx's theory of value lays the groundwork for theorizing the consequences to economic life of a commodity-economic logic organized around maximizing profit.

OUTLINE OF ARGUMENT

My argument will be presented in eight chapters. Chapter 2 will focus on Marx's theory of the commodity form, which, I shall argue, is his single greatest contribution to economic theory. Lukács and the Frankfurt School developed an overly totalized cultural theory based on Marx's theory of the commodity form, but few have explored in depth its importance for economic theory.[24] It is my contention that a general economic theory can only utilize mathematics when commodification of economic variables is complete, because otherwise relatively autonomous and qualitatively distinct economic and non-economic structures will alter quantitative outcomes such that there can be no purely mathematical precision in them.[25] And since at the level of history commodification is never complete, the study of economics at this level must always be multidisciplinary and include

24. See Albritton (2003a), "Superseding Lukács: A Contribution to the Theory of Subjectivity".
25. It may still be useful to study quantitative outcomes in connection with various types of power that determine them, but they would rarely if ever be outcomes resulting from fully commodified economic variables alone. My caution about the use of mathematics is aimed specifically at the use of equations in general theories that are presumed to be directly applicable to real historical economies. Employing statistics may always be useful when used with proper caution. See Marilyn Waring (1999) for an analysis of some of the distortions characteristic of National Accounts. Mathematical simulations are also problematic because their outcomes depend so much on the precise boundaries drawn between variables, boundaries that clearly do not exist in empirical reality. For example, Ross McKitrick "ran two simulations of the Canadian economy's response to a tax rise. The two projections shared the same Walrasian philosophy, used identical data and examined the same 10% tax on the purchase of services; they differed only in the way they clipped and pruned households and companies, giving different mathematical expression to the laws of demand and supply. But these subtleties of expression had profound effects. In the first of his simulations, the tax rise allowed government spending to increase by more than 60%; in the second, spending could rise by just 14%" (*Economist*, July 15, 2006, p. 69).

the study of different types of structures of power that are implicated in "economic" outcomes. Or, in other words, quantitative economic outcomes in history are always likely to have non-quantifiable structural determinants.

Marx recognized, correctly I shall argue, that the commodity form (the "cell-form" of capital's inner dynamic) is central to theorizing capital's inner logic.[26] Realizing the full import of this and all its theoretical ramifications is *key* to understanding Marx's theory and its particular strengths in theorizing capitalism. Nearly all mainstream economic theory simply takes complete commodification as a given, and hence ignores the problematics of absorbing social power relations into the commodity form.[27] Were the conception of commodification taken seriously by economists, there could be far less reliance on mathematics since all actually existing capitalisms are only partially commodified and this partial commodification is only sustained by economic, political and ideological supports (structures, practices or institutions) that usually need to be conceptualized structurally. Mainstream economists fail to understand how the commodity form reifies economic relations (they simply assume market-governed economies), producing a dynamic that prevails over the wills of individuals, and they also fail to understand how the commodity form hides the structural property relations that lie behind it. For example, because of the peculiar connection of the commodity form to the private ownership of the means of production, the commodity form tends to hide the power relations (class) that stand behind *quid pro quo* exchanges.

But complete commodification implies that the commodity form rules such that agency by capitalists only serves to reinforce a commodity-economic logic upon society as a whole. When commodification is complete, economic variables can vary internally and necessarily in relation to each other, but, at the same time, the resulting quantitative automaticity hides power relations that can only be effectively studied at more concrete levels of theory.[28]

26. "Two characteristic traits mark the capitalist mode of production right from the start. *Firstly.* It produces its products as commodities. ... The *second* thing that particularly marks the capitalist mode of production is the production of surplus-value..." (C III, 1019–20).
27. As Sekine has pointed out to me, mainstream economists assume that economic form and substance are always fused together, whereas such fusion only occurs under the historically specific conditions of capitalism.
28. At the levels of mid-range theory or historical analysis.

It is as if power relations are absorbed into the commodity form and thereby disappear from view. But arguably it is economic power that should be one of the central concerns of economic theory. By problematizing the commodity, Marx makes it possible to unpack the power relations that have been "disappeared" into numbers by generating more concrete levels of analysis, thus avoiding the extreme reductionism that would result from applying mathematical economic models to history.

Nearly all general economic theory produced historically has simply assumed the commodity form; whereas Marx both theorizes its fully developed capitalist forms and problematizes it. This is an absolutely fundamental and crucial difference distinguishing Marx from nearly all other economists. Because of the depth of his theory of the commodity form, Marx is able to demonstrate both the contradictory character of the commodity form at the level of abstract theory and its incompleteness in all actual capitalist societies. Its contradictory character underlies the periodic crises of capital in the theory of pure capitalism, and its incompleteness severely limits quantitative analysis and necessitates that economic theory become multidisciplinary as it approaches more and more closely to the analysis of history. And to the extent that the commodity form is not complete, it necessarily requires the support of economic, political and ideological power relations.

In Chapter 3 I argue that a second lasting contribution that places Marx head and shoulders above other economic theorists is his theory of surplus-value. While his theory of the commodity form is typically ignored or little understood, his theory of surplus-value tends to be dismissed by mainstream economists as either incoherent or "metaphysical" in the bad positivist sense of the word. In sharp opposition to nearly all economic theorists, it is my claim that a theory of price determination is not the highest achievement of an economic theory aiming to understand the deep structures of capital. This is because prices exist wherever there is money and are therefore not specific to capitalism, whereas a particular profit-making dynamic is central to capitalism. It follows that for a theory of capital's deep structures, a theory of profit and not price determination *is* the crowning achievement. And Marx roots such a theory in the private ownership of the means of production such that "surplus-value" synthesizes the structural relation of class with the quantitative economic variable "profit". Or, in other words, "surplus-value" connects the capitalistic organization of our labouring life energy with capitalistic profit.

The labour theory of value and surplus-value constitute the structural matrix out of which quantitatively determinate profits and prices arise. The theory of surplus-value roots all forms of profit-making (industrial profit, commercial profit, interest, rent) in total capitalistically organized labour considered as a homogeneous whole (simple, average, abstract labour), where the value produced by such labour in excess of the value of labour-power goes to the capitalist class considered as a homogeneous whole prior to any consideration of differences between types of capital or types of profit. The basic accomplishment of the theory of surplus-value is to present the fundamental capitalist class relation in its most clear and stark form, while at the same time connecting this relation to the internal relation of quantitative economic variables required to have a complete picture of the deep structures of capitalist profit-making. Indeed, the commonality (abstract labour) that makes for systematic variation amongst internally related economic variables is precisely what makes a *theory of value* possible.[29]

If what the theory of capital's deep structures ultimately needs to know is how the system of labour time relates to the system of profits, we need to develop a labour theory of value.[30] If successful, such a theory will explain how in a commodity regulated economy there is a system-dependent linking between labour time and the profits that stem from capitalistically produced commodities.[31] In capitalism (assuming a purely capitalist society)[32] this comes down to how we divide up our total life energy to produce the commodities that we consume, what gets produced and how it is produced, how it gets distributed, and who profits and how. And while a theory of price determination that is consistent with the theory of surplus-value is a necessary step in the theory of capital's inner logic, it is "surplus-value" that is the central concept.[33] The empiricism and formalism

29. Abstract labour is basically labour that can capitalistically produce any use-value. In this sense it is indifferent to use-value.

30. See Sekine (1997) for a powerful rendering of the labour theory of value including its relation to prices of production.

31. See Wiese (2003) for a representational theory of measurement.

32. A purely capitalist society is one in which commodification is complete such that socio-economic reproduction can be actualized through a commodity-economic logic alone.

33. For a clear theory of the relation between value and price see Sekine (1997, Vol. II).

of mainstream economics creates a point of view from which it is almost impossible to understand the centrality of "surplus-value" to grasping capital's deep structures.[34]

Yet another lasting contribution made by Marx is at least a partial realization of the importance of dialectical reasoning in theorizing capital's deep structures. I say "partial" because his theory of capital does not carry out the possibilities of dialectical reasoning systematically and in detail. It is in Chapter 4 that I address the issues posed by dialectical reasoning.

Going back to his heady left-Hegelian days in Berlin, Marx was exposed to Hegel's dialectical modes of reasoning, and contra Althusser (1969), I believe that if there is a break in the corpus of Marx's writings, it is from the simplistic dialectics of Feuerbachian humanism in his early works to a sort of dialectical reasoning closer to Hegel's *Logic* in *Capital*.[35] It is this that helps us to understand the sense in which *Capital* contains a theory of capital's *inner* logic, a logic that is a necessary unfolding of the commodity form as "cell-form", such that all fundamental capitalist economic categories are simply different forms of the commodity. In contrast, according to Feuerbach private property, religion and the state are all alienated expressions of the human essence that need only to be reabsorbed into that essence in order for humans to be happy and at home on earth. Such simplistic essentialism as a mode of thought produces romantic and quasi-religious theory that is likely to feed destructive millenarian modes of political practice.[36]

While Marx does not present his theory of capital as a rigorous dialectic, it can be so presented, and furthermore Marx's own presentation contains elements of such a presentation.[37] To understand this it is necessary to explore concepts such as: "sequence of categories", "contradiction", "necessary inner connection", "levels of abstraction within a theory", and "levels of abstraction between theories". Once a degree of understanding of dialectical reasoning

34. For example, Joan Robinson would consider "surplus-value" to be a metaphysical concept in the bad sense. She writes: "None of the important ideas which he expresses in terms of the concept of value cannot better be expressed without it" (1966, 20).
35. For the most complete theory of the relation between Marx's theory of capital's inner logic and Hegel's *Logic* see Sekine (1986). See also John Bell (1995, 2003); Stefanos Kourkoulakos (2003); and Albritton (1999).
36. However, the inversion of subject and object that was so central to Feuerbach does remain central to Marx's notion of capitalist reification.
37. The strongest such presentation is that of Sekine (1997).

is established, it becomes clear why a theory of price determination cannot be separated out from Marx's theory of surplus-value as the matrix out of which prices of production arise, and why at the same time a theory of price determination is not the central focus within the theory of capital's deep structural dynamics.

Chapter 5 will deal with the use of distinct levels of analysis to make connections between abstract theory and history. While Marx never explicitly theorized levels of analysis as levels of distinct degrees of abstraction between theories, such theorization is at least implicit in his writings. It is my contention that much of the confusion surrounding his theory might have been avoided, and his theory could have been enormously strengthened, had he consciously and systematically thought through the need for levels of analysis to mediate between abstract theory and historical analysis.

In *Capital* Marx explores the relations between capitalist economic categories when the commodity form and a commodity-economic logic are firmly in control. This inner logic of capital displays certain quantitative relations and certain abstract historical directionalities.[38] At this highly abstract level of theory, Marx suggests that periodic crises result primarily from the need to commodity-economically manage labour-power and fixed capital, and that such crises, by temporarily resolving contradictions, permit a continuation of capitalism.[39] All of this is to help us understand the deep structural dynamics or the core dynamics of capital in the abstract and in general. There is strong evidence that Marx would not consider that concepts like "rising organic composition of capital", "undercon-sumption", "profit-squeeze", or any other quantitative economic category derived from the theory of pure capitalism, could adequately explain by itself any actual capitalist crisis.[40] For example, when he discusses the causes of the economic crisis of 1847 in *Capital* volume III, it is quite clear that his explanation includes a variety

38. For example, periodic crises, increased productivity, concentration of capital and ongoing class struggle.
39. "Crises are never more than momentary, violent solutions for the existing contradictions, violent eruptions that re-establish the disturbed balance for the time being" (C III, 357).
40. This is not to say that in a very general sense some crises may not be predominantly underconsumptionist or profit-squeeze crises. While this may be, a full explanation would require an account of the major economic, political and ideological forces operating at an historical level.

of historically specific economic, political and ideological causes. Nor would he consider a concept like "equilibrium", a concept that he utilizes to clarify capital's deep structures, as a concept directly applicable to any actual historical capitalism.[41] Indeed, once we introduce the notion of levels of analysis, we can resolve many of the debates that continually revolve around Marxian crisis theory or around Marx's implicit and explicit use of "equilibrium".

While Marx goes in somewhat contradictory directions with regard to levels of analysis, it is easy to extract at least two distinct levels – abstract theory and historical analysis – in *Capital*. Given the distance between the theory of capital's deep structures and historical analysis, however, it is essential to have at least three levels of analysis that would include a mediating mid-range or mid-level theory. Indeed, elsewhere I (1991) have argued at length that we can utilize such a level to theorize the modes of capital accumulation distinct to different phases of capitalist development.

The conceptualization of levels of analysis utilized in this book is one of the areas in Marx's writings where there are confusions, contradictions and silences. And yet, I would argue that Marx's economic thinking is not only open to the theoretical possibility of distinct levels, but also invites some such resolution to the difficulties that he has connecting the theoretical with the historical. Furthermore, it is this resolution that may constitute the most important theoretical breakthrough in terms of enhancing the potentials that to some extent are lying dormant in Marx's *Capital*.

Chapter 6 deals with the conceptualization of class in Marxian political economy. This chapter utilizes levels of analysis to sort out some of the important debates that have swirled around "class" in Marxian political economy. Indeed, levels of analysis are particularly useful in theorizing the relation between phase-specific modes of accumulation and concepts like class, gender and race. Because the concept of class is so central to theorizing capital's deep structures, and because, in my view, there has been so much confusion around Marx's theorization of class, I devote a chapter to it. My discussion serves the double purpose of illustrating the use of levels of analysis

41. There are always equilibrating forces at work in historical capitalism; however, at the level of history these are always interfered with by extra-economic force and furthermore there is no evidence that historical capitalism has ever approached a state of equilibrium. Indeed, given the global uneven development of capitalism historically, equilibrium at this level would seem to be as rare as hen's teeth.

and of developing a theorization of class consistent with Marx's project of political economy as a whole. The aim is to achieve a clear and precise grounding for theorizing "class", while avoiding class reductionism at more concrete levels of analysis where economic power may articulate class, race and gender in complex ways.

Central to the position that I develop is the view that "class" as a structural relation of power is included in Marx's theory of capital's inner logic, while "class struggle" is not. This follows from the fact that Marx assumes total commodification in which human agency simply gives motion to the commodity form, whose motion channels that agency. And yet because the structural relation is antagonistic in the sense that all profits come from the exploitation of labour, where commodification is less than complete, one would always expect some degree of class struggle.

Chapter 7 deals with economic theory and ethics. Positivist philosophy with its fundamental distinction between empirical discourse that is cognitive and normative discourse that is emotive has generally promoted a conception of science that excludes ethics.[42] For at least some positivists, a cognitive ethics is impossible because all ethical discourse is seen to be emotive, and the aim of science is to be wholly cognitive, leaving the emotive realm to ethics.[43] To the extent that this way of thinking dominates social science, we tend not to develop traditions of discourse that can rationally and cognitively discuss ethical questions in connection with knowledge generated by the social sciences. And where effective rational debate is undermined, ethics do indeed become emotional, with the resulting hatreds fuelling a politics of violence. For example, capital values profits, but humans value many other things, and need to develop rational ways of deciding about many competing values or else a great deal of social life will be decided by the criteria of short-term profit-maximization that will not always advance human flourishing.

Since there are no strong mainstream traditions in economics that attempt to connect scientific and ethical discourse in economic theory,[44] our starting point must necessarily be somewhat primitive.[45]

42. See A.J. Ayer (1952) for the classic statement of logical positivism.
43. For a good account of the emotivist character of much modern ethical thought see MacIntyre (1984).
44. For example, "welfare economics" tends to be a peripheralized sub-discipline in most departments of economics.
45. Here I agree with MacIntyre (1984) on the lack of a developed tradition of moral discourse. I consider the work of Sen, Nussbaum, Roemer and others as lacking sufficient purchase on the severe injustices that we face.

I include a chapter that indicates some possible directions for economic ethics, realizing how difficult this will be until we have more theoretical and conceptual tools to carry out such a project. I call the approach that I advocate "negative ethics" for it would focus first on alleviating in practical ways injustices without being too concerned with what justice may be in the abstract and in general.

While not every economic theory need take on ethical issues, there needs to be a general recognition that all general economic theory has ethical implications and that in order to be scientific, economists need not avoid addressing ethical issues. We need to get clear what is the case before we can have productive debates on possible alterations that would advance social justice; hence, I am not suggesting that we collapse all distinctions between scientific and ethical discourse. If our interest in economics first and foremost concerns how the total labour of society is divided up to produce useful or wanted effects and how these effects are distributed, it would seem natural to want to discuss the fairness of the distribution of labour and of wanted effects. In other words, an economic theory that analyzes economic power invites discussion of distributive justice and the discussion of distributive justice raises most other ethico-political issues such as democracy, freedom, equality and rights. For example, outcomes that are not democratically arrived at could be considered lacking in at least one of the dimensions of justice.

To say that ethical considerations should be welcomed into academic economics is to propose radical change, for as presently constituted, academic economics generally ignores questions of economic power, offers little systematic attention to cognitive ethical issues as they relate to economics, and generally ignores the labour process. A labour theory of value not only can serve as a basis for discussing distributive justice, but also as a basis for discussing ecological issues, where environmental degradation may involve saving labour now only to make much more labour necessary for future generations (as in building huge dykes to prevent low-lying areas from being flooded by rising oceans). It follows that the "science" of economics should strive to be explanatory, and, at the same time, should not shy away from utilizing its explanations to clarify and contribute to ethical debate in the sense that issues of fairness of distribution can always be posed of any system of distribution (whether of work or of product) as can issues of long-term human flourishing.[46]

46. I do not mean to imply that every work of theory must combine both explanation and ethics. We must still work hard to determine as well as

Although there are critiques of mainstream economics scattered throughout, Chapter 8 engages more systematically with a few influential critical interpretations of Marxian economics. Here the main focus will be on the left Keynesian, Joan Robinson, both because she is sympathetic to Marx, and because she actively promotes the British empiricism of which her work is a clear example. My aim will be to point out ways in which, because of her empiricism, she has misinterpreted Marx and to indicate some of the strengths of Marxian political economy that she fails to recognize. This chapter will be brief because my main aim is to present previously underappreciated strengths of Marxian political economy and not deal with the enormous interpretive literature. The main purpose of critique in this chapter is to clarify some of the ontological and epistemological differences between the approach that I am advocating and more mainstream approaches, with particular emphasis on the difficulties empiricist approaches have connecting mathematical economics with historical analysis.

It seems to me that no economic theorist has come close to Marx's (C I, 163) realization that the commodity "is a very strange thing, abounding in metaphysical subtleties and theological niceties". And because they have failed to do so, they have unwittingly reproduced the metaphysics of the commodity form, when what they thought they were doing was producing empirical economic science. My aim in the next chapter, then, will be to explore some of the important dimensions of Marx's theory of the commodity form.

---

we can "what is the case"; however, in the social sciences we need to work even harder to determine what changes might most advance human flourishing. And I would add that this second step should be considered as invited by the first. And this implies a cognitive ethics.

2
The Theory of the Commodity Form

...for bourgeois society, the commodity form of the product of labour, or the value-form of the commodity, is the economic cell-form. (C I, 90)

All commodities are only transitory money... (G, 231)

...labour confronts capital not as a use value, but as the use-value pure and simple... (G, 295)

It is Marx's theory of the commodity form that most fundamentally places his theoretical achievements far above those of all other economic theorists.[1] No other economic theorist has even begun to give anything like the attention to the commodity form that is required in order to effectively theorize the deep structures of capital. Indeed, economic theorists from Adam Smith to Milton Friedman simply assume the commodity form, but this has the effect of making quantitative theorizing unproblematic and removes any serious consideration of how numbers might be unpacked in order to connect them with the analysis of history. Though Marx's theory of the commodity form or a refinement of it is absolutely crucial to any economic theory that has aspirations to understand either the deep structure of capital or the history of capitalism, in general you will find nothing like it in the introductory economic textbooks utilized by economics departments in North America or throughout the world. By not problematizing the commodity form, or in other words by not thinking deeply about what it is and how capital must operate because of what it is, commodities and markets are converted into ideological givens whose hegemony over us is simply accepted without ever being questioned.

A little reflection on Marx's *Capital* will bring out why the theory of capital's inner logic must start with the commodity and its most abstract and basic determinates. First of all, Marx (C I, 90, 125, 176) begins his theory with the economic category that, as the most simple and abstract category, has the fewest presuppositions, and,

---

1. I am indebted to Tom Sekine for much of my understanding of this point.

as his theory unfolds, this is demonstrated to be the commodity. Second, and closely related to the first point, is his desire to begin his theory with the least determined and most determining economic category, which the theory as a whole demonstrates to be the commodity.[2] Third, he shows that capital's essence can be revealed if we let the commodity form "take over" economic life, such that the fundamental economic categories are completely commodified.[3] The dynamics of capital's deep structures are then revealed as a commodity-economic logic that is self-expanding. This is crucial because it implies that the theory is less a matter of imposing a model on a subject-matter, than letting capital reveal itself by theoretically removing all interferences with its motions. Thus, capital perpetuates itself by subsuming economic behaviour to the price signals that emerge from its own commodity-economic logic and drive it to expand by maximizing profits. Fourth, and closely related to this last point, because the commodity form reifies and objectifies social relations by subsuming them to a commodity-economic logic, it is important to have a clear picture of a purely capitalist society in which social relations are objectified. In other words, it is important to understand the nature of a society, along with the ontological implications, in which economic subjects are objectified and capital as self-expanding value is subjectified.[4] Finally, it is important to understand commodification as a socio-economic process, that, while typical of capitalism, is only ever completed in the theory of capital's deep structures. And this implies that the inner integrity of capital's logic as a system of quantified qualities can only be assumed when commodification is complete.

For Marx, it is absolutely essential to understand what a full-fledged capitalistic commodity is and how the commodity form operates because of what it is. Thus, after a brief exploration of the basic features of the commodity, I shall consider the very sharp distinctions that Marx makes between the barter of products and the exchange

2. Marx's dialectical logic derives the money form from the commodity form and derives the capital form from the money form in process as self-valorizing value.
3. He continually insists on theorizing pure capitalism where all exchanges are *quid pro quo* (C I, 260, 268; C III, 252).
4. "In truth, however, value is here the subject of a process in which, while constantly assuming the form in turn of money and commodities, it changes its own magnitude, throws off surplus-value from itself considered as original value, and thus valorizes itself independently" (C I, 255).

of commodities, and between products of self-employment and capitalistic commodities. Next I shall consider the emergence of the commodity form out of private property in history. And following from this will be an examination of the theoretical import of the concept of commodification, which problematizes the commodity form by considering commodification to be always a matter of degree in history, a degree that is typically maintained by political and ideological supports that need to be included in any full account of historical outcomes. Arguably, "commodification" implies distinct levels of analysis based on different degrees of commodification and different spatial/temporal considerations. And finally I shall discuss some of the implications of the theory of the commodity form for subject formation.

WHAT IS A COMMODITY?

Marx's theory of capital is nothing else but the theory of the commodity form as it takes over and subsumes economic life. Or, put a little differently, the basic economic categories of capitalism are those required to think about the economic interconnections in a society that has become completely commodified. I refer to this most abstract level of theory as the theory of a purely capitalist society, the theory of capital's inner logic, or the theory of capital's deep structure, with each conceptualization emphasizing different aspects of the theory. Because commodification is assumed to be complete, the resulting commodity-economic logic can be theorized with considerable rigour. Thus the capitalistic concept "wage" arises from the commodification of labour-power, "rent" from the need for a commodity-economic logic to manage land, and "interest" from the commodification of funds that turns capital itself into an automatic interest-bearing force. Indeed, in the theory of capital's deep structural dynamics, all inputs and outputs of production must be completely commodified.[5] If this were not the case, there would

5. "The exact development of the concept of capital [is] necessary..." (G, 331); "...on the assumption that capital has conquered the whole of production – and that there a *commodity* (as distinct from a mere use-value) is no longer produced by any labourer who is himself the owner of the conditions of production for producing this commodity – that therefore only the capitalist is the producer of *commodities*... (S I, 158); "...we have to look at the phenomenon in its pure shape..." (C I, 203); "...it necessarily involves the exchange of equivalents, provided the phenomenon occurs in its purity" (C I, 260). "If we look at the creation

be no commodity-economic logic, capital could not be conceptualized as self-expanding value, and the economic as such could not be clearly distinguished from the political and ideological. It follows, then, that the commodity form only becomes fully developed in a purely capitalist society,[6] and in anything less than pure capitalism, many products that appear to be commodities may be only partially commodified or may not be specifically *capitalist* commodities.

Just as simple cells divide and differentiate in the formation of biological organisms, so does the commodity form divide and differentiate in the formation of capital as an integrated system of self-valorizing value (i.e. the continual production and reproduction of surplus-value). The theoretical starting point for Marx, then, is the simplest and most empty capitalistic commodity form, through whose development and differentiation the necessary inner connections of the basic economic categories of capital can be derived.[7] To say that all the fundamental categories of economic life are fully commodified, means that their quantitative or value side is not disrupted by their qualitative or use-value side with the result that as quantitative variables, they can all in principle be interrelated through the homogeneity of number. But unlike many

---

and the alteration of value for themselves, i.e. in their pure form, then the means of production, this physical shape taken on by constant capital, provides only the material in which, fluid, value-creating labour-power has to be incorporated" (C I, 323); "...a scientific analysis of competition is possible only if we can grasp the inner nature of capital..." (C I, 433). "Since we are essentially concerned here with grasping the pure, specific economic forms..." (G, 732). See also (S I, 160, 163, 167, 410; C I, 261–2, 269, 279, 494, 739, 763, 794, 811, 873, 899, 978, 1014; C II, 109, 186; C III, 117, 200, 241–3, 275, 291, 298, 311, 342, 344, 379, 428, 480, 516, 751, 755, 762, 927, 932, 954, 957, 970).

6. "In considering the essential relations of capitalist production it can therefore be assumed that the entire world of commodities ... are subordinated to the capitalist mode of production < for this is what is happening more and more completely..." (S I, 409).

7. "The *commodity* is the most elementary form of bourgeois wealth" (S I, 173). "The development of the product into a commodity is fundamental to capitalist production..." (S II, 423). "No analysis is possible ... if one failed to take the *value* of commodities in general as the point of departure" (S III, 111). "We start with the *commodity*, this specific social form of the product, as the foundation and prerequisite of capitalist production" (S III, 112). "Our investigation therefore begins with the analysis of the commodity" (C I, 125); "...the *form of the commodity* as the universally necessary social form of the product can only emerge as the *consequence of the capitalist mode of production*" (C I, 949).

other economists, Marx never forgets that the numerical thinking facilitated by the commodity form may consist of social power relations that can be thought as quantitative economic variables only because they have become commodified, objectified and reified.[8] In other words, political agency can only be pushed into the background to the extent that economic theory allows total commodification to take place in thought, and the only reason for following this theoretical path is to clarify the core structural dynamics of capital (or in other words, the economic) that would exist if capital were not interfered with by extra-economic practices. The aim of such a theory is to clarify capital's inner logic, its deep structural dynamics or, what is the same thing, the economic operating principles of a purely capitalist society.

With these notes in mind concerning the deep theoretical importance and extensiveness of the commodity form, it will be useful to outline some of its most basic characteristics. A commodity is first of all a thing (actually a unit of private property) that can be sold or bought, and, as such a unit, it is a social relation that entails exclusivity and power.[9] In the pure case, owners of private property have absolute control over their property including the right to sell it and the right to the total income that accrues from its sale. In a society where all production is the capitalistic production of commodities, ownership of the means of production entitles owners (capitalists) to appropriate the total product as their private property, even though the means of production only contribute a fraction

8. Marx is critical of the Physiocrats because "their general view of the nature of value ... is not a definite social mode of existence of human activity (labour), but consists of material things..." (S I, 46). "Bailey is a fetishist in that he conceives value, though not as a property of the individual object (considered in isolation), but as a *relation of objects to one another*, while it is only a representation in objects, an objective expression, of a relation between men, a social relation, the relationship of men to their reciprocal productive activity" (S III, 147).

9. "The fact that value – whether it exists as money or as commodities – and in the further development the conditions of labour confront the worker as the *property of other people*, as independent properties, means simply that they confront him as the *property* of the non-worker ... as a capitalist, he confronts them ... as the *subject* in which these things possess their own will, belong to themselves and are personified as independent forces" (S III, 476); "...value is here the subject. ... For the movement in the course of which it adds surplus-value is its own movement, its valorization is therefore self-valorization..." (C I, 255). "Conceptually, *competition* is nothing other than the inner *nature of capital*..." (G, 414).

of the value of the total output, and even though the value of the means of production is the result of previous labour. It follows that in a capitalist society, the commodity form, by virtue of its being a form of private property gives enormous structural power to the positionalities inhabited by capitalists.

Second, commodities have two sharply opposed characteristics: as values they differ only quantitatively and as use-values they differ qualitatively. The use-value of a commodity stems entirely from the qualitative material properties that make it useful; whereas value stems entirely from the social homogeneity of commodities whereby they differ only quantitatively.[10] Value must always be connected to a use-value wanted by someone, but value as capital strives to be indifferent to use-value in the sense that it would always prefer to focus single-mindedly on maximizing quantity in the form of profit. In order to behave according to the imperatives of capitalist rationality, capitalists must always be opportunistic (i.e. indifferent) towards use-values. If it suddenly becomes more profitable to produce whiskey than bibles, then capitalistic rational behaviour dictates a shift of production.[11] Profit forces capitalists to pay attention to use-value, but only as it serves the quantitative ends of profit-making. Since the overriding aim of capital is profit as pure quantity, it will never focus on the qualitative as an end in itself, but will only note use-value insofar as required to maximize profits.[12] Further, if not constrained by law, capital may engage in production that is destructive or dangerous to humans and the environment if it is

10. "As use-values, commodities differ above all in quality, while as exchange-values they can only differ in quantity, and therefore do not contain an atom of use-value" (C I, 128).

11. "Use-values are produced by capitalists only because and in so far as they form the material substratum of exchange-value..." (C I, 293). "For the use-value of labour-power to the capitalist as a capitalist does not consist in its *actual* use-value, in the usefulness of this particular concrete labour – that it is spinning labour, weaving labour, and so on. He is as little concerned with this as with the use-value of the product of this labour as such, since for the capitalist the product is a commodity ... not an article of consumption" (S I, 156).

12. "The objective content of the circulation we have been discussing – the valorization of value – is his subjective purpose, and it is only in so far as the appropriation of ever more wealth in the abstract is the sole driving force behind his operations that he functions as a capitalist, i.e., as capital personified and endowed with consciousness and will. Use-values must therefore never be treated as the immediate aim of the capitalist..." (C I, 254).

profitable to do so. This is part of what Marx means when he refers to "capital's indifference to use-value".[13] In a purely competitive capitalism, capital could not care less whether it is producing guns or butter, and will produce more of one or of the other entirely in accord with profit signals. It follows that in the fully developed capitalist commodity form, value subsumes use-value, or put a little differently, value manages use-value in accord with purely quantitative price and profit signals.[14]

Unlike neo-classical economists, Marx understands that in order to grasp the imperatives of capital expansion, the primary focus must be on the core profit-making activity of capitalists and not the final consumption of individual consumers. For this reason, he conceives the commodity from the point of view of the seller who is trying to make a profit and not the final individual consumer who is concerned equally with use-value and value.[15] From this seemingly small difference, stems two totally different worlds of economic theory. In the neo-classical "fantasy" world, classless sovereign consumers direct the economy by casting "dollar ballots" for use-values, thus ensuring that everyone's needs are maximally satisfied. In Marx's realistic theory of capital, the needs of consumers are met only

13. According to Marx, purchase and sale may be "spatially and temporally separate" and have a "mutually indifferent form of existence" (G, 148). "The reciprocal and all-sided dependence of individuals who are indifferent to one another forms their social connection" (G, 156). "Indifference towards any specific kind of labour presupposes a very developed totality of real kinds of labour..." (G, 104). "*Exchange* in and for itself gives these conceptually opposite moments an indifferent being; they exist independently of one another; their inner necessity becomes *manifest* in the crisis, which puts a forcible end to their seeming indifference towards each other" (G, 444); "...*the* use value which confronts money posited as capital, labour is not this or another labour, but labour pure and simple, abstract labour; absolutely indifferent to its particular *specificity* [*Bestimmtheit*], but capable of all specificities" (G, 296). "Firstly, capitalist production as such is indifferent to the particular use-values it produces. ... All that matters in any sphere of production is to produce surplus-value..." (C III, 297).
14. "And within the production process too – in so far as it is a valorization process – the means of production continue to be nothing but monetary value, indifferent towards the particular physical form, the specific use-value in which the exchange-value is clothed" (C I, 1012).
15. "...the commodity only becomes a commodity ... in so far as its owner does not relate to it as use-value. ... Appropriation through sale is the fundamental form of the social system of production..." (G, 881).

one-sidedly and generally in accord with enormous inequalities.[16] Capital has nothing to do with maximizing general welfare, rather it has to do with maximizing profits, which in turn generates class exploitation. Indeed, one can go further and claim that actually existing capitalism often has to do with what capitalists can get away with in terms of increasing profits by exploitation, oppression, environmental degradation and various forms of cheating, or, in general by forcing society to take on very large social costs generated by their profit-making.[17]

The aim of capital is to maximize quantity in the form of profit, and unless there is outside intervention, this aim will always override use-value considerations if there is an apparent conflict between the two. For example, if the profits of a capitalist bakery can be increased by adulterating bread (a not uncommon practice in Victorian England), then a capitalist baker will do so.[18] If, however, the result of this practice might be heavy fines (as a specific state intervention this is something that would not exist in purely competitive capitalism) that would reduce profits, then our bakery must no longer be indifferent to the reduced quality of its adulterated bread.

Marx makes it readily apparent that the competitive movement of prices in capitalism will not and can not maximize the social utilization of use-values, or, in other words, cannot maximize the quality of life of all citizens. Utilizing numerous totally unrealistic assumptions, neo-classical economics argues that the quantitative system of prices (it has no theory of value) will automatically maximize ("Pareto Optimality") the qualitative system of social well-being. In contrast, Marx demonstrates that even in a state of equilibrium, there

16. "The intimate connection between pangs of hunger suffered by the most industrious layers of the working class, and the extravagant consumption, coarse or refined, of the rich, for which capitalist accumulation is the basis, is only uncovered when the economic laws are known" (C I, 811).

17. "Here is some evidence of the broad limits within which clever directors can manipulate concepts [books] ... in the interest of their dividends" (C II, 259).

18. "Englishmen, with their good command of the Bible, knew well enough that man, unless by elective grace a capitalist, or a landlord, or the holder of a sinecure, is destined to eat his bread in the sweat of his brow, but they did not know that he had to eat daily in his bread a certain quantity of human perspiration mixed with the discharge of abscesses, cobwebs, dead cockroaches and putrid German yeast, not to mention alum, sand and other agreeable mineral ingredients" (C I, 359). See also (C I, 750, 1067).

will be systemic reasons, having to do mainly with class, why the value system will always cripple and degrade the use-value system. In short, the quantitative system of prices is inherently a poor manager of the qualitative system of human flourishing because underlying it is an indifference to use-value and a pronounced inequality of class that radically distorts demand.[19]

Besides his rigorous use of "commodity" as in capitalist commodity, Marx often uses "commodity" loosely to refer to products that have some commodity-like features in history, and he does the same thing with "use-value" when considered outside the capitalist mode of production.[20] Sometimes the concept "use-value" is used to mean about the same thing as "product", which may be the output of any mode of production or type of labour. In this usage, "use-value" simply refers to the qualitative material properties of any product, properties that make it wanted.[21] But this looser historical usage should not be confused with its usage in *Capital*, where value and use-value are always both connected and radically opposed such that the tension between the quantitative pursuit of short-term profit and the qualitative needs of society can be internalized as central to his theory (indeed one of the functions of periodic crises is to reduce the tension between value and use-value as a result of their becoming too divorced from each other). Thus the commodity form would quantitatively manage the use-value labour-power or the use-value land through the motion of value, but this quantitative management cannot avoid the massive unemployment associated with economic

19. "However the sale of commodities, the realization of commodity capital, and thus of surplus-value as well, is restricted not by the consumer needs of society in general, but by the consumer needs of a society in which the great majority are always poor and must always remain poor" (C II, 391); "'social need' which governs the principle of demand is basically conditioned by the relationship of the different classes and their respective economic position..." (C III, 282).
20. "Above all it will and must become clear ... to what extent use-value exists not only as presupposed matter, outside economics and its forms, but to what extent it enters into it" (G, 268).
21. "Use-value is not concerned with human activity as the source of the product, with its having been posited by human activity, but with its being for mankind" (G, 613). "Not only does the exchange-value not appear as determined by the use-value, but rather, furthermore, the commodity only becomes a commodity, only realizes itself as exchange-value, in so far as its owner does not relate to it as use-value" (G, 881).

crises, nor can it avoid the likely degradation of land resulting from its use in accord with short-term profit considerations.[22]

Value, then, is something social, or, to be more specific, it is the fundamental society-wide connector of capitalism based on a certain objectification or commodification of social relations. Commodities are products that are always produced to be exchanged for money that the capitalist hopes will accumulate as profit.[23] Barter in itself does not allow value to emerge as an objective society-wide category. The move that Friedman and nearly every other mainstream economist makes from barter to capitalist exchange is ideologically convenient because it pictures capitalism as a simple extension of a barter between consuming households or consuming hunters that get what they want through totally voluntary barter exchanges.[24] Marx is very clear on this. Barter is a thoroughly pre-capitalist category that can only confuse our thinking about the nature of the commodity form unless it is conceived initially as an external, impersonal relation between distinct communities that highlights at least one basic feature of the commodity form: the essential otherness of persons engaging in capitalist exchange relations (C I, 182). And even in this case, it only manifests the boundaries associated with the commodity form, for it cannot allow the key value property of capitalistically produced commodities to emerge. Commodity exchange creates a connection between selves that are other to each other.[25]

The commodity form is fundamentally a circulation form in the sense that it only becomes fully developed with the society-wide exchange of commodities for money. Marx continually refers to the exchange of commodities for money and money for commodities as a "metamorphosis" in order to underline the fact that in order to understand value, circulation must be assumed as a series of *quid*

22. There are many references in Marx on the tendency for capitalism to degrade the land: "...instead of a conscious and rational treatment of the land as permanent communal property, as the inalienable condition for the existence and reproduction of the chain of human generations, we have the exploitation and the squandering of the powers of the earth..." (C III, 948–9). See also (C I, 637–8, 752; C II, 252, 322, 431; C III, 216, 754, 757, 950).
23. "The concept of value ... is the most abstract expression of capital itself..." (G, 776).
24. Both Ricardo and Friedman conceptualize capital "merely as *instrument of labour* or *material for labour*" (G, 309).
25. See Sohn-Rethel (1978) for a fuller discussion of the "othering" force of the commodity form.

pro quo exchanges in which value does not change its quantitative content but only its form.[26] The origin of profit cannot be located in the realm of circulation because it cannot be based on the assumption that one group always voluntarily buys dear and sells cheap. It follows that the circulation form of capital, M-C-M' (M = money and C = commodity), where the second M is systematically larger than the first appears to be paradoxical, if not absurd. And it is this absurdity that drives the theory on to consider how capitalist circulation forms relate to capitalist production relations. M-C-M' can only make sense when it subsumes the labour and production process, and it is only the commodity labour-power that can systematically produce more value than it costs. In other words, C must be expanded into commodity inputs (including labour-power), a labour and production process, and commodity outputs containing surplus-value or profits that derive from the exploitation of labour-power. It is the commodity form that creates the conditions for capital's revolutionary dynamism that continually searches for more productive technologies and new commodities in order to maximize profits.

Once the basic production relation between capital and labour has been subsumed to the commodity form, it is then possible to theorize the division of surplus-value amongst industrial capitalists with differing capital intensities and between industrial capitalists and commercial capitalists, financial capitalists and landlords. Marx argues that these distribution relations are ultimately determined by the continual movement of capital from less profitable to more profitable sectors, which always pushes the profit rate towards an average.

When commodification is complete, Marx demonstrates that it is possible to construct a theory that presents the interrelations of basic capitalist economic categories as "necessary inner connections". This is because when the commodity form reigns all economic categories are either different forms of value, potential value (labour-power and the industrial reserve army), or structures that support capital as a self-expanding quantity. In other words it is the perfected commodity form that enables us to think socio-economic interconnections quantitatively and/or structurally, where the structures support

26. "The money-owner, who is as yet only a capitalist in larval form, must buy his commodities at their value, sell them at their value, and yet at the end of the process withdraw more value from circulation than he threw into it at the beginning. His emergence as a butterfly must, and yet must not, take place in the sphere of circulation" (C I, 269).

quantitative thinking. This culminates in an economy coordinated through price signals to maximize profits. In prosaic words, the result is a commodity-economic logic that is hell-bent on profit and nothing but profit.[27] At the same time as this theory reveals capital's deep structural dynamics in quantitative terms, it sharply poses the limits of mathematics, since no actual economy is completely commodified, with the result that mathematical outcomes will always be disrupted by power relations and human agency at more concrete levels of analysis.

BARTER AND THE COMMODITY FORM

From Adam Smith, to Jean Baptiste Say, to Milton Friedman, there is a tradition of economic thought that sees no qualitative difference between simple barter and the society-wide production of commodities for profit. For example, Nobel Prize winning economist Milton Friedman (1982, 14) claims that there is no substantial difference between an economy based on a fully developed capitalist economy and autonomous households voluntarily exchanging products through barter. As he puts it, "the central characteristic of the market technique of achieving coordination [without coercion] is fully displayed in the simple exchange economy that contains neither enterprises nor money". After all, isn't it obvious that if two households voluntarily agree to an exchange, it must be because they mutually benefit, and if a capitalist economy is simply an expansion of this, then its exchanges must also be free and mutually beneficial. According to Friedman (ibid.), money is simply "introduced as a means of facilitating exchange...", and enterprises are introduced to be "intermediaries between individuals in their capacities as suppliers of service and as purchasers of goods" (Friedman 1982, 13–14). It follows that, according to Friedman, the economic life of each individual or each household is totally free under capitalism, since capitalism is in principle a coercionless system coordinated entirely through mutually beneficial voluntary exchanges between individuals. Every one of these propositions advanced by Friedman is sharply and convincingly opposed by Marx. Friedman starts with voluntary barter between individual households, and by simple extension, arrives at coercionless capitalism. Marx starts with the

27. "He is fanatically intent on the valorization of value; consequently he ruthlessly forces the human race to produce for production's sake" (C I, 739).

commodity form, which by commodifying labour-power and nature and subsuming their use to short-term profit maximization results in the exploitation of labour-power and the possible degradation of nature.

In its fully developed form, the commodity must be always exchanged for money.[28] Barter is essentially an exchange of use-values by two consumers that does not allow value to emerge as a force that could subsume use-value.[29] Hence, it is qualitatively distinct from the exchange of commodities. In its simplest form a barter is an exchange of qualitatively different products between two individuals that may result in, say, an exchange of 50 pounds of gold for a cup of water. Such an exchange would indicate that the owner of the gold was very thirsty indeed and, in a nutshell, that is why barter is not a good indicator of value, which objectively equates all commodities irrespective of the strength of subjective desires in isolated contexts. With barter, exchange ratios may be a one-time-only ratio established according to the subjective desires or power relations of the individuals involved.[30] Furthermore, the abstract possibility of crisis that results from the fact that commodities may not succeed in being transformed into money, does not exist in the case of barter.[31] But for Marx value is not something purely subjective

28. "...the development of commodities necessarily leads to the formation of money" (S II, 164). Referring to Proudhon, Marx writes: "Thus, he has never understood that money is a necessary aspect of the commodity" (S III, 523).
29. "After the economists have most splendidly shown that barter, in which both acts [purchasing and selling] coincide, does not suffice for a more developed form of society and mode of production, they then suddenly look at the kind of barter which is mediated by money as if it were not so mediated, and overlook the *specific* character of the transaction" (G, 198). "Here the existence of capital is denied, in order to transform capitalists into people who carry out the simple operation C-M-C and who produce for individual consumption and not *as* capitalists with the aim of enrichment..." (S II, 534).
30. Remarking on a passage from Ricardo, Marx writes: "Here, therefore, firstly *commodity*, in which the contradiction between exchange-value and use-value exists, becomes mere product (use-value) and therefore the exchange of commodities is transformed into mere barter of products, of simple use-values. This is a return not only to the time before capitalist production, but even to the time before there was simple commodity production..." (S II, 501).
31. "The difficulty of converting the commodity into money, of selling it, only arises from the fact that the commodity must be turned into money but money need not be immediately turned into commodity..." (S II, 509).

and local. It is a result of all commodities expressing their values in relation to each other through money acting as universal equivalent, and as such, it has a certain society-wide stability and durability even as prices continually change.

If we go back far enough in history, then no society would have invented money and exchanges of products would presumably take the form of barter. Adam Smith (1993, 45) imagines such a situation as a kind of state of nature in which to ground his labour theory of value: "If among a nation of hunters, for example, it usually costs twice the labour to kill a beaver which it does to kill a deer, one beaver should naturally exchange for or be worth two deer." Let us compare this quotation with one from Marx (C I, 182):

Things are in themselves external to man, and therefore alienable. In order that this alienation [Veräusserung] may be reciprocal, it is only necessary for men to agree tacitly to treat each other as the private owners of those alienable things, and, precisely for that reason, as persons who are independent of each other. But this relationship of reciprocal isolation and foreignness does not exist for the members of a primitive community. ... The exchange of commodities begins [my emphasis] where communities have their boundaries....

From the point of view of Marx, Smith is reading back into a community of hunters, where even the barter of products would rarely occur much less the exchange of commodities, both nationhood and private property.[32] What Marx emphasizes is that in the first instance the commodity form entails the sort of impersonal relationship that can only develop between two communities or when private property creates boundaries between individuals. In other words, a product takes on its first commodity-like characteristic (i.e. otherness) when a community offers to barter it with a foreign community.[33]

Having said this, it is necessary to emphasize immediately that for Marx there is a world of difference between products being bartered and commodities exchanged. For example, let's say that in 1750 Hudson Bay Company traders exchanged one bottle of "fire water" to two Canadian indigenous hunters for 30 beaver pelts. This exchange ratio may have more to do with a certain addiction to fire water on the part of the hunters than with the quantity of labour embodied in the two products. Further, on the following day, the Hudson Bay

32. In most such communities there are status arrangements for dividing the product.
33. According to Weber (1978, 636): "the market is the most impersonal relationship of practical life into which humans can enter with one another".

traders may meet two different hunters who demand 5 bottles of fire water for 30 beaver pelts. In other words, without money acting as universal equivalent, barter ratios may not only be quite arbitrary, but may vary wildly depending on the subjective desires of the parties to the barter. In fact, unless it is subsumed to commodity exchange, barter can only be regularized by custom, for there would be no way to consistently equate labour time, which may differ enormously in skill. For these reasons, Marx does not try to derive the commodity form from barter, but instead begins his theory with the capitalist commodity form in its simplest and most basic outline. As I proceed, the sense in which his entire theory of capital fills in this outline and the sense in which the commodity form presupposes the money form from the beginning will become clearer. Suffice it to say here, that for Marx bourgeois economists tend to root the commodity in barter and this benefits them ideologically by denying the possibility of exploitation or of periodic crises, since with barter there are not typically huge stocks of commodities waiting to be bought.

Rooting the commodity in barter also makes it appear as if the commodity is a natural historical evolution and it papers over the radical break that distinguishes capitalism from all other modes of production. For while the commodity form may never in history (including capitalism) be totally in control of economic life, yet it is of central importance in capitalism, and it is precisely this that gives capitalism its historically unique character, and, as a result, explains so much that is central to the modern world.

THE COMMODITY FORM AND PRODUCTS

Marx makes a very sharp distinction between products and commodities.[34] Only those products that are capitalistically produced

34. "There are two points here which are characteristic of the method of the bourgeoisie's economic apologists. The first is the identification of the circulation of commodities with the direct exchange of products, achieved simply by abstracting from their differences. The second is the attempt to explain away the contradictions of the capitalist process of production by dissolving the relations between persons engaged in that process of production into the simple relations arising out of the circulation of commodities. The production and circulation of commodities are however phenomena which are to be found in diverse modes of production, even if they vary in extent and importance. If we are only familiar with the abstract categories of circulation, which are common to all of them, we cannot know anything of their *differentia specifica*, and we cannot therefore pronounce judgment on them" (C I, 209).

by commodified labour-power in a purely capitalist society are full-fledged commodities.[35] Products produced by self-employed persons, by slaves, by feudal peasants, or by voluntary unpaid labour are only partial commodities even if they are produced for sale on a market. And products produced by individuals for their own consumption are use-values but not values. A fully developed commodity is the output of a capitalist production process, produced for an indefinite and impersonal market, and produced for an exchange that the capitalist hopes will yield a profit.

Even at the start of Marx's theory of capital, the commodity form is conceived as that form whose logical development can become a fully developed capitalist commodity. For this to be the case, it must be conceived in the beginning from the point of view of the seller (value) and not of the consumer (use-value).[36] It must be conceived in a form that can commodify labour-power and will become the materialization of both value and surplus-value through the exploitation of labour. But in constructing a theory, patience is required, as it is not possible to introduce all distinctions at once. Marx allows what starts as a relatively empty form with minimum presuppositions to logically unfold towards completion as category after category becomes subsumed to the commodity form in its increasingly specified dynamic of expansion.

Starting with the simplest and most abstract commodity form, Marx moves logically to generate a sequence of economic categories that show how this form can bring all the most basic economic categories within its unfolding logic. The aim is to unveil the inner logic of capital as a logic internal to the commodity form, and this assumes that all production is a purely competitive capitalistic production of commodities. His theory explains what happens when the commodity form is allowed to completely take over economic life. By demonstrating the imperatives that are operative when capital is left to its own commodity-economic devices, Marx's theory can bring into focus the necessary inner connections amongst the economic categories of capital without the distorting interventions of extra-economic forces whether political or ideological.[37]

35. In discussing the third form of the circuit, the circuit of commodity capital, Marx writes: "...the valorized capital, in the shape of the total commodity product, forms the starting-point, and possesses the form of capital in movement, commodity capital" (C II, 173–4).
36. Sekine makes this point very clearly (1997, Vol. I, 26–7).
37. Marx uses various phrases to describe his theoretical object: "inner laws", "inner logic", "immanent laws", "economic relations in their purity",

It is unique in the social sciences to have a theory that can objectively present the fundamental nature of the economic under capitalism and therefore serve as a touchstone for thinking about situations where the economic is only relatively autonomous. And it is precisely by letting the commodity form have its way and by allowing it to generate the categories required for it to organize economic life according to its own logic that this unique degree of objectivity is possible. While it is beyond the scope of this book to explore the implications of this in depth, I will at least present a more extended discussion of the claim for objectivity in Chapter 4.[38]

Marx's radical break between capitalistically produced commodities and commodities produced by self-employed labour is particularly important given the ideological role of self-employment in mainstream economic theory. Schematically this distinction has to do with the differences between the circulation forms C-M-C and M-C-M' and the sorts of labour-and-production process typically associated with each. With C-M-C a watchmaker produces watches that are sold for money used to buy the conveniences of life. Because the watchmaker produces a particular use-value, this use-value is invested with her life-energy and skill, such that even if her income should decline perilously, it would be difficult to shift to a more lucrative product, say shoes. Further, the purpose of watchmaking in this case is to get other use-values that are needed to live the life expected of watchmakers. Should the watchmaker make more than this, she would presumably buy more use-values resulting in a more commodious living.

Capital is first introduced by Marx (C I, 256) as the circulation form M-C-M' (M = money, C = commodity and M' = M+ΔM, and ΔM = surplus-value), or the use of money to make more money as in buying cheap and selling dear. This circulation form is sharply contrasted with C_1-M-C_2, which involves exchanging an unwanted for a wanted commodity (C I, 250). This sharp contrast needs to be emphasized, for according to Marx it is one of the fundamental differences between all bourgeois economists, who want to conceive of capital in terms of coercionless satisfaction of need (as in C-M-C), and Marx, who emphasizes the pursuit of profit. There would be no

---

"capital in general", "society as economic structure", and "capital in its basic inner structure". This last expression is perhaps close to Chomsky's "deep structures" of language.

38. For a more extended discussion see also Albritton (1999) and Albritton (forthcoming [a]).

reason to carry out M-C-M since the starting point and end point are exactly the same unless the second M is larger than the first. In order to stress the importance of profit, Marx claims that M-C-M is totally indifferent to the use-value of C as long as it yields an increase in M, and will therefore opportunistically shift from one C to another to maximize surplus-value ΔM.[39] Third, C_1-M-C_2 comes to a halt when an unwanted use-value is exchanged for a wanted use-value; but in sharp contrast M-C-M', where the motive is profit, is in principle unlimited in the sense that the larger the profit the better.[40] Indeed, given the nature of money as pure buying power, M' would seem to be boundless.

In contrast with the petty commodity form C-M-C, which involves exchanging use-values not wanted with those wanted, M-C-M' is the circulation form specific to capital, in which the aim is unlimited money-making. In order to achieve this, ideally capital would move easily from less profitable to more profitable production processes, and this is significantly advanced by factory production which deskills and commodifies labour-power. Assuming in the main that capital needs unskilled labour and that this exists in a mobile industrial reserve army, by itself labour poses no obstacle to the mobility of capital in its pursuit of profit. It is the extension of the commodity form to labour-power and land, two commodities that cannot be produced by capital, that enables the commodity form to eventually subsume most of the labour-and-production process to M-C-M' in capitalist societies.

Where C-M-C is prominent, most labour is self-employed and skilled, and, most importantly, its aim is to attain wanted use-values. Such an economy will lack the mobility and dynamism of capitalism, such that shortages can easily occur as supply can only very slowly adjust to changes in demand. In this case the motion of value represented by M is constrained by use-value represented by C, and hence the motion of value cannot subsume economic life. But for the commodity form to become dominant, the motion of value must subsume use-value, and this is maximally achieved with

39. (C I, 254, 449, 612, 644, 739, 1001, 1012; C II, 48, 137, 159, 233, 297, 395, 427; C III, 134, 297, 351, 935, 967, 1019).
40. "...money is independent of all limits, that is it is the universal representative of material wealth because it is directly convertible into any other commodity" (C I, 231). "Use value in itself does not have the boundlessness of value as such. Given objects can be consumed as objects of needs only up to a certain level" (G, 405).

industrial capitalism. And yet, it must always be remembered that at the level of history commodification of all inputs and outputs is never as complete as Marx assumes in the theory of capital's deep structures, where capital is understood to be "self-expanding value", precisely because with self-expanding value political and ideological supports are pushed into the background and reduced to being passive reflections of the economic.[41] And while this abstract level of analysis is important for revealing capitalist social forms in their purest manifestations, more concrete levels of analysis that enable us to systematically unpack the social practices and power relations that have been absorbed into the commodity form in the theory of capital's inner logic are also required. Indeed, in Chapter 5 I argue for three levels of analysis: the theory of capital's deep structures, mid-range theory, and historical analysis.[42]

In its fully developed form, the commodity is a capitalistically produced commodity always intended to be exchanged for money. While in actual empirical situations commodities produced by self-employed persons often freely intermingle with capitalistically produced commodities, theoretically it is crucially important to distinguish the two. For just as barter is a pre-capitalist form of exchange, so is self-employed production a pre-capitalist or non-capitalist form of production. The obvious reason for this is that in a system in which most production is self-employed, the nature of capitalist profits cannot be grasped. Marx demonstrates that capitalist profits are based upon the exploitation of labour, and with self-employed labour no clear conception of surplus-value or rate of surplus-value can emerge. But there is also a deeper reason. Self-employed workers are typically very attached to the use-values they learn to produce through a long apprenticeship, and cannot with indifference shift to producing something completely different simply because they think they may make more money. Only with the greatest difficulty can a baker become a watchmaker or a spinster[43] a blacksmith. Whereas in competitive capitalism, where

41. "This juridical relation, whose form is the contract, whether as part of a developed legal system or not, is a relation between two wills which mirrors the economic relation" (C I, 178).
42. For a much fuller discussion of levels of analysis see Albritton (1991).
43. Since women typically did the spinning in cottage production and since spinning was one of the few ways a single woman could be self-employed, "spinster" has come to mean "single woman", while its original meaning has been forgotten.

there is mobility of capital and labour, and most production is the production of unskilled labour in factories, capitalists need only shift to buying different inputs (in practice there would be costs involved, but higher profits might well justify the costs) or possibly to investing their profits in a different industry or into financial paper with greater profits. The typical attachment of self-employed workers to use-value means that value cannot easily emerge and the economy cannot be governed by the rate of profit as it is under competitive capitalism. For this reason, economies based largely upon self-employed labour (have there ever been any?) only work when there is slow economic change or where they are subsumed to capitalism. It is possible to imagine a small local economy so organized, but not a large one, because lack of mobility associated with petty commodity production would imply prices that are only local.

THE COMMODITY FORM AND HISTORY

Although Marx begins *Capital* with the commodity form emptied of all but the bare essentials required for it to become, as the theory unfolds, the fully developed capitalistic commodity form, it must be remembered that in history the commodity form is rooted in and evolves out of the institution of private property. As Marx (C I, 272) points out, it is the enclosure of the commons in England that plays a crucial role both in the concentration of wealth that is a prerequisite to the private ownership of the means of production and in commodifying labour-power by divorcing it from the means of production and thus "freeing it up" to be employed by privately owned means of production.

Private property in its basic meaning entails a boundary within which the owner has total or exclusive control (except as constrained by law), and it entails a general recognition and enforcement of such boundaries. In other words, private property is a relation of exclusion constituted by a boundary, and it is a relation of power in the sense that within the boundary the owner has no opposition to his will. He is the all powerful sovereign, as in "a man's home is his castle". The owner has the absolute right to control the use made of his private property including its sale. Taking a factory as an example, insofar as private ownership is not constrained by laws or worker's organizations, the owner has the right to organize the productive activity that takes place within it including hiring, disciplining and firing at will, and has the right to the product of that labour even though it is not his labour that produced it. The commodity form, and its most fundamental offspring the money form, essentially act to mobilize private property towards the single goal of profit maximization. Each commodity is a piece of private property that can potentially be sold for a profit, and once the commodity form is in charge of social life, competition intensifies and the life energy of that society strains to maximize profits, creating an enormous dynamism that in its single-minded profit-orientation is often either blind to costly "externalities", or treats them as the unfortunate costs of doing business. Marx's *Capital* demonstrates that the theory of capital's inner logic is the theory of the commodity form having become totally hegemonic as a commodity-economic logic. In other words, when commodification is complete, the motion given the commodity by sellers and buyers creates a commodity-economic logic that can reproduce and expand capitalist socio-economic life.

In history the commodification of labour-power is never complete both because there is always expenditure of labour that is not commodified (self-employed, domestic labour, voluntary labour, forced labour, and so forth) and because that labour which is commodified is only partially so given that workers can and do resist having their labour-power completely commodified. Indeed, complete commodification implies being subjected to the arbitrary will of the capitalist, which further implies a total lack of job security. In unconstrained pure capitalism, each day each worker may or may not have a job, and if not, the subsistence income that he or she might have earned is forever lost. Further, given the cyclical vagaries of capitalism, massive unemployment and starvation (assuming no safety net) may always be just around the corner. Since such radical insecurity would be intolerable, workers have always tried to combine to multiply their powers of resistance against such insecurity within neighbourhoods, factories and states. The fact that the first anti-combination acts in England were legislated in the seventeenth century is one indication of how far back in the history of capitalism worker combinations were seen to be threatening.

From the point of view of capital, one of the most frightening spectres is an ongoing labour shortage, which would give workers enormous bargaining power. The main check on this occurring is the existence of a large industrial reserve army that by increasing the competition for jobs amongst workers can serve to keep wages down. Historically this demographic problem of capitalism has been solved by encouraging high birth rates, by the influx of workers from the agrarian sector, by legal and illegal immigration, by guest-worker programmes, and by moving production to regions with large impoverished populations. What I mean to emphasize here is that at the level of historical analysis there may be a variety of political and ideological factors that play an important role regulating relative surplus population both nationally and internationally. There may also be historically specific legislation or belief systems in particular countries that serve to either increase or limit the insecurity of workers. This means that labour-power may be commodified, decommodified, or recommodified.[44] To increase the minimum-wage, unemployment insurance and welfare would contribute to a process of decommodification; whereas to weaken trade unions, lower the social wage and increase competition for scarce jobs would constitute a process of recommodification (this is a central characteristic of neo-liberalism with its massive shift of wealth from the public to the private sector).

Fully commodified labour-power implies complete lack of organization of labour in its contracting with capital, and it implies a steady supply of labour-power to be drawn from an industrial reserve army. It also implies mobile workers competing for jobs and for wages such that workers will change jobs when higher wages are to be had until wages become more or less equalized across industries. Insofar as there is a good supply of workers, capitalists can focus purely on the use of labour-power to expand value, while being totally indifferent to use-value considerations such as the living conditions, health and well-being of workers. In *Capital*, Marx uses the example of the difficulties in getting legislation in nineteenth-century England to protect children from the brutal exploitation of capitalists to illustrate capital's indifference to use-value and its willingness to sacrifice even the most basic human decency on the altar of profit.[45] Fully commodified labour-power implies that capital can hire any labour that it wants and can exploit it to the limits of human endurance, and if workers do not like it, they can go look for another job or be fired.

To a certain extent organization is power, so that for workers to organize and assert their collective power already represents a step towards the decommodification of labour-power. Indeed, any

44. See Williams (2005) for an interesting discussion of various forms of decommodification in today's global economy.
45. "Competition with other capitalists, they said, did not allow them to limit the hours worked by children..." (C I, 381).

constraints or limitations placed on a purely competitive labour market can be conceptualized as a movement away from complete commodification. In England one of the first such steps was the Factory Acts of 1833 that placed limits on the length of the working day for children and women and limited the standard working day for adult males to 15 hours (from 5:30 am to 8:30 pm) (C I, 390).

The enclosure of the commons in England was a step towards the commodification of land, but land was too political and too basic to social stability to be fully subsumed to the hyper-mobility of the fully developed capitalist commodity form. Thus, while there was a small land market in early modern England, nearly all the great estates could only be inherited through accepting "strict settlement", which meant that future generations were always committed to neither dividing nor selling the land. It could be argued that strict settlement served indirectly to protect the land. Given capital's indifference to use-value and strong orientation towards short-term profits, but for the constraint of landlords there is no reason why capital should not despoil and desertify the land if it is profitable to do so. And today, a dawning awareness of the ecological hazards ahead has given a renewed impetus to protecting land against the often dangerous consequences of the free-wheeling commodity form.

Unlike labour-power and land, money in its commodity form can be capitalistically produced. Money in a purely capitalist society is a commodity (typically gold) that is qualitatively transformed by being set aside to function as universal reflector of value. In a completely commodified society there would only be gold and convertible paper money, or what might be called a simple gold standard. With gold-based money, presumably the over or under supply of money would be regulated by changes in the rate of profit in the gold producing sector. But even in Victorian England there was never a pure gold standard, as the state and the Bank of England intervened in various ways to prevent the excessive outflow of gold in certain situations. Hegemonic capitalist powers have generally had some political influence over the international monetary system in order to protect themselves from short-term balance of payments difficulties, and national monetary authorities have often had some influence on either the money-supply or interest rate because of their destabilizing potential. Once again, when we look at the example of money, we see that it has not been fully commodified in history, and that even an extreme neo-liberal like Friedman (1982, 42) does not advocate "a fully automatic gold standard" because in today's world it would lack the flexibility required of money.

While labour-power, land and money are assumed to be fully commodified at the level of the theory of capital's logic, it is readily apparent that at the level of historical analysis it is necessary to unpack the commodity form in order to explore the power implications of the interconnections amongst partially decommodified commodities. And while labour-power, land and money present perhaps the greatest challenges to complete commodification there are other candidates such as technology, agriculture, debt expansion, housing, infrastructure, production with large economies of scale, or very large investments that only pay for themselves over a long period of time.

If we look at the classic case of the development of capitalism in England, we see an increasing commodification of fundamental economic variables up to at least the mid nineteenth century. With the merger movement, increased state intervention, and imperialism in the late nineteenth century, commodification no longer feeds off itself as a self-deepening process. While more and more products take on the commodity form, in some areas of economic life power relations that had been at least partially displaced or absorbed by the commodity form re-emerge. For example, as workers become organized into trade unions and political parties, the state must more actively intervene to maintain the degree of commodification of labour-power required for capital accumulation to continue. Capitalism in the twentieth century, then, is no longer simply a progressive commodification of economic life, rather it is a mixture of commodification, decommodification and recommodification with regard to the variety of dimensions that make up economic life and the variety of economic formations that make up the globe.

WHY THE CONCEPTION OF COMMODIFICATION IS SO IMPORTANT

Not only do most economists neglect thinking deeply about precisely what a commodity is, they also tend to treat the commodity and other economic variables as simply given. In contrast, Marx tends to problematize all economic variables by seeing them first as social relations which only become completely commodified in pure capitalism.[46] Complete commodification implies that the commodity

46. "In this quite alienated form of profit and in the same measure as the form of profit hides its inner core, capital more and more acquires a material form, is transformed more and more from a relationship into a thing, but a thing which embodies, which has absorbed, the social

form is in charge to such an extent that value can expand itself without relying on extra-economic force. In such a situation it is the commodity form as the rate of profit that becomes the prime regulator. Thus resources continually shift from sectors with lower rates of profit to sectors with higher ones and the rate of expansion of value largely depends on the average rate of profit. Accurate numerical relations between economic variables depend on total commodification, because once commodification is partial and this partial commodification is partially supported by qualitative distinct institutions and human agency, it becomes difficult to determine the extent to which relatively autonomous political or ideological practices condition or determine quantitative outcomes. It may even be difficult to determine the weight of various causes where it is primarily economic power that is the focus. For example, does the high profit rate of a global monopoly producer come from shifting value from the Third World, from suppliers of inputs, from the retail sector, from the financial sector, competitive sector, state sector, from workers, or consumers? It is even more difficult to determine the effect of laws in England in the 1840s that made it dangerous to strike on the level of wages and profits, and yet more difficult to measure the impact of racist ideology on facilitating the East India Company's profits from its very significant opium trade with China.

From the point of view of the "autistic" economics of the mainstream, a concept like commodification would be subversive, for it suggests that the market is always to be bracketed.[47] Commodification, which always admits of degrees, invites the consideration of the role of political and ideological practices in maintaining types and degrees of commodification. It follows that markets in actual history are never purely economic phenomena. Markets are always more or less marketized, depending on degrees and types of commodification and on power relations that tend to artificially maintain or disrupt

---

relationship, a thing which has acquired a fictitious life and independent existence in relation to itself, a natural-supernatural entity; in this form of *capital and profit* it appears superficially as a ready-made precondition. It is the form of its reality, or rather its real form of existence. And it is the form in which it exists in the consciousness and is reflected in the imagination of its representatives, the capitalists" (S III, 483). And one might add the representatives of the capitalists in the academic discipline of economics.

47. In the theory of capital's deep structures, the market is in charge, but at more concrete levels of analysis, we can peel back its layers to expose the power relations behind it.

arenas of marketized practice. There are no pure markets in history, there are only impure markets.

With the concept "fetishism", Marx shows how social relations get disappeared into the commodity form in pure capitalism. And since pure capitalism never exists in empirical history, this should alert us to the need for economic analysis to unpack the commodity form, opening it to relatively autonomous political and ideological forces in the move from abstract theory to more concrete levels of analysis.[48] But this unpacking and opening up of the commodity form is bound to be resisted by capitalist ideologues, because markets would no longer have any hallowed status whatsoever, and we could freely consider every kind of intervention into every kind of market as required to democratically manage markets so as to serve the needs of social justice.

If the commodity is the primary socio-economic connector, then the degree of commodification will determine the degree to which social relations have become objectified or reified.[49] Fortunately social relations are never totally commodified in history because this would imply that insofar as they were economic, social relations would be totally determined by a commodity-economic logic and human agency would be reduced simply to propelling this logic. On the other hand, a price system can only be mathematically determinate insofar as economic objects alter their values in relation to each other in systematic ways. If instead of following the imperatives of a commodity-economic logic, human agency introduces relatively autonomous changes, then the price system becomes mathematically indeterminate. At the same time, the commodity-economic logic acting through existing institutions still exerts causal pressures, only now these pressures need to be thought in relation to causal pressures that cannot be traced back solely to this logic.[50] In short, complete commodification introduces the automaticity that makes quantitative theorizing possible, while at the same time it demonstrates the need for the theorization of relatively autonomous institutional practices at levels of analysis more concrete than pure capitalism.

48. "In its pure form, the circulation process necessitates the exchange of equivalents, but in reality processes do not take place in their pure form" (C I, 262).
49. "Capital, however, necessarily produces its product as a *commodity*. This is why as capitalist production, i.e. capital, develops, the general laws governing the commodity evolve in proportion..." (C I, 950).
50. "In reality the mobility of capital is impeded by obstacles which we cannot consider in the present context" (C I, 1013).

Remember that the theory of capital's deep structures is one in which *all* production is the capitalistic production of commodities. Such an assumption is required in order to get complete clarity on the dynamics of capital's commodity-economic logic. However, such a theory cannot account for self-employed labour, domestic labour, volunteer labour, indentured labour, slave labour, prison labour, or extra-legal or quasi-legal labour, to simply name some of the more prominent types of non-capitalist labour that may take place in any actual capitalist society. In order to think clearly about how these types of labour articulate with the dynamics of capitalist profit-making, it helps to first understand capital's inner dynamic. Any attempt to move from mathematical equations directly to empirical history, will necessarily be unable to adequately account for non-capitalist economic forces and for forces that are at least partially extra-economic. It follows that historical specificity can never be understood as a function of a mathematical equation.

The main point here is that the concept "commodification" opens up a way of moving theoretically from theorizing capital's inner logic to theorizing capitalist history without imposing the procrustean bed of mathematical models directly on history. This is because "commodification" invites the consideration of degrees, not only of commodification but of decommodification and recommodification. It enables us to understand why in the one case of complete commodification mathematical formulae are possible and why at more concrete levels of analysis the search for explanations based on mathematical equations is completely misplaced. It facilitates the theorization of how non-capitalist quasi-commodities and non-capitalist modes of labour articulate with capital's logic. It encourages us to think about the ways in which degrees and types of commodification are supported and opposed by relatively autonomous non-economic or quasi-economic practices. And all of this undermines the extreme reification of *the* market characteristic of nearly all mainstream economic theorizing. It opens the possibility of bringing the theorization of economic power and human agency back into economic theory, and of bringing to an end the fetishization of the market.

THE COMMODITY FORM AND SUBJECTIVITY

By theorizing the commodity form as complete, Marx invites us to consider the impact of capital on subject formation in its starkest terms. To put it a little differently, he invites us to consider which forms of subjectivity would be necessary to or at least would be encouraged by economic life in a purely capitalist society. Of course, in any actual historical society, the commodity form may not be the most important influence on the construction of some aspects of subjectivity, but insofar as capitalism is a dominant force in the modern world, we can expect a major impact of the commodity form on subject formation in general.

Hegel (1971, 40–6) begins his *Philosophy of Right* with the legal subject understood as the externalization of the will into the creation of private property.[51] Though Hegel is writing in an early phase of capitalist development in Prussia, his work interestingly foreshadows aspects of a more developed capitalism to come, while at the same time extending pre-capitalist traditions. For example, his legal subject is followed by a moral subject, who, through a process of internalization, develops a soul and conscience. Finally an ethical or political subject synthesizes the external and internal into institutions appropriate to the full development of both legal and moral subjects. The synthesis of the legal, moral and political subject can be called "the rational subject."

While his ideal of the rational subject has a certain appeal, from the point of view of capital Hegel's efforts fall short because he fails to understand the extent to which the legal subject in its highest perfection is not only specific to capitalism, but also, as the dominant subject form in pure capitalism, displaces altogether both the moral and political subject.[52] Further, far from being universal, his moral subject turns out to be an idealized Christian subject, and his political/ethical subject depends on a capitalism being constrained by "organic" feudal institutions (supposedly to counter the atomizing tendencies of civil society) that were already passing away as Hegel wrote his book in the early years of the emergence of capitalism in Prussia.

51. "Nothing could be more curious than Hegel's development of private property in land. Man as a person must give his will actuality as the soul of external nature, and hence take possession of this nature as his private property ... a man must be a landowner if he is to realize himself as a person" (C III, 752).
52. Capital as such does not produce and does not require moral or political subjects. Indeed, in history, more often than not the most moral or political subjects resist capital, attempt to reform it, or devote their lives to helping those damaged by capitalism.

Strictly from the point of view of capital in a purely capitalist society, only the legal subject must be recognized.[53] Class subjectivity is a structural position that capital does not recognize, and yet we and Marx recognize its potential impact on subject formation. But in this chapter the focus is on the commodity form and on capital's indifference to use-value which implies a non-recognition of moral, political or rational subjectivity. In a purely capitalist society all that is required is subjects capable of owning commodities, selling or buying commodities, or making contracts involving exchange transactions or transfer of ownership. Capital needs subjects who are free to enter contracts, to produce commodities and exchange them, and who can both embody and recognize property rights involving exclusive control over pieces of materiality. These legal subjects can have absolute rights over things and rights over the productive use of bodies limited by the rights of contract and exit that those bodies must have in order to be legal subjects (as opposed to slaves). From this point of view, the capital/labour relation is a relation between legal subjects who own and control the means of production and legal subjects that "freely" (insofar as they are single-mindedly thought of as legal subjects, as does capital in a purely capitalist society) sell their labour-power for the use of capital in return for a wage. From the point of view of pure capitalism, the only kind of subjectivity that need exist is free legal subjectivity: there need be no moral subjects or political subjects, and rational subjectivity is limited to the rules of survival in capitalism.

The reason that I started this section with reference to Hegel, is that I believe that he gets close to theorizing the basic form of legal subjectivity characteristic of capitalism.[54] Hegel's legal subject is the most abstract, formal and externalized subject form. It is basically the will of a person manifested in that person's private property. As the most shallow and contentless subject, for Hegel, it must be filled in by the dialectical unfolding of the moral and political subject. But capital in its inner logic cannot do this and has no interest in doing so. Indeed, were we to imagine that a purely capitalist society actually came into historical existence, the result would be a general hollowing out of the soul and an extreme externalization of the self into a commodity world. Selves would be nothing but differently appearing

53. See Pashukanis (1978) for a fuller account of legal subjectivity and the commodity form.
54. If Marx's interpretation is correct then we would need to expand private property from land to all commodities.

bodies plus the commodity accoutrement that they possess. They would be only differentiated from commodities by their capacity for self-movement, by their capacity for exclusive property rights against one another, and by their particular commodity equipage and consumption patterns.

I say "rights against one another" because a purely capitalist society is essentially atomistic and competitive, pitting individual against individual in the pursuit of profits or wages. Strictly speaking, other legal subjects are only of interest insofar as they can be used to improve one's economic position. It follows that legal subjects would gain recognition mainly by being productive or by capturing the outputs of other's productivity. "Disabled" subjects or subjects considered unproductive for whatever reason would have no standing to be recognized in such a society. For capital, existence is either the production of wealth or the possession of wealth.

An externalized subject is inherently decentred, since having a centre has always implied some kind of inner core whether called "ego", "soul" or something else. The legal subject of pure capitalism is radically decentred since such a subject is simply a collection of opportunistic profit-making capacities without any centre or inner connectedness. In this case the subject writ large is capital and individuals are only recognized as subjects insofar as they are useful to capital. It is the commodity form (and its variations) that provides the basic social connection, and it is the movement of commodities that ultimately determines the basic socio-economic outcomes. Thus the movements of legal subjects are ultimately determined by the movement of commodities in markets that through the quantitative movement of wages, prices and profits provide the signals that determine their actions.

In his influential essay "Ideology and Ideological State Apparatuses" Althusser (1971) argues that the most fundamental category of all ideology is the category "subject". He treats religion as the paradigm case of ideology since it is fundamentally through God as Subject writ large that each individual is called upon to be a subject. It is interesting to reflect that where Marx eschews theorizing "production in general" in favour of historically specific modes of production, in contrast Althusser theorizes "ideology in general" but not historically specific modes of ideology. Lacan (1977, 1–7) also tries to develop a general or universal theory of subjectivity. While both use a mirror metaphor somewhat differently, in both cases it plays a fundamental role in identity formation. It may well be that we spend our whole lives either believing that we are whole or striving to become whole (at least within the alienation of capitalist society), but, in my opinion, the important thing about the mirror is that we first see an image of wholeness reflected in a mirror as a capitalistically produced commodity and this produces the misrecognition that wholeness can be achieved through the possession of commodities or commodity-like persons. This suggests that a powerful starting point for understanding the human psyche under capitalism is not some imagined universal family structure or universal interpellation, but rather the historically specific capitalist commodity form.

Where capital in a purely capitalist society may be considered in some sense a Subject writ large, it is a different kind of Subject writ large than Althusser's God or Lacan's Father. Capital as subject has some distinct differences from Gods and Fathers or from God the Father. Capital collectivizes and quantifies individual actions sometimes pushing them along and sometimes blocking them, but in all cases it produces outcomes that no one intended and that can only be altered by powerful collectivist interventions. Capital is us, as we are objectified in the course of acting through the commodity form. It cannot act without our actions, but at the same time it adds up our actions into resultant prices and profits that drive the economy in directions that no one intended. Thus at the level of the individual, we are all supposedly free to engage in any exchange transactions that we wish, while at the level of the whole, most people experience sharp constraints relative to their positioning in the economy. A freedom of the individual and tyranny of the whole specific to capitalist commodity-economic logics heavily impacts on the main tendencies of capitalist ideology. For example, capitalist ideologues often play on the fact that for individuals in a capitalist society, it is much easier for them to think of themselves as free than it is for them to understand capital's logic that can make a travesty of their freedom. Ideologically capitalism always celebrates the individual freedom that it presumably promotes while ignoring the determinism that in a purely capitalist society ultimately trumps all individual actions with the overriding laws of motion of capital.

It is the commodity form that enables capitalism to present itself as free relative to slavery. Instead of buying the person of the labourer for life, the capitalist buys the use of the worker's labouring power for a determinate length of time. During that length of time the worker labours in a factory privately owned by the capitalist. This ownership gives the capitalist control over the factory including the organization of the labour that takes place. The difference between a slave plantation and a factory is the right of exit for the wage worker and the freedom to spend her or his wage on a "mess of potage" (C I, 382), gin,[55] or a bible (C I, 207). In short, outside of work time, the wage-labourer's time is "free-time" and decisions about how to spend the wage are "free" decisions. It follows that the commodification of labour-power is crucial not only for profit-making, but also for capitalist politics and ideology.[56] Friedman's (1982, 13–14) fantasy that I outlined at the start of this chapter reaches its most extreme point of unreality with his conception of the factory as an instrument utilized by sovereign individuals to connect their labouring capacity with their consuming capacity. It is a perverse world indeed in which such an ideologue can win a Nobel Prize.

The reification that accompanies the commodification of social life, puts a commodity-economic logic in charge of economic life. This means, for example, that even the smartest capitalist may go bankrupt as a result of a depression over which he or she has no control. Reification implies that although it is our agency that drives the economy, the price signals that result force our agency down certain paths. It is for this reason that Marx refers to capitalists and workers as personifications of economic categories.[57] It is not that they have no agency at all, but rather that in the theory of capital's deep structure their agency is sharply constrained by the motion of economic categories operating through a commodity form. A particular English capitalist in 1830 may not particularly like exploiting the labour of children, but because their labour is cheap and docile, he may be unable to afford not to if it means losing out to competitors. In short, in order to be a capitalist at all, he must make profits, and if exploiting children is a necessary part of this, then his choice is to exploit children or go out of business. Indeed, as Marx points out in *Capital*, it is precisely such reification that made

55. "Industry speculates on the refinement of needs, but it speculates just as much on their *crudeness*, but on their artificially produced crudeness, whose true enjoyment, therefore, is *self-stupefaction* – this *seeming* satisfaction of need – this civilization contained *within* the crude barbarism of need; the English gin-shops are therefore the *symbolical embodiments* of private property" (Marx in Tucker 1978, 98).
56. "In point of fact, capitalist production is commodity production as the general form of production, but it is so ... because labour itself here appears as a commodity" (C II, 196).
57. "...Monsieur le Capital and Madame la Terre, who are at the same time social characters and mere things" (C I, 969).

it so difficult to end the exploitation of children in England. And it is such reification that always leads to the "hard choices" that always place profits ahead of other human values. "Sorry we had to shut down the only company in the company town thus destroying the town, but it was no longer profitable." "Sorry we had to pollute the environment, but not to have done so would have increased costs too much." A great deal of the history of capitalism is people mobilizing to deal with such fallout, fallout that stems from the indifference to use-value (everything qualitative including human beings) that results from subsuming economic life to the commodity form.

Reification assumes a certain reversal of subject and object. Where commodification is complete the motion of commodities and money in the form of capital takes on some characteristics of subjectivity, while persons who fill certain economic subject positions are objectified.[58] Unskilled workers are particularly objectified because from the point of view of capital they are simply commodity inputs that hopefully will not be too demanding.[59] In other words, capital primarily hires a number of workers: ten, fifty or a hundred. Similarly, without legal or trade union constraints, capitalists can fire workers at will. "Sorry, due to bad times, we are forced to lay off 1,000 employees." Workers can be discarded like any other commodity input that is no longer needed. Of course workers have always struggled against such objectification, but to this day it persists, and in parts of the world in its most extreme forms.

The value of a commodity started out as the relation between one commodity and all other commodities, and can be called a "social relation between things" (C I, 166). In order to become transformed into M-C-M', or "self-valorizing value",[60] it must now entail a commodified relation between persons, in which workers give over the use of their labour-power to capital for profit-making production in return for a wage.[61] Thus, reification in this case invests

58. "Hence the rule of the capitalist over the worker is the rule of things over man..." (C I, 990).
59. "As capital, therefore, it is animated by the drive to reduce to a minimum the resistance offered by man..." (C I, 527).
60. "Self-expanding value" and "self-valorizing value" are expressions used frequently when Marx wants to emphasize the automaticity of capital. I give only a small sample of references here. (CI, 255–6, 342, 425, 449, 612, 711, 954, 1040; CII, 125, 131, 137–8, 180, 299, 427; CIII, 124, 459, 516, 727).
61. "...the simple forms of exchange-value and money latently contain the opposition between labour and capital etc" (G, 248).

the movement of commodities and money in markets with the characteristics of subjectivity while investing the actions of persons with the characteristics of being objectified.[62] In other words, M-C ... P ... C'-M' (P = production) exactly maps the circuit that capital must take, setting in advance the paths individuals must follow in order to participate in this circuit. If the profit M' for an individual capitalist turns into a deficit, bankruptcy will soon follow, forcing that capitalist out of the circuit. If a depression ensues, not only will many capitalists cease operating, but many workers will not be able to sell their labour-power, and those who do will have to accept lower wages. It is this that Marx means to emphasize when he refers to capitalists and workers as "personifications of economic categories".[63] The course of economic life and the path of individual wills is dictated by price signals generated in markets, or in other words, socio-economic life is market-governed and market-driven (or more precisely driven by profits generated by markets). Thus, when the commodity form subsumes the labour-and-production process, it finds within itself the wellspring of value expansion which makes it possible for a commodity-economic logic to encompass the material reproduction of a society and for capital to become self-valorizing value. When Marx refers to the "immanent laws"(C I, 381; C III, 298) of capital or to capital as an "independent force" (C II, 195; C III, 753), he means to strongly emphasize the fact that the circuit of capital has a built-in dynamic such that the forces of competition continually drive capital to maximize short-term profits even in the face of a looming economic crisis which may produce a destructive war of attrition amongst competing units of capital. Marx (C III, 298) makes it clear throughout the three volumes of *Capital* that the more competitive the economy, the closer it approaches pure capitalism. It is competition that drives the economy, that reifies the economy, and that atomizes the economy pitting capitalist against capitalist and worker against worker.[64]

62. "What is also implied already in the commodity, and still more so in the commodity as the product of capital, is the reification of the social determinations of production and the subjectification [*Versubjektifierung*] of the material bases of production which characterize the entire capitalist mode of production" (C III, 1020).
63. CI, 92, 179, 254, 342, 424, 739, 991, 1003, 1015, 1058; CII, 196–7, 207, 550; CIII, 403, 727, 958.
64. "Men are henceforth related to each other in their social process of production in a purely atomistic way. Their own relations of production therefore assume a material shape which is independent of their control and their conscious individual action" (C I, 187).

Reification forces workers to confront everyday what capitalists only have to confront in deep crises. For while workers may be out of a job on any given day, capitalists are forced out of business in large numbers only during depressions, and even then many have the resources to ride it out. More often than not, reification enables capitalists to make excuses for doing things that their workers or their communities would prefer that they not do. Needless to say, the total human costs can become immense. By allowing capital to be a semi-subject, not only are we reduced to being capital's semi-objects, but also to reacting to capital's continual rain of damaging fallout. "Sorry. To have provided safe working conditions would have been too costly."

The reification that causes capital to be indifferent to use-value creates conditions that work against the struggle for a better quality of life for most people. And even those who make enormous profits may not have a good quality of life because they live in a society and a world that has been degraded. Even gated communities and other cleansed spaces will not necessarily protect the rich from war, from environmentally induced cancer, and from the fallout of global warming.

It has often been noted that the commodity form promotes a radical kind of individualism that Marx (C I, 187) refers to as "atomization". Indeed, legal subjectivity is grounded in the boundary that surrounds one's private property, and freedom for such a subject consists in the absence of impediments to his will that exists within the boundaries of his private property.[65] To maximize freedom is to maximize private property, and other individuals always represent potential trespassers rarely forgiven by criminal law. Private property for such individuals is not only the basis for freedom but also for security. Workers, who generally have as much debt as they do property, are radically insecure without some kind of community support. For the majority of the people in the world, the highly touted individual freedom of capitalism comes down to little more than radical insecurity.

The general indifference of capital's commodity-economic logic to use-value requires that people continually fight against capital to improve their quality of life. The sad contradiction is that the atomizing tendencies of the commodity form that produces radical insecurity generally undermine the ability of people to sustain effective solidarity over time. Not that significant gains have not

65. The famous liberal definition of negative freedom is to be found in Hobbes' (1969) *Leviathan*.

been made in some parts of the world in constraining the destruc-
tiveness of unbridled capitalism, yet these gains are always subject to
considerable reversal as long as the economies of dominant powers
are not democratized far beyond what has so far been achieved. We
no longer live in a world where we can afford to have our future
dictated by enormous concentrations of private power whose goal is
nothing but profit-maximization and economic empire-building.

CONCLUSIONS

While Marx's theory of capital's inner logic begins with the
commodity form, the theory should not be thought of as the
progressive imposition of an alien form on to content. In *Capital*
the commodity form is precisely that form required by a substantive
content which is capitalist. If Marx begins *Capital* by considering
the commodity, money and capital primarily as circulation forms,
it is not because circulation forms are the core of capital, rather it is
because dialectical reason requires this sequence. Using a dialectical
logic Marx generates the money form from the commodity form
and the capital form from the two previous forms.[66] Marx makes it
clear that none of these circulation forms can be complete without
the commodification of labour-power and the exploitation that
necessarily follows.[67] Production relations and not circulation forms
are at the core of capitalism, but these relations cannot be clearly
articulated without the prior articulation of capital's basic circulation
forms. Some interpreters believe that, given the importance of class
to the understanding of capital, this concept should come first. But
the order of concepts is not necessarily determined by how core they
are, rather it is determined by how they can be most clearly presented

66. According to Marx the money form is simply the fully developed value-
    form of the commodity (C I, 90). Furthermore: "the money-form is merely
    the reflection thrown upon a single commodity by the relations between
    all other commodities" (C I, 184). Marx argues that the movement of
    money "is in fact merely the movement undergone by commodities while
    changing their form" (as in M-C-M) (C I, 212). And finally, Engels argues
    "commodities and commodity exchange must give rise to the antithesis
    of commodities and money..." (C II, 99).
67. In criticizing Garnier, Marx writes: "[he]... considers *inessential* the feature
    which makes this production capitalist – the exchange of capital for
    wage-labour..." (S I, 187). "Now wage-labour, however, is a *commodity*.
    It is even the basis on which the production of *products* as *commodities*
    takes place" (S II, 397). "What he sells to the capitalist is not his labour
    but the temporary use of himself as a working power" (S III, 113).

in relation to other important concepts, and Marx believes the basic class relation that emerges from the theory of surplus-value cannot be clearly and persuasively presented prior to clarifying the basic categories of circulation even though they have more to do with capital's appearances than its essence. For Marx, the more capitalist a society is, the more clear and distinct the economic becomes.[68]

Taking the commodity form as the economic cell-form is key to Marx's crucial conceptualization of the reification associated with capital. For Marx capital is a powerful reifying force in history in the sense that by its own logic and dynamic it tends to both deepen the penetration of the commodity form into social life and to spread it into new areas of social life and new areas of the globe.[69] In other words, capital as an historical force forces global history to increasingly fall into line with its own imperatives, but only up to a point. And while Marx is aware that pure capitalism has never existed and will never exist in history, he sometimes mistakenly seems to believe that capital's reifying forces will produce a capitalist history that is a close approximation to capital's inner logic.[70]

Marx's understanding of the reified character of economic categories sharply distinguishes his conceptualization of the economic from mainstream bourgeois economics. In his theory he never simply posits or assumes the existence of commodities, money, prices or profits.[71] Rather he generates them by logically thinking through the implications of the process of commodification, and this is a process of subsuming social power relations to the commodity form such that power relations are converted into numerical relations. Numerical relations, then, are never simply given for Marx, but are always problematized in terms of the power relations that can so

68. "*Free competition* is the relation of capital to itself as another capital, i.e. the real conduct of capital as capital. The inner laws of capital – which appear merely as tendencies in the preliminary historic stages of its development – are for the first time posited as laws; production founded on capital for the first time posits itself in the forms adequate to it only insofar as and to the extent that free competition develops..." (G, 650).
69. "The constant enlargement of his capital becomes a condition for its preservation" (C II, 159).
70. See the discussion of this point in Chapter 5.
71. "Ganilh is quite right when he says of Ricardo and most economists that they consider labour without exchange, although their system, like the whole bourgeois system, rests on exchange-value. This however is only due to the fact that to them the *form* of product as commodity seems self-evident, and consequently they examine only the *magnitude of value*" (S I, 205).

easily disappear when thought becomes engrossed in the movement of numbers as is common in mainstream mathematical economics. At the same time, because reification makes quantification possible by converting power relations into commodified structures, the inner structural dynamics of capital can be thought as a set of necessary inner connections. But since this necessity is a product of capital's reifying power that we extend in theory in order to better understand capital, it is not a necessity that we need to accept in history. Indeed Marx's use of "reification" problematizes every economic category in terms of the power relations that it tends to reproduce. And this opens up economic thought to considerations of the democratization of economic life, social justice and social flourishing, such that every capitalist objectification of a social relation is exposed to critique. Reification is two-sided. It makes possible the clear theorization of capital's inner logic and it makes possible the critique of every social relation that becomes objectified by this logic. Breaking the spell of reification in our thinking is important if we are going to effectively alter capitalism in practice.

In the next chapter I shall examine how the commodity form can sink deeply into the materiality of social life once it can systematically produce surplus-value by subsuming the labour and production process. And a thorough discussion of Marx's theory of surplus-value will necessarily lead to a defence of the labour theory of value.

3
The Theory of Surplus-Value

The objective content of the circulation we have been discussing – the valorization of value – is his subjective purpose, and it is only in so far as the appropriation of ever more wealth in the abstract is the sole driving force behind his operations that he functions as a capitalist, i.e. as capital personified and endowed with consciousness and will. Use-values must therefore never be treated as the immediate aim of the capitalist. (C I, 254)

…it thus becomes transformed into an automatic subject. … For the movement in the course of which it adds surplus-value is its own movement, its valorization is therefore self-valorization. (C I, 255)

The driving motive and determining purpose of capitalist production is the self-valorization of capital to the greatest possible extent, i.e. the greatest possible production of surplus-value, hence the greatest possible exploitation of labour-power by the capitalist. (C I, 449)

It is generally the case that within the modern academic discipline of economics the crucial test for any general economic theory is the strength of its theory of price determination. And, as a corollary, because Marx's labour theory of value is seen to lack an adequate way of transforming values into prices, Marx's entire theory of capital is dismissed. But what if this emphasis is totally misplaced? What if the key to understanding capitalism is a theory of profit determination and not a theory of price determination, and what if Marx's theory lays the groundwork to succeed in this, while nearly all other major theories fail miserably? Indeed, because profit determination is typically only considered (if at all) in mainstream economics as it enters into price determination, the resulting explanations have often been superficial. For example, profits as "opportunity costs" are little more than a "souped up" (utilizing the languages of mathematics and marginal utility theory to cook the soup) abstinence theory that Marx so thoroughly discredited over a century ago.[1] One theorist is

1. "Someone may castigate and flagellate himself all day long … and this quantity of sacrifice he contributes will remain totally worthless" (G, 613).

so impressed by Sraffa's theory of price determination – even though it cannot determine the extent to which profits are based on the exploitation of labour – that he claims that we should simply drop the question about where profits come from (Keen 2001, 286). Is profit nothing but the value of commodity outputs exceeding the value of commodity inputs? But what if the most important question to address in a general theory of capital is precisely the question of where profits ultimately come from?[2] Or what if the key question of economic theory is how does capitalist profit-making impact on the utilization of human life energy in the form of labour? In these cases, Sraffa's theory is of little or no use compared to Marx's.

Indeed, Marx makes an extremely powerful case that if it is the specificity of capital that we want to understand, then profit determination (grounded in the theory of surplus-value) must be the central focus of economic theory and price determination should be a subsidiary or secondary concern. After all, prices exist wherever money exists and can therefore appear in the most diverse modes of production in connection with almost any property relations, whether slave, feudal, petty commodity production, capitalist, socialist or any hybrid of these. From the point of view of price, the only difference between capitalism and any other mode of production is the purely quantitative distinction that apparently more things have prices because more things are managed by markets. And presumably between petty commodity production and capitalism there would be no difference. Further, the focus on price tends to focus attention away from the realm of production on to markets and circulation forms, when it is precisely the realm of production that is key to the origin of profits.[3] Price is at the same time both a nearly universal and superficial or lazy way of tying together and identifying those phenomena to be labelled "economic". As a category it almost immediately invites formalistic and mathematical thinking that tends to disconnect from anything historically specific. But if prices circulate titles to property, then it is crucial to understand what the structure of property relations is, how it is perpetuated, and how in

2. "The other side of the crisis resolves itself into a real decrease in production, in living labour – in order to restore the correct relation between necessary and surplus labour, on which, in the last analysis, everything rests" (G, 446).
3. "If we are only familiar with the abstract categories of circulation, which are common to all of them, we cannot know anything of their *differentia specifica*" (C I, 209).

general the circulation of titles and the organization of production is shaped by this structure.[4] A theory of price determination that is simple, elegant, and most importantly (for "economic science") is made up of mathematically solvable equations (for example, Sraffa's), is, by itself, of little use or interest, if what it is we are interested in understanding is the specificity of capitalism and its historical development.[5] If the driving force of capitalism and the goal of capitalists is profit, then surely a theory of profit determination must be central to any theory whose aim is to understand capitalism. Contrary to many interpreters of Marx's *Capital* who dismiss his category "surplus-value" as defective and even "metaphysical" (in the bad positivist sense), I want to argue that it is both absolutely central to his theory and should be absolutely central to any theory aiming to understand the nature of capitalist profits.

THE CENTRALITY OF "SURPLUS-VALUE"

Marx entitles his monumental three volume critique of all important political economists *Theories of Surplus Value* for a very good reason. "Surplus-value" is *the* crucial concept for developing an adequate theory of capital's deep structural dynamics, and it is the concept that the best classical economists, Smith and Ricardo, approach closely only to avert their eyes at the last moment. It is not surprising, then, to find the first words of *Theories of Surplus Value*, volume I to be: "All economists share the error of examining surplus-value not as such, in its pure form, but in the particular forms of profit and rent" (S I, 40). In other words, a theory of capital's deep structures requires a theory of the common source and interconnectedness between all the basic forms of profit and interest on the one hand and rent on the other. Exactly what is surplus-value "as such, in its pure form"?

A good place to start in answering this question is to remember that for Marx the major class-based modes of production – slavery, feudalism and capitalism – are differentiated primarily by the type of property relations that enable the dominant class to system-atically appropriate society's surplus labour. "Surplus-value" is the concept that enables us to think how it is in a "freely" competitive,

4. "The capitalist exists in a dual form – juridically and economically" (S III, 458). See also (G, 194).
5. While of little interest in itself, the theory of price determination is essential in a larger theory that relates price to property relations and labour.

fully commodified society (that is, a purely capitalist society) that a capitalist class without utilizing extra-economic force can systematically appropriate surplus labour. Or in other words, "surplus-value" represents the result of a theoretical effort to understand how total surplus labour can be appropriated through the commodity form without reliance on the sort of strong political and ideological supports required of slavery and feudalism.

In order to present the relation between the capitalist class as a whole and the working class as a whole in its most clear and precise form in *Capital*, Marx first conceives of them as homogeneous classes confronting one another. And in this case homogeneity means that the capitalist class as an undifferentiated whole draws its profits from the surplus-value created by the working class as an undifferentiated whole: surplus-value being the difference between the total new value created by the labour of the working class and the value of labour-power, or, what is the same thing, the value of the commodities required for the working class to reproduce itself at a particular historically given standard of living. To avoid distorting the theory with irrelevancies and in order to grasp the capital/labour relation in its clearest most basic form, Marx (C I, 306) assumes that all labour is simple average abstract labour (unskilled labour of average intensity and indifferent to use-value), and initially that all capital has the same ratio between constant capital (the portion of value that goes to material inputs) and variable capital (the portion of value that goes to living labour-power).

Marx would not consider these abstractions to be "violent abstractions",[6] because as labour was becoming increasingly commodified in history up to the time of his writing, it also was tending to become more equalized and homogenized as simple, abstract labour. Hence, as a theorist he was simply extending to completion in theory, the process of commodification that was happening before the eyes of all with the development of capitalism. While there was no historical tendency deriving from the forces of competition for the

6. "This inner connection [between surplus-value and profit] is here revealed for the first time. ... all economics up till now has either violently made abstraction from the distinctions between surplus-value and profit, between rate of surplus-value and rate of profit, so that it could retain the determination of value as its basis, or else it has abandoned, along with this determination of value, any kind of solid foundation for a scientific approach, so as to be able to retain those distinctions which obtrude themselves on the phenomenal level" (C III, 268–9).

ratio between variable and constant capital (essentially the "organic composition of capital") to become more equal amongst distinct sectors of productive capital, this is not important to the theory at a point where it is the relation between capital as a whole and the general pool of surplus-value that is being considered.

Marx made these abstractions to clarify the fundamental forms of exploitation that are central to profit-making in capitalism.[7] And in doing so, he was totally aware of the fact that in no actual capitalist society is it the case that all labour is engaged in the capitalistic production of commodities, nor that the labour so engaged is all simple average abstract labour. Absolutely crucial to his entire theory is the view that every form of profit, whether industrial profit, commercial profit or interest, as well as rent in its basic capitalist form, all derive from surplus-value. It follows that the concept "surplus-value" must be fully grounded theoretically prior to its serving as a matrix out of which the various forms of profit and rent can be specified. There is thus a logical sequence of categories that move from the less specified to the more specified. This being the case, the forms of profit theorized in volume three of *Capital* are simply more fully specified forms of surplus-value, and prices of production should be viewed similarly as more fully specified values.[8]

THE LABOUR THEORY OF VALUE

Following the work of Sekine in interpreting Marx, I believe that the labour theory of value claims that in a state of equilibrium one hour of labour engaged in the capitalistic production of commodities will on average produce the same value as any other hour of such labour.[9] And when supply and demand approach an equilibrium, it follows that no labour is wasted and each commodity is produced by socially necessary labour time only.[10] Since at this level of abstraction the

7. "All this conceals the true nature of surplus-value more and more, concealing therefore the real mechanism of capital" (C III, 967).
8. See Sekine (1997, Vol. II, Ch. 7) for a fuller development of this approach to the transformation problem.
9. "The same labour, therefore, performed for the same length of time, always yields the same amount of value..." (C I, 137).
10. "The total product – that is to say, the value of the total product – is in this case therefore not equal to the labour-time contained in it, but is equal to the proportionate labour-time which would have been used had the total product been in proportion to production in other spheres" (S I, 232). "If the market cannot stomach the whole quantity at the

aim of the theory is to understand the fundamental class relation between homogeneous capital and labour in commodity-economic terms, a price is nothing but the money expression of value.

In *Capital* volume one, Marx moves from theorizing the commodity, money and capital as circulation forms, to exploitation in the realm of production where the focus is in the first instance on the relation between two variables: variable capital (value of labour-power) and surplus-value (the difference between new value created by labour-power and the wage when it equals the value of labour-power). A third variable, constant capital, is discussed briefly. It refers to material inputs that, according to Marx, cannot contribute to surplus-value because they cannot add more value to the product than they already contain. Other than a brief introduction to the ratio c/v (constant/variable capital), which Marx refers to as "organic composition" insofar as changes in "value composition" reflect changes in "technical composition", there is little systematic attention given to the concept "constant capital".

In *Capital* volume two, Marx breaks constant capital down into circulating and fixed material inputs, where the difference is that the entire value of circulating material inputs (such as cotton in the production of textiles) is passed on to the product in one turnover of the circuit of capital (he assumes no change in value between the moment of production of the input and the moment of its incorporation in the new product), while fixed capital (typically machinery) remains in the sphere of production for more than one circuit. Thus, fixed capital passes on its value gradually until the machinery (in this case) is replaced. But what is to ensure that the life-span of fixed capital exactly corresponds to the value that it is supposed to gradually give over to the product? Marx does not give enough attention to this issue, writing little more than the claim that the periodicity of crises corresponds to the average life (in value terms) of fixed capital. It is Sekine who to my knowledge best handles this problem by arguing that large new investments in fixed capital will be made when the old fixed capital is fully depreciated in the trough of a depression, and that after a few such cycles the average life-span of fixed capital during which it would pass on all its value

---

normal price ... this proves that too great a portion of total social labour-time has been expended in the form of weaving. The effect is the same as if each individual weaver had expended more labour-time on his particular product than was socially necessary" (C I, 202). See also (S II, 521; C III, 774).

to the product would tend to correspond to the periodicity of crises. That is, capitalists would tend to hang on to their fixed capital until it was fully depreciated, and they were forced by the extreme competition, and invited by the general depreciation of all capital in a depression, to invest in new more productive machinery. Sekine's (1997, Vol. I, Ch. 6) distinction between widening (where more of the same technology is bought) and deepening (where more productive technology is bought) phases of capital accumulation helps to clarify and strengthen Marx's brief comments on the relation between fixed capital and periodic crises. And the objection that this is not the way it usually happens in empirical reality ignores the fact that this is not a crudely empiricist theory, but rather, it is a theory aimed at showing how a commodity-economic logic could in principle manage the expanded reproduction of a society in which all inputs and outputs are completely commodified.

It is not until volume three of *Capital* that Marx drops the assumption of homogeneous capital and considers the more empirically real situation of heterogeneous capital where different sectors have different ratios of c/v. This means that prices of production are simply more fully specified values, and it is not a question of transforming a fully developed mathematics of value into a mathematics of price. Indeed, the more abstract conceptualization of value can only be definitively quantified simultaneously with prices of production.[11]

An important aspect of "surplus-value" is that it is a *value category*. Insofar as we focus on purely capitalist economic structures, value is *the* social connector. If, as Marx (G, 265) claims, "Society does not consist of individuals, but expresses the sum of interrelations, the relations within which these individuals stand", then from the point of view of the forms of value, the relations within which individuals stand are exchange relations. As values, commodities are qualitatively the same, differing only quantitatively as they are connected by that purest external representative of value, money. Thus the social relation in pure capitalism is a "cash nexus", and individuals find themselves standing within networks of prices. But behind these prices is a division of labour, and, if we follow Marx on this, each price is ultimately an objectification or materialization of abstract simple labour. The labour theory of value, then, points us towards a consideration of how society organizes its total labour-power.

11. See Sekine (1997, Vol. II, Ch.7) for a clear statement on the relation between the labour theory of value and prices of production.

I want to argue against all those mainstream economists, who, mesmerized by mathematics, so easily dismiss the labour theory of value, when it is potentially the most humanly relevant focus of economic theory. Taking the strongest exception to mainstream economics on this point, I want to argue that a labour theory of value should be central to any economic theory worth taking seriously because economics ought to be about how our life energy is utilized to provision ourselves. For the vast majority of people throughout history, provisioning takes a large majority of their life energy, and therefore how this provisioning is organized will have an enormous impact on quality of life. It is perhaps not too strong an emphasis to say that as long as working time is most of our life time, who we are will largely depend on how we work, what income we get from our work, and what we do with our working income. Marx demonstrates that these things are heavily impacted by property relations, which are ultimately class relations modified in historical contexts by more specific power relations. This means that central to any meaningful economic theory, we need a means of moving from mathematical variables to structures of class and power at the most abstract level of theory, and we need to be able to analyze the complexities of power and agency at more concrete levels of analysis. Far from being ends in themselves, quantitative equations should be viewed as mere stepping stones, useful only to the extent that they can clarify economic/political/ideological relations of class and power. But Steedman (1977, 207), who thinks that everything is achieved with a theory of price determination, writes off the labour theory of value as nothing but confusing and misleading excess baggage. After all, why have a theory of value at all if it is not mathematically required for the derivation of prices? There are many reasons.

First, we can pose a question of Steedman. By itself, what use is a highly abstract theory of price determination? If economics were to reorient itself to focus on economic power relations and their impact on human flourishing, Steedman's theory is useless unless it is embedded in a larger theory of social relations that could provide a basis for developing theoretical mediations that could ultimately connect it to history. And this is precisely what Marx's integration of the theory of the commodity form and theory of class does. It provides a social matrix or social setting out of which a theory of price arises such that quantities are always connected back to structural property relations and quantification itself is problematized by the commodity form. Quantification can only effectively displace power relations by a reification based on complete commodification. Understanding this is absolutely key to a systematic unpacking of quantitative economic variables necessitated by the sort of institutional analysis required in the move from the theory of capital's deep structures to more concrete levels of analysis. It follows that a theory of value serves to map out the structures of socio-economic relations that provide the conditions of possibility for a system of prices.[12] At the same time it provides the matrix that can guide our thinking about more concrete levels of analysis.

Second, an understanding of how the economy channels people's life energy into labour activities and what this means to their life chances, would be extremely important to members of society. To achieve this, economic theory would need to make connections between economic variables and the channelling of our energies, and this would seem to require either a labour theory of value or something quite like it. The great achievement of Marx's labour theory of value is that it demonstrates how it is possible for the commodity form to systematically capture surplus labour and place it in the hands of the capitalist class in the form of surplus-value. It is a theory that tightly integrates a structural theory of property relations with a quantitative theory of value. Since billions of people around the world experience daily the soul-destroying discipline of capitalist and quasi-capitalist labour processes, one would think that an economic theory would find a way of linking these experiences to the centrality of profit-making in the theory of capital's deep structure. Lengthening the working day, intensifying labour and displacing labour with machinery are things that workers experience in ways that are all too real throughout the history of capitalism with little or no letting up to this day.

Third, the concepts "surplus labour" and "surplus-value" directly connect value-formation with profit-formation, thus grasping that the driving force central to capitalism is not the provision of use-values to consumers but the maximization of profits by capitalists. This is an extremely important corrective to nearly all mainstream economic theory that proposes some sort of "consumer sovereignty".

12. The common insistence on the separation of quantitative economics from "political sociology" or "historical materialism" is precisely what Marx's value theory avoids. For example, Roemer's (1988, 133) "property relations approach" to exploitation is an effort to separate a theory of exploitation from value theory, an effort that is diametrically opposed to Marx's efforts.

Marx presents a most convincing case that capitalism is the most extreme channelling of life energy into profit-making ever devised, and not to place this at the centre of economic theory is a travesty.

Fourth, the labour theory of value focuses attention on the realm of production as the key to understanding profit-making. And while the commodity form in its undeveloped forms goes back very far into our primal past, its historically specific developed capitalist form converts capitalism into a radically distinct mode of production. It is the commodification of labour-power and with it profit-making based on the systematic exploitation of labour-power that makes capitalism such a unique way of organizing economic life. Marx (S I, 44) praises the Physiocrats, calling "them the true fathers of modern political economy", because they were the first to see through the realm of circulation to the realm of production where surplus-value is created. Their mistake and that of all other bourgeois political economists was to consider "the capitalist form of production an eternal, natural form of production". And the failure to conceive capitalism "...in its *specific historical* form...", means that "...one cannot get beyond inanities..." and "...talk about 'civilization'"(S I, 285). More often than not, talk about civilization is not only vague but has the racist undertones that come from the civilization/barbarism binary that has played a central role in many of its historical usages.

Fifth, the commodification of labour-power is the *sine qua non* of capitalism, and the labour theory of value places proper emphasis on this fact. Without a substantial commodification of labour-power, not only would a labour theory of value not be possible, but capitalism itself could not exist. This subsumption of human labour to the commodity form has enormous implications for subject formation and for human flourishing, for it subjects worker's energy flow at every moment of the working day to sudden and arbitrary blockage – either from being "fired" or "laid off" – and it exposes our security and very survival to the vagaries of the labour market and the threat of falling into the industrial reserve army. Indeed, the commodification of labour-power requires a pool of underemployed and/or unemployed, and, of course, in pure capitalism, the threat of unemployment may be a "death threat". To exclude such realities from having a central place in economic theory could possibly stem from an ideology shaped by the indifference to use-value that is so characteristic of capitalism itself that it has infected and compromised the "objectivity" of economic "science".

It is clear that capital as M-C-M' can only be theoretically presented after the commodity form and money form as basic circulation forms are theorized, and that surplus-value is already embedded in the first theoretical appearance of capital as a circulation form. From the point of view of circulation, M-C-M' is inexplicable, since Marx argues that the fundamental nature of capitalist profits can only be understood if we assume equal exchange.[13] On this assumption the only way in which the second M can be larger than the first, is if there is some C that can create new value. And it is this theoretical quandary that propels Marx's theorization of the commodification of labour-power. Indeed, this is crucial to the entire theory that centres on the nature of profit as derived from the exploitation of labour. To make sense, M-C-M' must be expanded into the formula M-C ... P ... C'-M' (C = means of production and labour-power purchased as inputs into a production process, ... marks the interruption that P makes in the circuit, P = labour and production process, C' = the commodity output of the production process with surplus-value embedded, and M' the profit made upon the sale of C'). Since according to Marx, the means of production can only pass on their value to the product, the increase of value must come from living labour. In other words, M-C-M' must subsume the labour and production process in order to become a generalized form of economic activity, and the key to this is the commodification of labour-power.[14] And since the commodification of labour-power entails a class of persons who have nothing to sell but their labour-power, it follows that the generalization of the commodity form entails a class relation between capital and labour. For Marx, to say that capitalism is commodity production generalized thus entails the notion of class.[15]

Sixth, the focus on property, class and power, though of great interest, poses further questions about distributive justice and human flourishing. For power relations may be "empowering" or "disempowering", democratic or authoritarian, and may open up space for self-development or close it off. Individuals are born into social relations within which they are supposed to learn to stand, but which, on the contrary, may make it difficult for them to get off their

13. The assumption of equal exchange is often asserted. A few examples: C I, 252, 260–3, 268, 270, 301, 417–18, 431, 678, 710, 729–30, 747.
14. "...capitalist production is commodity production as the general form of production, but is only so, and becomes ever more so in its development, because labour itself here appears as a commodity..." (C II, 196).
15. Marx says as much in many places.

knees. And these considerations point us towards ethical and moral considerations, considerations which have been largely excluded from economic theory because positivist assumptions label ethical theory as unscientific and because market outcomes are often assumed to be in some sense socially optimal. As a result, in western capitalist societies we lack a tradition of academic and public discourse that would connect rational ethical discourse with substantive economic theory.[16] For example, consider how little public discourse there is about the justifiability of various kinds of inequality and what might be done to alter forms of inequality that are not justifiable. Market outcomes are seldom questioned, even though these outcomes are nearly always skewed by power relations and nearly always by themselves generate increased inequality. The potential space for public debate on distributive justice and economic ethics tends to be filled with legalism on the one hand and increasingly cultural reactions such as religious fundamentalism on the other. And any policy slightly approaching the redistribution of wealth, is usually only achieved by an immense struggle over extended periods of time, and tends to be quickly rolled back by capitalist interests at the first possible opportunity.

The basic point is that economics cannot avoid taking up questions having to do with human flourishing: questions of distributive justice, freedom, equality and democracy. As Marx (G, 172–3) puts it: "…in the case of an individual, the multiplicity of its development, its enjoyment and its activity depends on the economization of time. Economy of time, to this all economy ultimately reduces itself." In other words, time for us is ultimately our lifetime, and if most of our lifetime is devoted to mind-numbing labour, then little energy will be left to develop our caring, generous and creative potentials.

The labour theory of value is a way of connecting quantitative economic variables with the expenditure of life energy. And, as Marx utilizes it, it illustrates how, through commodification, economic power structures can be translated into economic variables that vary systematically in relation to each other. While such variables tell us a great deal about capital's deep structural dynamics – knowledge that is essential for clear thinking about alternatives to capitalism

16. It would not be too inaccurate to say that little headway has been made in ethical theory since Aristotle, and that probably much of this has to do with the split between religion and science, resulting in ethics being largely handled by religion, or in a positivist world by "normative discourse".

– they also demonstrate the class exploitation and oppression that is inherent to capitalism and thereby invite the consideration of mapping paths to freer, more democratic and egalitarian future economic arrangements, mapping that requires a movement away from quantitative variables to more concrete qualitative variables that reveal the complex articulation between economic, political and ideological power relations.

A labour theory of value can play a central role in connecting a critical, ethical dimension of thought to economic theory. For example, in a purely capitalist society, one hour of one worker's labour is worth one hour of another's. This would suggest the need for a continual discussion on issues of distributive justice, since any inequality of income would need to be justified. And as a result, one would think that a post-capitalist economic world would move towards much greater equality, since it is difficult to imagine a rational ethical theory that could justify the enormous inequalities that have been generated by capitalism. Further, a labour theory of value can serve to develop an ecological ethics, because forms of production and consumption that are unsustainable will increase the labour of future generations. And finally since working life takes up most of our waking hours, the ways in which this life is organized must have a deep impact on our quality of life. Numerous questions follow: How does the organization of work life impact on the raising of children? How does it support the development of social virtues such as mutual aid and generosity? How does it foster the development of reason and creativity? How can work be made more pleasurable? How can its more unpleasurable forms be reduced or shared in more equitable ways? Finally how can we better relate non-work time with work time so that leisure time is both more equalized and less a sort of escape from the trials and tribulations of work?

CAPITAL AS SELF-VALORIZING VALUE

The theory of surplus-value and labour theory of value might seem to represent theoretical work based on Weberian extreme-type concepts. The difference is that in this case it is the motion of capital itself that develops a strong enough directionality in history to lead our thought towards these conceptualizations. In history, once the commodity form combines with the dynamism of factory production, there is a qualitative leap forward in the reifying forces of capital. The result of this is that areas of social life that are partially commodified become more commodified, new areas become commodified to greater or lesser extent, and the rapidly increasing productivity of capitalism undermines pre-capitalist modes of economic life. The tendency for the circuits of capital to become more capitalist through their own motion can be called self-reification. Or in other words, self-reification is the tendency for the commodity form to both spread and deepen by its own dynamic, and it is a tendency that picks up enormous momentum after the industrial revolution.

Marx's continual reference to capital as "self-valorizing value" brings out a number of aspects of capital in its relation to surplus-value. First is the sense in which capital takes on a life of its own, acting as an "automatic subject" which drives the economy towards profit maximization until a periodic crisis causes a sudden contraction (C I, 255). But, as Marx argues, capital works best when it continuously expands, such that the discontinuity caused by a crisis must be seen by capital simply as a "correction" that brings quantitative variables that have wandered astray back into line (C II, 133, 182). And ideally this will be achieved without state intervention, proving that capital can manage itself and the economy that it dominates by a commodity-economic logic that does not need to rely on extra-economic force. It is only then that capital is truly *self*-valorizing value, value that can expand itself without relying on outside supports. In other words, self-valorizing value implies that the commodity form has sunk so deeply into economic life and commodification is so complete that the commodity form can operate without interference.[17]

Second, self-valorizing value implies that the aim of capital expansion is not use-value and quality of life, but profit no matter what the cost unless groups of citizens rise up to limit the costs.[18] Given the immense power of the profit drive, placing effective limits on it in history usually requires the mobilization and resistance of large numbers of people over a considerable period of time. As previously mentioned, the example that Marx explores at some length in *Capital* is the extraordinary resistance of capital in Britain to efforts by citizens to place limits on the exploitation of children in the first half of the nineteenth century. If children can be paid less and offer less resistance to work intensification, then a capitalist cannot afford to give up the practice of exploiting child labour, if this will place him at a competitive disadvantage vis-à-vis those who do.

17. C I, 711; C II, 128, 131, 180, 185, 291, 299.
18. C I, 254, 612; C II, 137, 138, 159; C III, 297.

Even after protective legislation was passed against the protests of capitalists, the practice continued for some time because there were not enough factory inspectors to enforce the legislation.

Third, the conceptualization of capital as self-valorizing value is meant to emphasize the fact that individual units of capital and hence capital as a whole has a built-in dynamic to continually expand (C II, 159). The aim of each unit of capital is to maximize profits, but in the long run this is best achieved by becoming more productive than one's competitors, so that one can sell below their price and still make more profit. But increased productivity fundamentally means that the same amount of labour can produce more product in the same amount of time. And in general this will mean a proportionally larger investment in machinery and other material inputs per worker, such that the ratio c/v will rise and along with it the rate of profit will fall (C III, 317–19, 329). While in a purely capitalist society we do not know how fast this might occur or what its precise consequences might be, a falling rate of profit points to the ultimate mortality of capitalism.[19] According to Marx, at the level of historical analysis, a fundamental tendency of capital and the state that supports it is to find ways of countering this tendency. And while one might imagine many ways of doing this, Marx (C III, 349) places particular emphasis on the centralization of capital into larger and larger units.

Fourth, an important way that capital can maximally valorize itself is to speed up the circuit of capital so that the rate of turnover of capital increases (C II, 328). Here the shrinkage of space occurs as a result of technologies that subsume its traversal and management to decreased time, and the shrinkage of time occurs by speeding up the rate of turnover of capital.[20] Insofar as capital plays a dominant role in social life, one would expect significant increases in the rate of turnover of capital to increase the pace of life generally. And since

19. "The rate of profit ... is particularly important for all new off-shoots of capital that organize themselves independently. And if capital formation were to fall exclusively into the hands of a few existing big capitals, for whom the mass of profit outweighs the rate, the animating fire of production would be totally extinguished" (C III, 368).

20. "Thus, while capital must on one side strive to tear down every spatial barrier to intercourse, i.e., to exchange, and conquer the whole earth for its market, it strives on the other side to annihilate this space with time, i.e. to reduce to a minimum the time spent in motion from one place to another. The more developed the capital ... the more does it strive simultaneously for an even greater extension of the market and for greater annihilation of space by time" (G, 539).

value in the case of capital is pure quantity, both space and time tend to be subsumed to quantity such that both become linear and sequential. It is then easy to consider time as a dimension of space as Marx (G, 399) notes: "But the working day, regarded spatially – time itself regarded as space – is *many working days alongside one another.*" And capital conceptualized temporally is a social relation in process attempting to maintain continuity, expansion and an increasing rate of turnover.[21]

SURPLUS-VALUE AND PROFIT

As previously argued, Marx first considers surplus-value in a highly abstract context in which the following assumptions are made:

1) All production is the capitalistic production of commodities, such that there are two and only two classes: capital and labour (C II, 422).
2) All exchanges are equal exchanges[22] and any labour applied to a commodity in excess of social demand is wasted (is not value forming); hence an equilibrium of supply and demand is assumed so that all abstract simple labour is embodied in commodities.[23]

21. "When it is said that capital 'is accumulated (realized) labour..., which serves as the means for new labour (production)', then this refers to the simple material capital, without regard to the formal character without which it is not capital. ... According to this, capital would have existed in all forms of society. ... since every form of labour ... presupposes the product of prior labour. ... [and capital would be] a necessary condition for all human production ... [and would be] conceived as a thing, not as a relation. ... Capital is not a simple relation, but a process, in whose various moments it is always capital" (G, 257–8). "This independent existence becomes even more evident in capital, which, in one of its aspects, can be called *value in process* – and since value only exists independently in money, it can accordingly be called *money in process*, as it goes through a series of processes in which it preserves itself, departs from itself, and returns to itself increased in volume" (S III, 137).
22. "The formation of surplus-value ... can consequently be explained neither by assuming that commodities are sold above their value, nor by assuming that they are bought as less than their value" (C I, 263). And this also applies to the commodity labour-power. See also (C I, 260–3, 268, 301).
23. "We assume throughout, not only that the value of an average labour-power is constant, but that the workers employed by a capitalist are reduced to average workers" (C I, 418). See also (C I, 202).

3) All labour is abstract simple labour, and the working class receives the full value of labour-power, while the value that they create in excess of this is appropriated by capital as surplus-value. Thus homogeneous living labour creates both the total value of labour-power and the total surplus-value.[24]

4) Capital is homogeneous in the sense that Marx has not yet introduced the idea that different capital's may have different organic compositions. Thus, at this point, all we know is that capital as a whole appropriates the surplus-value as a whole, but we know nothing about how it is divided up between fractions of capital, capital's of different composition, sectors of capital, or individual capitalists.[25]

5) Marx has not yet introduced any considerations of how changes in value over time can act back upon previously formed values. Thus surplus-value is initially created by homogeneous labour and appropriated by homogeneous capital at a point in time.[26]

Following the work of Sekine on this, the concept of profit emerges when Marx introduces elements of heterogeneity into capital that competition cannot get rid of.[27] First to be introduced is the idea that capitals may have different organic compositions (ratios of constant to variable capital c/v), which competition has no tendency to get rid of, whereas competition does create a tendency for capitals of the same size to converge towards an average rate of profit since those capitals making less than an average profit will tend to reinvest into those sectors making above average profits.[28] Thus the tendency will be for surplus-value to be distributed in accord with total capital invested, c + v, and not in accord with the size of v by itself. Many interpreters of Marx believe that this creates a "transformation problem" requiring values to be mathematically transformed into prices of production. On this reading, no such problem exists because

24. C I, 306, 417–18, 747; C III, 241–2, 774, 971.
25. Concerning the apparent contradiction between the rate of surplus-value and the rate of profit at this point in the theory Marx writes: "For the solution of this apparent contradiction, many intermediate terms are still needed..." (C I, 491).
26. "The value of any commodity ... is determined not by the necessary labour-time that it itself contains, but by the *socially* necessary labour-time required for its reproduction" (C III, 238).
27. Sekine (1997, Vol. II).
28. C III, 261, 273, 297–8, 310, 488.

prices are nothing but more specified values.[29] At such an abstract level, values cannot be quantitatively expressed except as the direct money expression of value. While values cannot be fully determined quantitatively prior to the determination of prices, once prices are determined, we can derive value quantities from them because values are simply less specified prices.[30] Values then are like the shadows of prices projected backwards, only in this case, it is the shadow that gives substance to that which casts the shadow.

So what is the point of value categories if not the derivation of prices? Value categories reveal how economic power relations get absorbed into the commodity form, and by revealing this, we can understand how prices and profits can be related back to the deep power structures that they tend to make disappear. They provide an avenue connecting quantitative variables with the qualitative structures of property relations, class and power. Without this sort of connection, the movement from mathematical equations to real economic life is a leap in the dark, and formalistic economics emerges triumphant.[31] By itself, therefore, the category profit can play a deeply mystifying and ideological role.[32] And from the point of view of economic theory, if, like Ricardo, we assume that surplus-value and profit are identical, we will not only lack a way of adequately theorizing the relations between different forms of surplus-value, but will also be unable to theorize how "...*with a given surplus-value*, various factors may raise or lower and in general influence the rate of profit" (S II, 378).

EQUILIBRIUM

I include a brief discussion of equilibrium here because I have claimed that Marx assumes equilibrium, at least at the start of his theory, and

29. A fundamental point for Marx is that the value of labour-power is an historically constructed subsistence, and not simply the result of supply and demand. This is important because actual wages may fluctuate above or below the value of labour-power (C I, 419).
30. Both Robinson (1966, xi) and Sekine (1997, Vol. II) agree on this.
31. "In itself, the value of the total capital stands in no inner relationship to the amount of surplus-value, at least not directly" (C III, 137).
32. "On the other hand, the simple, fundamental form of the process of accumulation is obscured both by the splitting-up of surplus-value and by the mediating movement of circulation. And exact analysis of the process, therefore, demands that we should, for a time, disregard all phenomena that conceal the workings of this inner mechanism" (C I, 710). See also (C III, 134–40) for a full discussion of the mystifying properties of the category profit cut free from surplus-value.

there are few categories more castigated these days by those critical of the "static equilibrium" of neo-classical economics.[33] And yet without the competition that fuels tendencies towards equilibrium, any general theory of capital would be simply a violent abstraction with very little explanatory power and would more likely oversimplify and distort than advance substantive understanding of capitalism. It is only because there are equilibrium tendencies that Marx is able to theorize capital's deep structural dynamics, and yet in recent years "equilibrium" has become a kind of conceptual scapegoat for all that is wrong with neo-classical economics. In part this is because that concept has been associated with ideological theories claiming that the closer to perfect competition, the closer to equilibrium, and the closer to equilibrium the closer to optimal distribution of all economic values.[34] And in part it is because "equilibrium" has been associated with statics that seem totally divorced from the dynamics that is history. What is seldom considered is the possibility that an historically specific quasi-statics (structures that have only the most general directionalities) may be a starting point for moving towards the understanding of historical dynamics.

I use the term quasi-statics in the sense that the theory of capital's deep structures is a theory of structural relations that do not themselves change though the variables embedded in these structures do. For example, insofar as capitalism exists, capitalists continue to own the means of production, but this ownership tends to become more centralized in the sense that units of capital become larger. Further, while the enduring structural dynamics have a certain abstract historical directionality, we cannot directly derive from them historical specificities or the rate of historical change. We know that capital will always generate class struggle in history, but we do not know what forms this will take. Similarly we know that capital will centralize, but we do not know at what rate and in what organizational forms. We know that capital will be prone to periodic crises, but we do not know their precise causes, their depth and duration, their geographical impact, and the nature of the recovery. We know that capital will always need to find ways to counter a falling rate of

33. For example, see Aglietta (1979), Farjoun and Machover (1983), Freeman and Carchedi (1996), Fullbrook (2003), Keen (2001), Robinson (1964, 1966).

34. Marx chides "orthodox economics" for "...the dogma that misery springs from an absolute surplus population, and that equilibrium is re-established by depopulation" (C I, 861).

profit and its accompanying general growth of unemployment or underemployment, since any long-term significant fall in the rate of profit would lead to the demise of capitalism, but we do not know what means will be used in specific historical contexts.[35]

Marx assumes that in a purely capitalist society the forces of competition, the mobility of capital and labour, and the availability of credit will promote powerful equalizing tendencies.[36] He argues that if supply and demand are in equilibrium, no labour will be wasted, all commodities will be produced with necessary labour only, and wages will equal the value of labour-power.[37] The reason that Marx assumes an equilibrium of supply and demand is that he initially wants to think value categories as a relation between homogeneous capital and homogeneous labour independently of the movement of supply and demand.[38] For him, supply and demand enter the theory as outer constraining categories and not as inner determining categories.[39] For example, they do play a role in determining the rate of interest, which is the most externalized category in the theory. To explain the source of profit in exploitation in the clearest possible terms, Marx initially assumes that the total wages of the working class equal the full value of labour-power and that all commodities exchange at value so that surplus-value will equal total value created by labour-power minus total wages. Having clarified the fundamental class relation of capitalism, he then moves in *Capital* volume two to consider issues of temporality such as how circulation costs and turnover time impact on surplus-value. Later, in volume three, the consideration of variations of organic composition between

35. In my opinion one of the most common errors in the use of Marx's *Capital* is to directly connect parts of the theory to history prior to thinking the value interconnections of the theory as a whole.
36. A huge number of citations could be listed to support this point. Here are a few: C I, 261, 262, 268, 270, 431, 678, 710; C III, 241–2, 273, 275, 275, 291, 297, 298, 310, 774, 1004.
37. "This is in fact the law of value as it makes itself felt, not in relation to the individual commodities or articles, but rather to the total products at a given time … so that not only is no more labour-time devoted to each individual commodity than necessary, but out of the total social labour-time only the proportionate quantity needed is devoted to the various types of commodity" (C III, 774). See also (C I, 179, 201–2; S I, 410).
38. S III, 97; C I, 419.
39. "Where, as here [rate of interest], it is competition as such that decides, the determination is inherently accidental, purely empirical, and only pedantry or fantasy can seek to present this accident as something necessary" (C III, 485).

different capitals requires that he introduce prices of production as more specified conceptions of value. The outer limit of his theory of price determination occurs when supply and demand conditions as constrained by value relations determine whether the more productive or less productive technique determines a market price that is above or below the price of production for that commodity;[40] whereas the outer limit of his theory of profit determination is where the rate of interest is determined by the supply and demand of funds as constrained by movements of the rate of profit. Gradually Marx modifies his initial statics with more dynamic considerations. For example, the value of fixed capital that has been around for some time is the socially necessary labour time to reproduce that capital given existing levels of productivity and not the socially necessary labour time that was initially required. Further, wages will rise above the value of labour-power when expansive prosperity dries up the pool of unemployed, and wages will fall below the value of labour-power in the trough of a depression. It follows that a purely capitalist society would approach closest to an equilibrium at a point early in the prosperity phase when average wages would equal the value of labour-power. Thus a theory that starts out assuming equilibrium develops into a theory where equilibrium is only approached during a particular phase in the cycle of capital. And this is not a contradiction, but a movement from the abstract-in-thought to the concrete-in-thought in which an initial simplicity alters as a dialectical logic unfolds ever more concrete concepts.

Although Marx continually refers to the equalizing tendencies of competition, he never assumes that capitalism in history comes at all close to fluctuating around an equilibrium point. While competition would tend to equalize the average rate of profit in pure capitalism, in history this averaging would never converge on an equilibrium point.[41] Marx (C III, 291) emphatically claims that: "In actual fact, demand and supply never coincide, or, if they do so, it is only by chance. ... Why then does political economy assume that they do coincide? In order to treat phenomena it deals with in their law-like form, the form that corresponds to their concept, i.e. to consider

40. "If supply and demand coincide, the market price of the commodity corresponds to its price of production, i.e. its price is then governed by the inner laws of capitalist production..." (C III, 477).
41. Marx argues that "this constant equalization of ever-renewed inequalities is accomplished more quickly, (1) the more mobile capital is ... (2) the more rapidly labour-power can be moved..." (C III, 298).

them independently of the appearance produced by the movement of supply and demand." In other words, clarifying capital's inner logic, which requires the concept of equilibrium, is a necessary prerequisite to understanding actual capitalism which would only by accident ever even approach a state of equilibrium. It is only crude empiricism that would find difficulties in utilizing a concept of equilibrium to theoretically shed light on an empirical reality where equilibrium tendencies always fall far short of their goal. For it makes perfectly good sense in the case of historical capitalism to use the concept "equilibrium" to understand a situation where equilibrium tendencies are continually interfered with and would only accidentally reach a point where supply and demand balanced in every type of market simultaneously. Indeed, I would argue that Marx's use of "equilibrium" is rather unique. Not only is it used in different ways at different levels of concreteness within the theory of pure capitalism, it is also used differently between the theory of pure capitalism and concrete history. While the concept of equilibrium is necessary in order to clarify the necessary connections between the core categories of capital, the theory of capital's inner logic ultimately moves away from utilizing the concept of equilibrium as the concept of periodic crises is developed. If the concept of equilibrium plays an important role in the theory of pure capitalism, it plays an attenuated role at the levels of mid-range theory and historical analysis. In other words, it falls into the background when unpacking the power relations that stand behind the quantitative categories of capital's deep structures, because such power relations need to be theorized in a context where commodification is partial and where human agency intervenes, disrupting any commodity-economic logic that would on its own produce equilibrium.

CONCLUSIONS

In this chapter I have defended some of the most frequently attacked and/or dismissed concepts of Marx's political economy. I have argued for the importance of the theory of surplus-value and its corresponding labour theory of value for getting at the deep structural dynamics of profit-making in capitalism. I have argued that the labour theory of value can be given a clear and coherent quantitative formulation, but even more importantly, it can serve as a basis for unpacking the power relations that quantitative formulations distil and/or hide. Used in this sense it is key to moving from the most abstract levels of theory where commodification is assumed to be complete to more concrete levels, including historical analysis, where commodification is never complete and is always to some extent maintained by an array of forces which may not all be simply economic forces.

For Marx the theory of capital in the abstract and in general is essentially a theory of how surplus-value is created, circulated and distributed. For him, capital is a commodity-economically organized profit-oriented force. And while its inner logic may in some cases be far removed from empirical reality, it is this logic that can give the best orientation to more concrete levels of analysis. Indeed, capital, as self-valorizing value may display "…endless variations and gradations in its appearance, as the result of innumerable different circumstances, natural conditions, racial relations, historical relations acting from outside, etc., and these can only be understood by analysing these empirically given conditions" (C III, 927–8). And "analysing these empirically given conditions" is enormously improved, I would argue, through the support of three theoretical levels of analysis including at least the theory of capital's deep structure, mid-range theory and historical analysis.

Not far from the end of *Capital*, volume three, Marx (969–70) makes a particularly clear statement about the primary object that he is theorising.

In presenting the reification of the relations of production and the autonomy they acquire vis-à-vis the agents of production, we shall not go into the form and manner in which these connections appear to them as overwhelming natural laws, governing them irrespective of their will, in the form that the world market and its conjunctures, the movement of market prices, the cycles of industry and trade and the alteration of prosperity and crisis prevails on them as blind necessity. This is because the actual movement of competition lies outside our plan, and we are only out to present the internal organization of the capitalist mode of production, its ideal average, as it were.

In other words, in *Capital* Marx is not primarily concerned with conjunctural analyses of movements of markets and cycles, because actual historical analysis "lies outside our plan" (in other words with a level of analysis that cannot be absorbed into the theory of capital's logic). I think that I have presented a convincing case that "the internal organization of the capitalist mode of production" refers to a commodity-economic logic according to which capital can become self-expanding value. And "ideal average" implies that the equilibrium conditions assumed in theory for the sake of letting the commodity form take charge are an "ideal" that while necessary for theoretical clarity would never likely exist in actuality. For example, while competitive pressures would push capital towards an average rate of profit, in reality we would never expect a close approximation in any actual economy to a situation in which each capitalist in each sector would earn an average rate of profit. It is in this sense that the "average rate of profit" is an "ideal average".

And I must admit that my defence of the labour theory of value has been rather offensive, since my aim has been less to make Marx's formulations acceptable to mainstream economics, than to propose a complete reconstruction of economic theory, a reconstruction that would place many of Marx's most attacked conceptualizations at the centre. Thus, for example, the problem is not with Marx's labour theory of value, but with those who have misunderstood its power and have dismissed it, rather than placing it at the centre of economic theory where it belongs. The problem is not with Marx but with how mainstream economics has conceived of the economic in formalistic, uncritical and capital-friendly ways.

So far I have at times used the language of dialectics without focusing specifically on how Marx utilizes dialectical reason. It is my view that along with an adequate appreciation of Marx's theory of the commodity form, an adequate appreciation of his use of dialectical reason is another major reason why so many have failed to fully appreciate the enormous strengths of his theory. I turn next to a condensed and introductory excursion through the demanding topic of dialectical reason in Marx's *Capital*.

4
Reasoning Dialectically

Thus in capital the independent existence of value is raised to a higher power than in money. (S III, 131)

Capital runs through the cycle of its transformations, and finally it steps as it were from its inner organic life into its external relations, relations where it is not capital and labour that confront one another, but on the one hand capital and capital, and on the other hand individuals as simple buyers and sellers once again. (C III, 135)

Whatever shortcomings they may have, the merit of my writings is that they are an artistic whole, and that can only be attained by my method of not having them printed until they lie before me in their entirety. This is impossible with the Jacob Grimm method [instalments] *which is in general more suited for writings that are not dialectically constructed.* (Marx 1979, 199)

Unfortunately Marx's desire to have *Capital* before him in its entirety never came even close to fulfilment. It is also clear, however, that though the three volumes of *Capital* were not completed by Marx, and he (C I, 106) even had the intention of rewriting the one volume that was completed (volume one), his theory of capital's inner logic, even in its unfinished state, is presented as a totality informed at least to some extent by dialectical reasoning. It is the work of Tom Sekine that has most effectively brought out the dialectical reasoning lying dormant in *Capital*, but precisely because Marx's use of dialectics was sporadic at best, Sekine (1997) has had to reconstruct the sequencing and presentation of categories. In so doing, he has reconstructed capital's logic as a dialectical logic, converting it into arguably the most powerful theory in all of the social sciences.[1] Indeed, it is primarily Sekine's work that informs my explication and analysis of Marx's use of dialectic.[2]

Besides the failure to understand the full significance of Marx's theorization of the commodity form, another major reason that mainstream social scientists have often misinterpreted Marx's *Capital*

1. See Albritton (1999), Bell (1995), Kourkoulakos (2003).
2. His earlier work on the dialectic of capital has a fuller and more explicit treatment of the parallels between Hegel's *Logic* and the theory of capital (Sekine, 1986).

is that they approach it so steeped in empiricist epistemology that they fail to pick up on the important elements of dialectical reason in his theory. Ever since Bertrand Russell (1963) dismissed Hegel's dialectical mode of reasoning as sheer "mysticism", empiricists have paid it little attention. But Marx's object of knowledge can be described as capital's inner logic, and without an appreciation of dialectical reason, it is unlikely that an interpreter could fully understand the sense in which capital could have a logic that is internal to it and that in principle can be fully set forth in theory. Coupled with Marx's understanding of the key importance of the commodity form, it is precisely the opening towards dialectical reason that makes his theory potentially so powerful.

The rigorous kind of dialectic that I have in mind requires an object that can be theorized as a set of necessary inner connections between categories that are simply different forms of the same substance. Further, there must be a primary category containing a fundamental categorial opposition that can propel reasoning forward until all basic categories required for the object to have a complete logic can be internalized into the primary category as simply different forms of it. The primary category, which Marx refers to as the "cell-form", is the commodity form with its inner contradiction between value and use-value.[3] For Marx, dialectical reasoning utilizes the contradiction between value and use-value to drive forward a logic that moves from less specified economic categories to more specified until the interconnections between all the basic economic categories of capital are clarified. The least specified, most general economic category, and therefore the starting point that can encompass the whole that is to be known, while requiring the fewest presuppositions, is the commodity form with its internal contradiction between value and use-value.[4] Dialectical reason utilizes this contradiction to move thought from the most abstract and indeterminate to ever more concretely specified economic categories.[5] Thus the dialectic

3. "Capital, however, necessarily produces its product as a commodity. This is why as capitalist production, i.e. capital, develops, the general laws governing the commodity evolve in proportion..." (C I, 950).
4. "As the commodity form is the most general and the most undeveloped form of bourgeois production..." (C I, 176); "...the exchange of commodities implies contradictory and mutually exclusive conditions. The further development of the commodity does not abolish these contradictions, but rather provides the form within which they have room to move" (C I, 198).
5. It is important to distinguish the dialectical "concrete-in-thought" from the empiricist "real concrete".

can be conceived as value overcoming and subsuming successive use-value obstacles until value can, as self-valorizing value, achieve indifference to use-value precisely in the sense that capital can shift from producing one use-value to another with only short-term profit criteria in mind. And this indifference is maximally expressed in M-M', the form of interest-bearing capital, which represents the commodification of capital itself and has the liquid form of being immediately investible in any promising profit-making activity, thus closing the circle that started with the commodity form and making it appear that value in its externalized form of money can really expand itself indefinitely and think of itself only in mathematical terms without any reference to social relations.[6]

THE UNIQUE ONTOLOGY OF CAPITAL

In other writings, I have argued at length that the sort of dialectical reasoning employed by Marx may only be truly effective in theorizing capital's inner logic because of the unique ontology of this particular object of knowledge.[7] The uniqueness in this case has to do with social relations that become absorbed into a commodity-economic logic such that though the logic is propelled by human agency, social relations become self-objectifying and self-abstracting, and hence theorizable dialectically as an unfolding of a set of necessary inner connections. And while large parts of capital's inner logic can be theorized in this peculiarly powerful manner, there are points that escape strict dialectical reasoning.[8]

As a self-reifying set of social relations, capital is, for that very reason, also self-abstracting. In other words, capital's commodity-economic logic is self-expanding and self-deepening such that historical capitalism manifests movement from less commodified

6. "We started with money as the converted form of the commodity. What we arrive at is *money as the converted form of capital*... (S III, 467). "The formation of interest-bearing capital, its separation from industrial capital, is a *necessary* product of the development of industrial capital..." (S III, 471).

7. I take ontology to refer to the study of the basic properties of an object, properties that in this case make a dialectical theory both possible and desirable.

8. Though the necessity for the commodification of labour-power can be dialectically derived its actual commodification is a long historical process. Similarly, an industrial reserve army is necessary, but it too is an historical construct which may take diverse forms.

to more commodified societies. But because the form of value treats qualitatively different things as the same except as they differ quantitatively, it abstracts from difference with the result that a certain homogenizing abstractness rules social life. Social relations become abstract insofar as they are absorbed into the commodity form such that they relate as economic variables. And while this self-abstracting movement of the commodity form never comes close to completion in history, such completion can be achieved in theory.[9] The result is a society completely subsumed to the movement of the commodity form, and it is only because of this completion that economic variables can accurately be theorized in quantitative terms and at the same time be theorized dialectically as a set of variables that can be unfolded in a necessary sequence of inner connections. Thus in theorizing capital as a dialectic our aim is to trace capital's own self-abstraction through the commodity form, and not to simply impose a model on it that we have invented.[10] And capital is perhaps a unique object of knowledge in the degree to which it manifests a powerful self-reifying and self-abstracting dynamic in history. Or in other words, the built-in motion of capital deepens the commodity form by increasing the degree of commodification and expands the commodity form by subsuming more and more of economic life to its logic.

I shall present this uniqueness by noting some of the differences between the cell-form as primary concept of biology and the commodity form as primary concept of capitalist economics (one could say simply "economics", since it is only with capitalism that economics becomes a set of distinct relatively autonomous practices). Despite certain surface similarities between the two, making the analogy useful for Marx, a fundamental difference is that it is not possible from the cell-form to dialectically derive an inner logic of living beings (plants and animals).

In order for such a dialectical inner logic of biology to be theorizable the following conditions would need to hold.

1) Living organisms would constitute a biological totality whose basic interconnections would be theorizable in the abstract and in general by a limited set of biological categories (core categories).

9. "...individuals are now ruled by *abstractions*, whereas earlier they depended on one another" (G, 164).
10. Sekine makes this point very forcefully in all his writings.

These categories could all be generated from a basic contradiction within the cell-form.

2) Further the categories would be simply different forms of an underlying homogeneous substance such that their interconnections could be understood quantitatively.

3) Biological evolution would result in a self-expanding and self-reifying movement that would cause the totality of biological organisms to increasingly manifest (at least up to a point) the core categories. In other words, evolution, though incomplete, would present a directionality that would enable completion in theory.

4) By theoretically extending this movement to completion, the core categories would reveal necessary inner connections, that, as different forms of the same substance (differing only quantitatively), could be thought mathematically and in a necessary sequence from abstract-in-thought to concrete-in-thought (or from the less specified to the more specified).

5) Theorizing the mathematical interconnections of the core categories would reveal a built-in logic that would explain how the core variables must interrelate in the expanded reproduction of the totality of biological organisms. The result would be a theory of the inner logic of biological organisms.

Though not a biologist myself, I would be surprised if the above propositions would hold for biology. If they do not, as I suspect, then there can be no dialectical inner logic of living organisms. And yet, because of capital's unique self-reifying ontology, I would argue that they all hold for theorizing capital's inner logic.

The above five points can be summarized by claiming that historical capitalism, by its own built-in logic, tends to a significant extent to become *more* capitalist, thus indicating to the theorist by extension how to think the *most* capitalist. But the "most capitalist" turns out to have an inner logic precisely because it implies a situation in which the commodity form has taken over economic life totally such that this form, propelled by human agency, can reproduce itself, deepen itself and expand itself as if it had a life of its own. This commodity-economic logic reveals the essence of capital precisely because no outside force interferes with it in the context of pure capitalism. It is not the logic of the capitalist state or of the worker's movement or of organized capital. It is capital's logic and only capital's logic. Furthermore, this logic can be thought quantitatively because the core economic categories are as value all simply different forms of homogeneous human labour or objectified abstract labour.

On the one hand, Marx is not fully cognizant of the above points and hence does not theorize capital's inner logic as a rigorous dialectical logic. On the other hand, both implicit and explicit elements of dialectical reasoning are scattered through the three volumes of *Capital*. In what follows I shall draw out and analyze some of these elements.

CONTRADICTION AND NECESSITY

In a dialectic we know in a general way where we want to go conceptually, but instead of simply positing concepts, we try to let their necessary inner connections emerge as a logical unfolding. For example, the class relation emerges necessarily from the basic opposition between value and use-value when it becomes clear that self-valorizing value requires the exploitation of labour.[11] By letting categories emerge in their necessary sequence (e.g. "money" cannot come before "commodity"), dialectical reasoning at the same time fills in the meaning of previous categories. We start with the commodity form, but we only subsequently learn that for it be a capitalistic commodity form, both the money form and capital form are required. Indeed, at the end of the theory we learn that not only are all the basic economic categories necessary in order to completely fill in the commodity form if it is to be fully capitalist, but also that all of these categories have necessary ways of interrelating. And the necessity may be quite strict, as in the commodity form strictly requiring the money form, or it may be looser, as in the rate of profit necessarily constraining movements of the interest rate.

How does dialectical reasoning work? First, it emphasizes what is most opposing between two categories, and treats this opposition as a contradiction that must be resolved through the production of a more concrete category (concrete in the sense of more specified) that temporarily resolves the contradiction until a new contradiction arises that pushes the dialectic yet further. The two basic categories of

11. "As soon as production by way of wage-labour becomes general, commodity production must be the general form of production" (C II, 119); "...capitalist production is commodity production as the general form of production, but it is only so, and becomes ever more so in its development, because labour itself here appears as a commodity" (C II, 196).

the dialectic of capital, value and use-value, are mutually exclusive, and yet they mutually condition and constrain each other.[12] Value is what makes all commodities the same, differing only quantitatively as members of the homogeneous community of number. It constitutes a commodity's sociality or interconnection or indeed sameness with all other commodities. Use-value represents a commodity's materiality or its qualitative difference from other commodities. In the ideal of those who support capitalism, the motion of value is directed by "consumer sovereignty" to ensure that use-values are distributed so as to maximally meet social needs. In sharp opposition to such a position, Marx demonstrates that while in capitalism the motion of value can subsume the fundamental use-values of economic life, its accomplishment of this is at great social cost. This is because it creates an economy where social needs are systematically sacrificed if they do not fit the requirements of short-term profit considerations, where one class is systematically dominated and exploited by another, and where all are dominated by the violence of things.[13] And all of this is mapped out theoretically by a logic that moves forward because of the contradictions between value and use-value.

Since it is commodity as form of value that is central to unfolding capital's inner logic, for the dialectic to proceed it must generate a new category by which value can subsume ever new use-value obstacles until all the main use-values of economic life are subsumed. For example, it proceeds to find a logical way to show that the money form is always-already contained in the commodity form as necessary to its development towards becoming a fully filled-in capitalist commodity form. In short, dialectical reasoning demonstrates that for the commodity form to evolve into self-valorizing value, it presupposes the money form from the beginning, but we cannot thereby simply posit money, rather we must derive it logically from the commodity form such that the money form becomes a qualitative differentiation that takes place within the commodity form. And as with money, so it is with other economic categories with the partial

12. For example, Marx writes: "The relative form of value [the commodity form as value form] and the equivalent form [ultimately the money form] are two inseparable moments, which belong to and mutually condition each other; but, at the same time they are mutually exclusive or opposed extremes..." (C I, 140).
13. "Hence the rule of the capitalist over the worker is the rule of things over man, of dead labour over the living, of the product over the producer" (C I, 990).

exception of the commodification of labour-power and the commodification of a surplus population in the form of an industrial reserve
army, since neither of these can be strictly derived from the logic of
the commodity form, but rather require a definite historical condition
(mainly the separation of workers from the means of production).

A dialectic is a kind of theoretical bootstrap operation.[14] The further
development of a more abstract category requires a more concrete
category, such that though a fully formed capitalist commodity
presupposes the entire theory, as the most abstract category with
fewest presuppositions the commodity form also constitutes the
beginning.[15] Thus while in order to be a commodity, a product
must always exchange for money, we cannot theoretically generate
the money form without first starting with the commodity form.[16]
The dialectical movement from commodity form to money form is
one of the most important for the entire theory because it liberates
value from its enclosure in the commodity, giving it the externalized
form of money – a palpable object that as universal equivalent is
hyper mobile (as in liquid funds) and relatively autonomous from
the commodity.[17] Indeed, in order for us to reach a conceptualization of capital as self-valorizing value, value must first achieve the
"independent selfhood" that becomes a potential with the money-
form.[18] Marx (C I, 152–3) derives the money form from the commodity

14. "Money and commodities as such are therefore latent capital, potential
    capital; this applies to all commodities insofar as they are convertible into
    money, and to money insofar as it is convertible into those commodities
    which constitute the elements of the capitalist process of production.
    Thus money – as the pure expression of the value of commodities and
    of the conditions of labour – is itself as capital antecedent to capitalist
    production" (S III, 475).
15. "Hence if the *commodity* appears on the one hand as the premise of the
    formation of capital, it is also essentially the result..." (C I, 950).
16. In criticizing Proudhon (it could just as well be Ricardo) Marx writes: "he
    has never understood that money is a necessary aspect of the commodity"
    (S III, 523).
17. "Exchange, however, produces a differentiation of the commodity into
    two elements, commodity and money, an external opposition which
    expresses the opposition between use-value and value which is inherent
    in it" (C I, 199).
18. According to Marx money "...is the first form of appearance of capital"
    (C I, 247); "...all new capital, in the first instance, steps onto the stage
    – i.e. the market, whether it is the commodity-market, the labour-market,
    or the money-market – in the shape of money, money which has to
    be transformed into capital by definite processes" (C I, 247). See also
    (C I, 255).

form by showing the necessity for a particular commodity to be set aside from all others in order to serve as universal value reflector. Or, to put it otherwise, money is a commodity whose use-value serves to express value so that all other use-values can be subsumed to the motion of value. All use-values are material properties that are wanted for some purpose; whereas since money can buy any use-value, it is wanted for all purposes.[19]

With the commodity form and money form theorized, it is possible to generate the next most concrete category: the capital form. Since the basic form of capital is the circulation form M-C-M' (presumably buying cheap and selling dear), clearly it is a theoretical expression that presupposes a certain grounding of the commodity form and the money form as a prerequisite. But in a closed society of equal exchanges M-C-M' could not exist. If everyone bought cheap and sold dear, in the end circulation would equalize and no one would profit. In order to be systemic, M-C-M' would seem to require unequal exchange facilitated by markets sufficiently isolated from one another to have different prices for the same commodity so that one could continually buy cheap in one market and sell dear in another. But one of the main tendencies of capitalism is to break down the isolation of markets such that the tendency is towards one and only one market price for each type of commodity at each point in time. Indeed, this is precisely what is assumed to be the case by Marx where there are no obstacles to competition. Thus, it makes no sense to try to explain profits in the theory of capital's deep structures through a mechanism of systematic unequal exchange.

On the assumption of equal exchange, the only way in which the second M can be larger than the first, is if there is some C that can create new value. And it is this theoretical quandary that propels Marx's theorization of the commodification of labour-power. Indeed, this is the *sine qua non* of the entire theory that centres on the nature of profit as derived from the exploitation of labour. To make sense, M-C-M' must be expanded into M-C ... P ... C'-M', and since the means of production can only pass on their value to the product, the increase of value must come from living labour. In other words, M-C-M' must subsume the labour and production process in order to

19. "This contradiction between the quantitative limitation and the qualitative lack of limitation of money keeps driving the hoarder back to his Sisyphean task: accumulation. He is in the same situation as a world conqueror, who discovers a new boundary with each country he annexes" (C I, 231).

become a generalized form of economic activity, and the key to this is the commodification of labour-power.[20] The expanded second M' is the excess of the total value created by social labour over the value that labour receives in the form of a wage, or "surplus-value". And since the commodification of labour-power entails a class of persons who have nothing to sell but their labour-power, it follows that the generalization of the commodity form entails a class relation between capital and labour. For Marx to say that capitalism is commodity production generalized, thus entails the notion of class. The precise sense of Marx's claim that "...in capital the independent existence of value is raised to a higher power than in money" should now be readily accessible. In the form of money, value can buy anything that has a price; whereas in the form of capital value can continually expand itself and thus buy more and more. The value of a commodity which started out as the relation between that commodity and all other commodities, and can in this sense be called a "social relation between things" (C I, 166), in order to become transformed into M-C-M', or "self-valorizing value", must subsume the labour and production process.

Dialectical reasoning can demonstrate the logical necessity for labour-power being commodified, but its actual occurence is a result of a long historical process in which private property enclosed the commons and divorced labour from the means of production.[21] It is also the case that once the commodification of labour-power develops to some extent, the self-expansion of capital will tend to further divorce labour from the means of production by undermining self-employed labour. In this sense capital in history is a self-commodifying and self-reifying force, such that once it gets its foot in the door, it creates the conditions for its own further expansion, and this tendency is carried to completion by Marx in his concep-tualization of self-valorizing value.

Dialectical reason continually returns to deepen our understanding of the commodity form as it moves forward. At first it focuses primarily on circulation forms. Then it shifts to the basic production relations between capital and labour as these are subsumed to the

20. "...capitalist production is commodity production as the general form of production, but is only so, and becomes ever more so in its development, because labour itself here appears as a commodity..." (C II, 196).

21. "It [capital] arises only when the owner of the means of production and subsistence finds the free worker available, on the market, as the seller of his own labour-power. And this one historical pre-condition comprises a world's history" (C I, 274).

circulation forms. Finally, it shifts to distribution relations which examine the distribution of the surplus-value resulting from the marriage of circulation forms and production relations. According to Marx (S III, 56), "the relations of distribution are only the relations of production seen from a different aspect". He can make this claim because all of the categories involved are different forms of value and thus are connected inwardly. All the forms of profit and rent are thus surplus-value expressed in more concrete and externalized forms, but still interconnected. And we proceed this way until capital itself, as interest-bearing capital, is subsumed to the commodity form.

Marx attempts insofar as possible to present the inner connections amongst value categories as necessary connections.[22] Thus the money form is necessary to the commodity form and these two forms are necessary to the capital form.[23] Similarly the commodification of labour-power is necessary to the further development of the capital form as self-valorizing value. And the theory of relative surplus population and periodic crises are necessary to understand how the commodification of labour-power is maintained relative to the needs of self-valorizing value. Inner necessary connections are often contrasted with outward appearances, which may mislead. Sometimes Marx utilizes the term "competition" to refer to the realm of empirical appearances, and this needs to be kept in mind in order not to get confused with his use of "competition" to refer to one of the basic conditions of pure capitalism. In the empirical world of competition, economic phenomena appear as discrete perceptions without any connections other than constant conjunction. For Marx, one of the main tasks of theory is to clarify the inner connections that stand behind these outward appearances.

For example, from the point of view of capital, the cost-price for producing a commodity is a very important category, because profit appears as the difference between cost-price and selling-price. And yet cost-price makes it appear as if profit arises equally from total cost-price. By breaking down this category into $c + v$, Marx makes it clear that profits arise totally from v and not at all from c.[24] Economists

---

22. "...the simple form of value automatically passes over into the more complete form" (C I, 154).
23. "Money as a measure of value is the necessary form of appearance of the measure of value which is immanent in commodities, namely labour-time" (C I, 188).
24. "...cost price does ... in the economy of capital, present the false semblance of an actual category of value production" (C III, p. 119). "Capital runs through the cycle of its transformations, and finally steps as it were from

see the appearance of capital "in its mere material existence, independently of its social relation to labour ... an autonomous source of surplus value alongside labour and independent of it" (C III, 135). The specificity of the capital/labour relation is further obscured by the wage-form, which makes it appear that what is being paid for is a quantity of labour rather than the use of labour-power for a certain amount of time (C I, 682). With the category "profit" "*capital appears as a relationship to itself*" and with this appearance the source of all profit in surplus-value cannot be thought. And the extreme of this appears with interest-bearing capital represented as M-M'.

A further assumption of Marx's theory of capital's deep structure is that exchanges are on average equal exchanges. There are scores of quotations that could be used to back up this interpretation, and for Marx it is important because capitalist profit-making is rooted in the realm of production, and if unequal exchange were systemic in theory, then profits might just as well come from the realm of circulation.[25] In the first instance he wants to explain exploitation on the assumption that on average workers receive the value of their labour-power. Further, the theoretical push from M-C-M' to the theory of exploitation is precisely the fact that in a closed society it is not possible for everyone to buy cheap and sell dear, and if one group does so systematically at the expense of another group, it can only be explained through the use of extra-economic force and not by the operation of a commodity logic.

Lest one consider this an unrealistic assumption, Marx argues that the self-reifying force of capital has generally increased the strength of the commodity form in economic life such that his abstractions simply follow to completion this commodification. And since commodification converts social relations into quantitative relations that abstract from qualitative difference, if capitalism is self-commodifying,

---

its inner organic life into its external relations, relations where it is not capital and labour that confront one another, but on the one hand capital and capital, and on the other hand individuals as simple buyers and sellers once again ... surplus-value itself does not appear as having been produced by the appropriation of labour-time, but as the excess of the sale price of commodities over their cost price..." (C III, 135).

25. "...all that happens in exchange is a metamorphosis." "In so far, therefore, as the circulation of commodities involves a change only in the form of their values, it necessarily involves the exchange of equivalents, provided the phenomenon occurs in its purity" (C I, 260). See also: (C I, 252, 260–3, 268, 270, 301, 417–18, 431, 678, 710, 729–30, 747, 1009; C II, 109, 153, 428; C III, 252).

it is also self-abstracting. Hence Marx's theoretical abstractions follow the real abstractions that arise in capitalist history, and insofar as the focus is on the purely economic structure of capitalism, the social connector is value. Or as Marx (S III, 147) puts it: "… [value] is only a representation in objects, an objective expression, of a relation between men, a social relation, the relationship of men to their reciprocal productive activity". I would add that value is ultimately a set of power relations (class) in which the power can easily disappear into what appear to be purely quantitative relations between things.

In a theory presented in accord with dialectical reason, the sequence of categories is a necessary unfolding from an initial category whose content is gradually filled in. And to the extent that the dialectic works, the sequencing presents inner connections amongst the categories that are necessary. Joan Robinson (1966, 10) exposes her British empiricist roots when she writes: "It seems, certainly, perplexing as we follow the uphill struggle of Marx's own mind from the simple dogmatism of the first volume of *Capital* to the intricate formulations of Volume III." For dialectical reason requires that volume one precede volume three, and furthermore by letting the economic categories find their necessary inner connections, dialectical reason is far less prone to dogmatism than empiricism, which tends to simply assert formal models on the one hand and let the "facts speak for themselves" on the other.

A dialectical theory is a layered theory, moving from the simple-in-thought to the complex-in-thought or from the abstract-in-thought to the concrete-in-thought. Theorizing the relation between homogeneous capital and homogeneous labour is not dogmatic as claimed by Joan Robinson, but is a simplifying clarification supported to some extent by the self-abstracting tendencies of capital itself. And Marx himself is fully aware of the fact that in history class relations are significantly more complicated.

Another much misunderstood and sometimes maligned category of dialectics is "contradiction". The use of "contradiction" in dialectical reasoning does not violate the law of non-contradiction in formal logic. To say that within the commodity form there is a contradiction between value and use-value is to say that they are mutually dependent and mutually opposed semi-autonomies. Mutual dependency implies that a value must always be attached to a use-value, and mutual opposition implies that as pure quantity, self-expanding value must overcome the difficulties posed by incorporating use-value as pure quality. Value must incorporate use-value without compromising its self-expanding quantitativeness, which it does by producing a sequence of categories that overcome and subsume successive use-value obstacles. For example, money is generated when a particular use-value becomes the universal value reflector. Money becomes that commodity whose use-value is to embody pure quantity so that it can be immediately exchanged (in sufficient quantity) for any use-value whatsoever.

Understood in this way, it is contradiction that propels the unfolding of categories in a dialectical logic. In the first instance, the only kind of change associated with contradiction is conceptual change, and later I shall argue at some length that it is only through the mediations of other levels of theory that bring in the consideration of non-capitalist economic practices and non-economic social practices that the conceptual changes of the dialectic of capital may contribute to our understanding of historical changes. For example, because capital expands value as an end in itself, there is always a tendency for value to become too autonomous and hence out of phase with use-value, and it is this tendency that underlies periodic crises.

According to Marx (S II, 513): "Crisis is the forcible establishment of unity between elements that have become independent and the enforced separation from one another of elements which are essentially one." And while it is clear that there are numerous points in the theory in which value could in history become too independent from use-value, thus triggering a crisis, Marx also gives an account of why periodic crises would even occur in pure capitalism. In any actually existing capitalism, the contradictions within the dialectic of capital can help us sort out and think through the causes of a particular crisis, which may include non-capitalist economic causes and non-economic social causes. And while I claim that no actually existing capitalist society ever approximates pure capitalism, yet the more capitalist the society, the stronger the explanatory power of the theory of capital's logic, and furthermore, it is that theory that serves as the reference point to determine just how capitalist a society is.

Another concept that Marx often uses in a dialectical sense is "necessity".[26] When used dialectically, "necessity" refers to a particular kind of deductive entailment that resolves a contradiction in the only way that it can be resolved. The basic contradiction of the dialectic of capital is between value and use-value in the sense that self-valorizing

---

26. I wish to thank Stefanos Kourkoulakos for clarifying this point.

value can only be achieved when potential use-value obstacles are subsumed to the commodity form, and this can only be achieved by mobilizing value. In other words, value must be mobilized through expanding the commodity form until the basic economic categories of capitalism can all be interconnected and operated by a commodity-economic logic. Initially both value and use-value are locked up within a single commodity, but the commodity form requires the money form since a basic property of all commodities is to be sold for money, and furthermore, value must necessarily become a society-wide set of stabilized quantitative exchange relations. The challenge for dialectical reason in this case is to generate the money form from the commodity form. The task is to show that the contradiction between value and use-value within a single commodity necessarily entails a logical movement of thought that results in the emergence of the money form. Without going through all the steps that Marx follows in this case, it must be emphasized that the contradiction can be resolved *only* by generating the money form from the commodity form. Essentially this is achieved by setting aside a single commodity (gold) that serves as a universal value reflector that can quantitatively equate all capitalistically produced commodities as differing systematically in quantitative terms. Money serves to externalize value that is initially locked up within commodities such that it can become a social system. Without this step in the dialectic of capital, the theory could not get off the ground, for the sociality of value could never be expressed. The movement of dialectical reason is thus a necessary movement required to unfold the categories that are to constitute a totality.

TOTALITY

Since "totality" is a much despised concept these days, I shall sketch the precise sense of this concept when applied in this case. It is Marx's purpose to understand all of the most abstract and general economic categories of capitalism as different objectifications of one basic substance: value, or, what is the same thing, abstract, homogeneous labour. All of the basic quantitative economic categories: "price", "profit", "interest", "wage", and "rent" are understood as simply different forms of value, and, as such, their connections are "inner" connections.[27] In order to make the theory as clear as possible,

27. Marx criticizes Smith because: "he constructs the exchange-value of the commodity from the values of wages, profit and rent, which are

he assumes that commodification is complete and that all labour is engaged in the production of capitalist commodities. Labour is assumed to be unskilled and abstract in the sense that labour can easily be shifted indifferently from producing one use-value to another as required by capitalist profit maximization.

If we call the totality that Marx theorizes a purely capitalist society, then we should understand the "purification" as a self-purification of capital brought to completion by Marx the theorist for cognitive purposes. The action of the commodity form reduces power relations to a structural dynamic in which the inner connections of the structures can be numerically expressed in forms of value. Marx is completely aware of the fact that pure capitalism will never exist in history, but he also believes that historical capitalism is self-purifying to such an extent that the law of value can help a great deal in understanding the actual tendencies of historical capitalism. He continually refers to this actual historical capitalism as "competition",[28] and though he sometimes writes as though he planned to theorize this more concrete level, his health declined and his life was cut short. It follows that the theory of pure capitalism is a sort of realistic thought-experiment made real precisely by capital's powerful self-abstracting tendencies. The object is an inner logic of the motion of value that absorbs all basic socio-economic relations into the commodity form. It is an exclusionary totality in the sense that with the completion of the dialectic, capital can ignore all use-values that do not impinge on profits. In other words, it is capital's logic that is exclusionary and not the theorist of capital who simply attempts to trace capital's self-abstractions. And this exclusion is summarized by Marx as capital's indifference to use-value (or quality).

---

determined independently and separately. Instead of having their source in value, they become the source of value" (S II, 217). "The form of revenue and the sources of revenue are the *most fetishistic* expression of the relations of capitalist production. It is their form of existence as it appears on the surface, divorced from the hidden connections and the intermediate connecting links. Thus *land* becomes the source of *rent*, *capital* the source of *profit*, and *labour* the source of *wages*" (S III, 453).

28. That "competition" has multiple uses in Marx's *Capital* has led to considerable confusion. Three basic uses are: 1) As a fundamental condition for the existence of capitalism; 2) that of volume three as opposed to volumes one and two, because in volume three competition over how total surplus will be divided must be conceptualized; and 3) actually-existing historical capitalism as opposed to the theory of capital's inner logic.

While any totality in the strong sense must include some sort of closure, the closure in the case of value theory invites more concrete levels of analysis. Marx's closure or completion is not so final as Hegel's Absolute, for by demonstrating the tenuousness of the commodity-economic management of the interest rate, it invites us to think of ways of moving to more concrete levels of theory that lack the degree of commodification required for a dialectical logic to be workable. For the dialectic of capital closes with the commodification of funds, thus turning capital itself into an automatic interest-bearing force, and what is important in this case is that value cannot fully determine the rate of interest, rather it only strongly influences it and confines its movement within certain limits. Such a weak closure suggests the need to move to more concrete levels of analysis where qualitative institutional forces are required to understand the impact of capital's logic in particular circumstances. The degree of com-modification assumed in the theory of pure capitalism never exists in actuality such that the stabilization of social structures required for them to be absorbed by the commodity form and thus converted into quantitative economic variables must be translated ultimately into processes and structures of power and agency as we move from abstract theory to more concrete levels of analysis.

Marx, for example, makes it clear that the category "rate of interest" is not a pure value category, but rather is formed from power relations constrained by value. A further example would be the category "fictitious capital" as developed through stock markets. While in the context of pure capitalism, it is possible to imagine markets where paper is traded based on expected future earnings, little more can be said at this level of analysis and this is because stock markets are largely shaped by historically specific legislation and other rather specific institutions which may vary considerably as between time and place (hedge funds, swap markets, and so forth). Thus Marx is only interested in theorizing the independent value forms of interest-bearing capital, of bank capital, and of fictitious capital and not their actual functioning in some particular context. But since these are things that we would naturally want to explore, there is a built-in imperative driving us to theorize more concrete levels of analysis. And Marx makes note of this throughout *Capital* by referring to dimensions of economic life that cannot be fully subsumed to the commodity form. Hence, the notion of levels of analysis is continually implied by Marx's theory, but the fact that he neglected to ever systematically approach this issue has left a gaping theoretical lacuna subsequently filled with the most diverse inter-pretations of how to relate the logical with the historical in Marxian economics. Indeed, Marx himself sometimes seems to think that the historical is increasingly becoming to a large extent a function of the logical, and at other times, in sharp contrast, the emphasis is placed on the need to develop theoretical mediations, which could include distinct relatively autonomous levels of analysis to relate the logical and the historical theoretically.

In Marx's conception of totality the sequence of categories often, but not always, unfolds in accord with dialectical reasoning. For example, as a rough approximation there is a parallel between Hegel's sequence of the doctrines of Being, Essence and Notion in the *Logic* and Marx's sequence of the theory of circulation forms, production relations and distribution relations in *Capital*. For Marx, the realm of circulation is the realm of forms *par excellence* because all that can happen in this sphere is that value can change its form from commodity to money to capital or vice versa. In other words, value cannot augment itself in circulation but can only change form; hence Marx's frequent use of the metaphor "metamorphosis" in connection with circulation to underline this point. For him this metaphor implies change of form without change in the quantity of substance passing through various forms, or one could say it implies equal exchange. Value only takes flight in its butterfly form or capital form when it is capable of self-valorization.[29] But since the basic form of capital as M-C-M', or using money to buy a commodity cheap and sell it dear, is inexplicable in a system of equal exchanges, our dialectical reasoning is necessarily forced beyond the realm of circulation to the realm of production relations. It only becomes possible to find a basis for profit to the extent that circulation forms can subsume a set of production relations. And the first step facilitating such a move is the commodification of labour-power.

Since capital in the abstract and in general only relates to labour in order to profit and since there are a number of forms of profiting, it is necessary to produce a category that provides the content for these forms and that clearly grasps the fundamental relation between homogeneous capital and homogeneous labour. This is the category "surplus-value", and, as previously argued, along with the commodity it is the most important category of Marx's theory

29. "His emergence as a butterfly must, and yet must not, take place in the sphere of circulation" (C I, 269).

because it demonstrates that the swirl of numbers that appear in markets are all fundamentally connected to the capital/labour relation or to the way in which a basic undifferentiated capital form subsumes the labour and production process to constitute a capitalistically organized labour and production process. The immense significance of the category "surplus-value" suggests that any general theory of capitalism that lacks such a category must be considered fundamentally defective. For this category must be fully developed before it is possible to move on to the theory of distribution relations where we can consider how surplus-value becomes differentiated into industrial profit, commercial profit, rent and interest.

THE BOUNDARY PROBLEM

If the concept "totality" does not include everything, then its usage implies at least some distinction between inside and outside. For Marx, the inside or "inner" are the fundamental economic categories of capitalism, plus categories such as "surplus-value", required to think their interrelations. But "inner versus outer" are not rigid categories for Marx. I have already argued that the closure of the dialectic with "interest-bearing capital" at the same time is an opening that invites more concrete levels of analysis, levels that should not be inner to the dialectic, but are a necessary supplement if the dialectic is to effectively inform our study of history. Furthermore, one can claim that there are levels of analysis within the theory of capital's inner logic. Indeed, since the dialectic starts with the simplest, most abstract and most empty category (commodity) and gradually fills it in with more and more determinations, each move in the dialectic can be considered a move towards greater concreteness (not empirically concrete, but concreteness in terms of greater specification). For example, the move from value to price is an important step towards greater concreteness. Thus, looking back at the quotation at the beginning of the chapter, we see Marx writing metaphorically of the "inner organic life" where homogeneous capital confronts homogeneous labour in contrast to "external relations" where capital confronts capital and individuals confront each other as buyers and sellers. Here, Marx is emphasizing the greater innerness of value categories relative to price categories within the larger totality of pure capitalism, or, in other words, the greater theoretical concreteness of price categories. It follows that there can be totalities within totalities.

Marx (S I, 409) writes: "In considering the essential relations of capitalist production it can therefore be assumed that the entire world of commodities, all spheres of material production ... are (formally or really) subordinated to the capitalist mode of production for this is what is happening more and more completely...". First it is necessary to make an aside, for this quotation exemplifies Marx's frequent over-estimation of the extent to which history might come to resemble the theory of capital's deep structures. The main point I want to make, however, has to do with Marx's notion: "essential relations". Precisely what sort of totality is constituted by essential relations or what Marx elsewhere refers to as "inner logic"?[30] In other words, how do we determine the boundary, the inner versus outer, of Marx's theoretical totality?

In my view two categories most clearly indicate the boundaries of self-valorizing value: rent and interest. For Marx the fundamental form of capital is industrial capital, where surplus-value is embedded in the commodity output.[31] Rent is a boundary concept because it arises from subsuming an alien feudal landlord class to the motion of self-expanding value and because land cannot be capitalistically produced.[32] Interest is a boundary concept because though the rate of interest is constrained by the law of value, it is not fully determined by it.

The landlord class is essentially an alien class that becomes domesticated and subsumed to capital as passive junior partners.[33]

30. "An exact analysis of the process, therefore, demands that we should, for a time, disregard all phenomena that conceal the workings of its inner mechanism" (C I, 710). "The further we trace out the valorization process of capital, the more is the capital relationship mystified and the less are the secrets of its internal organization laid bare" (C III, 139). "The real inner laws of capitalist production clearly cannot be explained in terms of the interaction of demand and supply..." (C III, 291).
31. "Where capitalist production has developed all its manifold forms and has become the dominant mode of production, interest-bearing capital is dominated by industrial capital, and commercial capital becomes merely a form of industrial capital, derived from the circulation process" (S III, 468). "Those who consider the autonomization [*Verselbstständigung*] of value as a mere abstraction forget that the movement of industrial capital is this abstraction in action" (C II, 185).
32. "...modern landed property is in fact *feudal* property, but transformed by the action of capital upon it..." (S II, 153).
33. "Landed property thus receives its purely economic form by the stripping away of all its former political and social embellishments and admixtures..." (C III, 755).

Marx theorizes rent in connection with agriculture, the most extensive form of capitalist production that utilizes land. In its pure form capitalist agricultural production involves a landlord class that owns the land, a capitalist class that pays rent to the landlords for access to the land, and a working class that receives a wage for its agricultural labour. As Marx (C III, 751) puts it, "...the farmer produces wheat, etc. just as the manufacturer produces yarn or machines". In other words, he (C III, 762) argues that it is important to analyze rent "...in its pure form and free from all adulterations and blurring admixtures...". Now if rent is essentially "...a part of society's surplus labour as tribute"(C III, 911), then Marx's task is to explain rent consistent with self-valorizing value. Since the key to understanding the distribution of surplus-value is the average rate of profit, rent must also be consistent with this. So, for example, landlords receive differential rent in relation to fertility differences and other factors that generate surplus profits that must be absorbed if capitalist farmers are to earn the average rate of profit like all other capitalists. In principle it would be possible for landlords to charge exorbitant monopoly rents, but then capitalist farmers would migrate to other sectors of capitalist production where they could earn average profits and landlords would get no rent at all. A monopoly rent, then, cannot be explained by the law of value because it "...is determined neither by the price of production of the commodities nor by their value, but rather by the demand of purchasers and their ability to pay, consideration of which belongs to the theory of competition, where the actual movement of market prices is investigated" (C III, 898).[34] And Marx makes it clear time and again that the actual movement of prices in any particular time and place lies outside the theory of capital's inner logic.

Rent, then, is a boundary concept because "land" (including all monopolizable natural resources) cannot be capitalistically produced and because land of the worst quality must yield an average rate of profit with the result that all better quality land will yield surplus profits. And since these surplus profits cannot be reabsorbed through competition as with new technologies that only yield profits until the competition catches up, they would permanently undermine the overall regulating force of the average rate of profit were they not transformed into rent. It follows that land has use-value properties that can only be subsumed to self-valorizing value through the

---

34. In this instance, the theory of competition refers to empirical-historical analysis which lies outside the theory of capital's inner logic.

category rent, and it is easy to imagine situations where rent would not systematically absorb such surplus profits with the result that the regulating function of the average rate of profit would be undermined and with it so-called "capitalistic rationality".

Marx's conceptualization of rent cries out for more concrete levels of analysis because agriculture in actual history has almost nowhere been organized like purely capitalist agriculture, as he describes it. A three-class agriculture with capitalist farmers acting just like industrial capitalists comes closest to realization in England in the 1860s, but even in this case, only part of agricultural production was so organized and capitalist farmers could never achieve the mobility and indifference to use-value that was achieved by industrialists. In short, this example suggests that in actual history "land" has always been resistant to complete commodification, and hence, even its partial commodification has usually been accompanied by significant political and ideological supports.

Marx uses the formula M-M' for interest-bearing capital: money is lent and then paid back with interest. As with rent, Marx theorizes interest as it relates to the average profit made by industrial capital. Interest is a sub-division of the profit of enterprise that accrues to the ownership of capital over time. If the annual average rate of profit of enterprise is 10 per cent and rate of interest is 5 per cent, then for a capitalist who does not borrow any money, the total profit will be 15 per cent. It is as if he lent his capital to himself and earned 5 per cent. For Marx the percentage of this division between profit of enterprise and interest is determined by the rate of profit, custom, legal tradition and competition amongst capitalists for loanable funds. In the long run the main influence on the rate of interest is the average rate of profit; hence, the law of value strongly influences the rate of interest without determining it. In this sense, it represents the outer limits of the law of value. As the most externalized form of self-valorizing value, interest is the most removed from its source in the exploitation of labour.[35] While the rate of interest is constrained by the rate of profit it is not determined by it since ultimately it is determined by competition between lending and borrowing capitalists. As Marx (C III, 485) claims, "Where, as here, it is competition as such that decides, the determination is inherently accidental, purely empirical,

35. "...separated from its inner essence by a mass of invisible intermediate links, [interest-bearing capital] reaches ... the form of absolute *externalization*" (S III, 486).

and only pedantry or fantasy can seek to present this accident as something necessary."

What Marx means here is that the availability of loanable funds and what capitalists will pay for their use is determined both by purely empirical conditions and by the inner logic. In other words, there is no inner logic to fully determine the ratio between profits of enterprise and interest as there is to determine what portion of total surplus-value goes to industrial capital as a whole as opposed to say the surplus-value that is transformed into rent that goes to landlords. In a purely capitalist agriculture, landlords will necessarily receive the differential rent that is required in order to absorb the surplus profits generated by qualitative differences between pieces of land. In contrast the rate of interest can vary within limits, and there is no commodity-economic necessity determining a particular level in short-run.

Because interest-bearing capital seems to make the mere ownership of capital the basis for capital expansion and because it is this form of "profit" that is most palpable and immediate to everyday sense perception, it is also the form in which capital presents its happiest and most illusory face. For Marx (C III, 515–16), M-M' is the most fetishized form of capital because it appears that a thing, money, simply expands value out of itself without any reference back to the capital/labour social relation. Hence, "interest" is a favourite category for bourgeois political economists who want to think profit without exploitation.

Behind the misrepresentations of capital's most externalized packaging in the form of interest-bearing capital are many layers. The first and simplest form is the commodity form, but it is not simply any commodity. It must be a commodity form through whose unfolding we can reach the commodity that is the product of self-valorizing value.[36] Or, in simpler words, it will eventually become a capitalistically produced commodity. Similarly, not only is the money form derived from the commodity form, but also it is not just any money, it is money that can be conceptually unfolded to become the liquid form of capital. It is money on its way to becoming capital. And M-C-M' is not simply the capital of a merchant who takes advantage of market differentials to buy cheap in one market and sell dear

36. "As the product of capital, the commodity embodies the total value of the capital together with the surplus-value, unlike the original commodity which appeared to us as an autonomous thing. *The Commodity* is a transfiguration of capital that has valorized itself..." (C I, 954).

in another, it is a dominant, society-wide process of profit-making that only becomes possible to the extent that M-C-M' subsumes the labour-and-production process. It turns out that C cannot be a capitalistically produced commodity without M, M-C-M', and M-C ... P... C'-M'. This means that from the beginning, we must know where we need to go theoretically, while at the same time we can only get there by unfolding the more simple, abstract and formal categories that are the prerequisites for theorizing the more complex, concrete and contentful categories.

It is clear that surplus-value is a key category because it expresses in value terms the social relation between capital and labour. And since the creation of surplus-value occurs in production, the realm of production is at the centre of the theory. This means that not only is the realm of circulation more external, but the forms of capital that operate in the realm of circulation (commercial capital and interest-bearing capital) are also more external. Indeed, to the extent that these more external forms are not tied theoretically to the core capital/labour social relation, they generate misleading economic theory. That is why it is so important for Marx that even though theorizing the circulation forms must come first in the theory, these forms must from the beginning be theorized as those circulation forms whose content will become a capitalist labour and production process.

CRITIQUE OF CLASSICAL POLITICAL ECONOMY

This outline of some of the dialectical features of Marx's thinking can now help us to understand the character of the criticisms that he makes of the classical political economists that he most respected, Smith and Ricardo. A term that Marx sometimes uses to describe their failings is "crass empiricism", a term that can be broken down into at least the following:

1) Uncritical use of everyday language.[37]
2) Taking as given what needs to be problematized.[38]

37. "He too remains a captive of the economic categories as he finds them" (C II, 95).
38. "Ganilh is quite right when he says of Ricardo and most economists that they consider labour without exchange, although their system, like the whole bourgeois system, rests on exchange-value. This however is only due to the fact that to them the *form* of product as commodity seems self-evident, and consequently they examine only the *magnitude of value*" (S I, 205).

3) Producing theoretical terms by violent abstraction immediately from empirical phenomena or applying theoretical terms directly to empirical phenomena without considering the need for mediations.[39]

4) Lack of attention to systematic inner connections amongst theoretical categories.[40] Or lack of attention to the possible systematicity of a theory of deep structures.

5) Lack of attention to the need for mediations between theoretical categories or between theoretical categories and empirical history.[41]

6) Lack of attention to the distinction between form and substance and to the issue of the diverse forms substance may take.[42]

In referring to the post-Ricardian, Rodbertus, Engels (C II, 95) writes: "He too remains a captive of the economic categories as he finds them. He too christens surplus-value with the name of one of its particular subordinate forms, rent...". And the same can be said for Smith and Ricardo, who fail to see that different forms of profit, rent and interest are all simply different forms of surplus-value. No doubt several of the above mentioned aspects of crass empiricism are mutually supportive in producing these results. And while both Smith and Ricardo manifest elements of crude empiricism, there are also important differences between them.

39. "With all later bourgeois economists ... lack of theoretical understanding needed to distinguish the different forms of economic relations remains the rule in their coarse grabbing at and interest in the empirically available material" (S I, 92).

40. "One of these conceptions fathoms the inner connection, the physiology so to speak, of the bourgeois system, whereas the other takes the external phenomena of life, as they seem and appear and merely describes, catalogues, recounts and arranges them under formal definitions. With Smith both these methods of approach not only merrily run alongside one another, but also intermingle and constantly contradict one another" (S II, 165).

41. "Here the contradiction between the general law and further developments in the concrete circumstances is to be resolved not by the discovery of the connecting links but by directly subordinating and immediately adapting the concrete to the abstract" (S III, 87).

42. "However, let us remember that commodities possess an objective character as values only in so far as they are all expressions of an identical social substance, human labour, that their objective character as values is therefore purely social" (C I, 138–9). "We therefore have to consider the whole process in its formal aspect, that is to say, the change in form or the metamorphosis of commodities through which the social metabolism is mediated" (C I, 198–9).

Marx argues that Smith radically shifts perspective between exploring the inner connections of value and "crass empiricism".[43] Without actually conceptualizing it, Smith's theory often implies the existence of something like "surplus-value".[44] But because he never nails it down with a concept, it is easy for him to slide away from thinking through his labour theory of value as it interconnects wages, profits and rents, and instead think of these categories as they appear to the senses as simply separate revenues that go to labour, capital and landlords. Conceived in this latter way, the exploitative class relation between capital and labour disappears, and instead of starting with a society-wide interaction of capitalistically produced commodities, Smith starts with three groups of people (capitalists, landlords and workers), who presumably receive income (profit, rent and wages) in proportion to their contributions to capitalist production – capital thereby becomes a harmonious and happy family. Instead of constructing a general theory that would trace the inner connections between profit, wages and rent, Smith resorts to the immediacy of three empirical groups who are assigned these revenues in fair proportion to their contributions. As Marx puts it: "The form of revenue and the sources of revenue are the *most fetishistic* expression of the relations of capitalist production. It is their form of existence as it appears on the surface, divorced from the hidden connections and the intermediate connecting links."[45]

While Smith slides away from the labour theory of value when it suits him, Ricardo clings to it with a vengeance, producing a kind of economic geometry by immediately deducing all other economic concepts from it. As a result Ricardo (as does Smith), completely ignores the crucial importance of the commodity form and its necessary unfolding into the circulation forms of money and capital

43. "As Adam Smith resolves surplus-value not only into profit but also into the rent of land – two particular kinds of surplus-value, whose movement is determined by quite different laws – he should certainly have seen from this that he ought not to treat general abstract form as directly identical with any of its particular forms. With all later bourgeois economists ... lack of theoretical understanding needed to distinguish the different forms of the economic relations remains the rule in their coarse grabbing at and the interest in the empirically available material" (S I, 92). See also (C II, 269, 276, 282, 304–5).

44. "Because Adam Smith makes what is in substance an analysis of surplus value, but does not present it explicitly, in the form of a definite category, distinct from its special forms; he subsequently mixes it up directly with the further developed form, profit" (S I, 89). See also (C II, 458).

45. S III, 453; see also (C III, 953).

for understanding capital and the labour theory of value.[46] Thus not only does Ricardo lack an adequate theory of circulation, but also an adequate theory of the social forms in general that stand behind the quantifications of economic categories.[47] For example, instead of theorizing the commodification of labour-power, he immediately quantifies labour as wages. In other words, instead of presenting the social forms that commodification rests on, Ricardo simply assumes the existence of commodities and proceeds to think quantitatively.[48] Quantification thus becomes completely unproblematic, power relations disappear, and formalistic mathematical economics is born.[49] But this papering over of the class relation between capital and labour goes back at least to Locke. For "the general juridical notion from Locke to Ricardo is always that of *petty-bourgeois ownership*, while the relations of production they describe belong to the *capitalist mode of production*" (C I, 1083). And furthermore, this failure to address social forms leads Ricardo to claim universality for his theory instead of theorizing capital in its socio-historical specificity. Finally his failure to address the commodity form with its contradiction between value and use-value leads him to deny in theory that capitalism is prone to periodic crises.[50] Because of his tendency towards formalistic abstractions connected both to each

46. "...Ricardo says here: wealth consists of *use-values* only. He transforms bourgeois production into mere production of use-value, a very pretty view of a mode of production which is dominated by *exchange-value*" (S III, 54).
47. "...to them the *form* of product as commodity seems self-evident, and consequently they examine only the *magnitude of value*" (S I, 205). See also (S II, 168, 527; C I, 994).
48. "But *Ricardo does not examine* the form – the peculiar characteristic of labour that creates exchange-value. ... Right from the start he is only concerned with the *magnitude of value*..."(S II, 164).
49. Ricardo is a prime example of "the dogma that misery springs from an absolute surplus population, and that equilibrium is re-established by depopulation" (C I, 861).
50. "If Ricardo thinks that the *commodity* form makes no difference to the product, and furthermore, that *commodity circulation* differs only formally from barter, that in this context the exchange-value is only a fleeting form of the exchange of things, and that money is therefore merely a formal means of circulation – then this is in fact in line with his presupposition that the bourgeois mode of production is the absolute mode of production, hence it is a mode of production without any definite specific characteristics, its distinctive traits are merely formal. He cannot therefore admit that the bourgeois mode of production contains within itself a barrier to the free development of the productive forces, a barrier which comes to the surface in crises..." (S II, 528).

other and to empirical reality without adequate mediations, Ricardo is also prone to crude empiricism.[51]

Marx (S I, 89) claims that "Crass empiricism turns into false metaphysics, scholasticism, which toils painfully to deduce undeniable empirical phenomena by simple formal abstraction from the general law, or to show by cunning argument that they are in accordance with that law." Implied here is the need to carefully consider theoretical inner connections systematically before thinking the mediations that might make them useful to historical analysis as opposed to the direct moving back and forth between theoretical categories and empirical analysis that can only do violence to both. One way of expressing this is to say that the horizontal relation amongst all the basic capitalist categories that are subsumed to the commodity form must be thought systematically before thinking the vertical relation between the theory of capital's deep structures and capitalist history.[52] And since this way of proceeding requires thinking the relation between the totality of the theory of a purely capitalist society and actual historical capitalist societies, mediating levels of analysis are required.

According to Marx (S II, 106) Ricardo represents an advance over Smith in the sense that he does focus consistently on the inner "laws as such". But, on the one hand, Ricardo's theory is not abstract enough in the sense that he never understands surplus-value as the inner connection between rent and profit, and, on the other hand, his abstractions are formal, violent abstractions in the sense, for example, that he slights issues of social form and fails to develop the mediations that would connect his theoretical category "profit" to his labour theory of value or connect the "laws as such" with empirical reality. Indeed, at one point Marx (S II, 169) claims that Ricardo's entire theory can be reduced to one fundamental law.

CONCLUSIONS

It is now possible to make a stronger claim about the importance of the theory of the commodity form. The subsumption of the expanded reproduction of socio-economic life by the commodity

51. Marx refers to "Ricardo's ... arbitrary attempt to make concrete relations directly fit the simple relation of value" (S III, 124).
52. "But he misses the point because, right from the beginning, he is concerned with the explanation of a *particular* phenomenon (ground rent) and not with the establishment of a general law" (S II, 63).

form represents a self-objectification of capitalist social relations. And since this self-objectification can be theorized as a dialectic logic or a necessary unfolding of economic categories, the result is an objective theory of capital's inner logic. The importance of having such an objective touchstone for the social sciences can hardly be overstated. Indeed, the self-reifying force of capital is such that in the long run it tends to have at least some impact on all other social relations; and in many cases of multiple causality, it tends to be the strongest causal force. Thus given the objectivity of the dialectic of capital and capital's reifying force, it makes good sense to theorize such things as the "capitalist state" or "capitalist ideology".

Marx's great achievement with regard to dialectical reason was to theorize the expanded reproduction of capital's deep structure as the dialectical movement of value subsuming those use-value obstacles attached to the core economic categories of capital. The result was a systematic theory of the material reproduction of an entire society made into an abstract economic totality by the completion of the commodity form. And, following the lead of Japanese political economist Tom Sekine, I believe that because the dialectic of capital constitutes a totality, it neither makes good sense to think of capitalist history as a function of this theoretical totality, nor to isolate pieces of it and apply them directly to history. What does make sense is to maintain three levels of analysis, in which the middle level once again theorizes the material reproduction of an entire society, but in this case where the use-value obstacles are specific to a mode of capital accumulation that is most characteristic of an entire phase of capitalist development, where the lack of complete commodification requires political and ideological supports, and where capitalist social relations articulate with quasi-capitalist and non-capitalist social relations.

While Marx never explicitly theorizes levels of analysis, such an approach clearly makes the best sense of his theory, particularly when his theory of capital's inner logic is understood to be a powerful horizontal dialectic. In the following chapter, I shall gather together all the hints that point towards levels of analysis as the best solution for relating a dialectical theory of a deep structure to historical specificity.

5
Levels of Analysis

This does not prevent the same economic basis – the same in its major conditions – from displaying endless variations and gradations in its appearance, as the result of innumerable different empirical circumstances, natural conditions, racial relations, historical influences acting from outside, etc., and these can only be understood by analysing these empirically given conditions. (C III, 927–8)

While it is not our intention here to consider the way in which the immanent laws of capitalist *production manifest themselves in the external movement of the individual capitals … a scientific analysis of competition is possible only if we can grasp the inner nature of capital.* (C I, 433)

A perennial problem in all social science and particularly in economics with its highly abstract and mathematical theory is how to connect abstract theory to complex processes of historical change. Are mathematical economic variables to be lowered directly into history, and if so, how are we to think their interaction with both economic and non-economic structures, processes and agencies that are partially qualitative and not convertible into quantitative variables? This is the basic problem with empiricist approaches to economics that want to think in purely quantitative economic categories at both the level of theory and history. The aim in both cases would be to achieve a close approximation (verification or falsification) between theory and empirical data. In economics this approximation is seldom achieved because the simplicity and formalism required for a theory to be mathematically workable generally places it at a considerable distance from history. And although making sense out of empirical data requires that the data be already theoretically or at least ideologically informed, such presuppositions are seldom explored. Furthermore, for theorists to successfully integrate data collections into meaningful historical analyses, they need to be explicit about how they are theorizing history so that we can know the implications of the data for the unfolding of history. The scholastic discipline of economics tends to fail on both counts: abstract models are left hanging in mid-air, and data collections are left under-theorized as if they could speak for themselves.

Recently, many voices that would reform mainstream economics blame its failures on adopting "static equilibrium models". The collective demand of the reformers is for "dynamic theory", but this is easier said than done. For dynamic theories that would make economics more historical face irresolvable dilemmas stemming from their simultaneous commitment to empiricist epistemologies and to quantitative theorizing. In their pursuit of dynamism they become almost immediately too complex to be mathematically manageable, or they become egregiously economistic by reducing history to being a function of "dynamic economic variables", or finally, they give up all theoretical and mathematical hubris of trying to understand the bigger picture and content themselves with particularistic studies aiming to make sense out of very particular economic institutions in particular times and places. What they tend not to address is the severe limitedness of mathematical economics and the need to think in interdisciplinary power terms about how economic practices inform and are informed by non-economic or partially-economic social practices.

Hegelian-informed approaches tend to develop layers and levels both within theory and between theory and empirical reality. While, as already suggested, Marx did explicitly theorize layers of abstraction within the theory of capital's inner logic, he did not systematically theorize levels of analysis mediating abstract theory and historical reality. And as is usually the case in theoretical work, Marx's vagueness on this issue is filled with all sorts of formulations that point in rather different directions. It is therefore not surprising to find interpreters of Marx arriving at a host of different solutions. In this book one of my main aims is to argue for the superiority of a particular neglected solution: one that in many ways seems most in keeping if not with the letter (which is vague on this point) of Marx's theory, at least with the spirit. And if widely adopted, the solution that I will propose would tend to reorient not simply Marxian economics, but economic science in general, away from fetishizing mathematics, towards a very specific way of theorizing institutional power.

I have argued that Marx's theory of capital's inner logic is a unique theory in the social sciences in being able to think simultaneously both dialectically and quantitatively about a large number of socio-economic variables, all of which vary systematically in relation to each other. And this extraordinarily powerful theory is only possible when we conceive of economic categories as reified social relations that are managed entirely by the logic of the commodity form, for otherwise qualitative variables would intervene disrupting the quantitative logic. As the dialectical logic of the commodity form unfolds, it subsumes those use-value obstacles that would otherwise prevent value from being self-expanding. The aim of the dialectic is to maximally free the pursuit of profit from being tied to any particular use-value so that it can freely produce whatever use-value will be most profitable regardless of whether it is opium, leopard-skin coats, or carcinogenic chemicals. This is what Marx means in the first instance when he refers to capital's "indifference to use-value". But indifference to use-value as indifference to the qualitative side of the commodity is extremely far reaching in a society basically governed by the commodity form. For it implies that without human resistance and human intervention the tendency of capital will be to always sacrifice qualitative considerations when a choice must be made between profit and the quality of human life. It is my contention that a good deal of capitalist history is precisely a history of trying to limit or overthrow capitalism's destructive dialectic of placing profits above all other considerations. And very often capital either finds ways of circumventing the constraints placed upon it, or it moves into new arenas where constraints have yet to be constituted.

CAPITAL'S DEEP STRUCTURE AND HISTORY

While the quantitative dialectic of capital's inner logic is enormously useful in clarifying how capital as such would behave if not interfered with, in fact, in history, it is always interfered with. The problem that this poses for theory is how to move from a situation where human agency is always channelled by a commodity logic, to history where human agency may interfere with or compromise that logic in all sorts of ways. While Marx does not solve this problem himself, he is aware of it, and his theory offers the concepts that can contribute to a solution.[1] Marx's quasi-dialectical logic commodifies social relations precisely so that the motion of value as pure quantity trying to

1. For example, critical of James Mill he writes: "Here the contradiction between the general law and further developments in the concrete circumstances is to be resolved [by Mill] not by the discovery of the connecting links but by directly subordinating and immediately adapting the concrete to the abstract" (S III, 87). Marx's complete rejection of Mill's logical-historical method could not be more clear.

expand itself can be theorized without being disrupted by qualitative differences such as one might find, for example, between land and labour. It is clear that for Marx the basic contradiction of his theory of capital is between value and use-value, with value ultimately overcoming the resistances of use-value in order to become self-valorizing value. But as we move away from the dialectic of capital and the triumphant commodity form to more concrete levels, value is never self-valorizing since commodification is never complete. Not only are there areas of economic activity that are not commodified, but also the partial commodification that does exist is often both politically and ideologically supported and at the same time contested and resisted.

In history the motion of value (capital) must find ways to deal with use-value configurations that it cannot completely subsume or control. In an early phase of capitalist development in England, the dominant manufacturing sectors were organized as putting-out systems in which, for example, merchants provided wool to cottagers who would spin and weave it for a piece wage. This particular configuration of use-value production posed quite different commodification problems for the motion of value than say competitive cotton-factory production, monopolistic steel production, or the mass production of consumer durables. This suggests that thinking more concretely about use-value configurations and the sorts of political and ideological supports required for value to manage them could be a useful way of utilizing the theory of pure capitalism to help conceptualize capital accumulation at more concrete levels of analysis. Or, to put it a little differently, the motion of value itself can only manage use-values to the extent that they are commodified. But outside of pure capitalism commodification is never complete, forcing us therefore to supplement quantitative analysis with analysis that is qualitative and multidisciplinary.

So how does Marx's theory of capital in the abstract and in general help us to think about capitalist economic life at more concrete levels? The theory demonstrates what is required in order for a consistent commodity-economic logic to operate. By clarifying the necessary inner connections amongst completely commodified basic economic categories, we are aided in thinking about interconnections amongst those categories where and when commodification is not complete. For example, in pure capitalism, in the first instance, the capitalist class appropriates all the surplus-value (though ultimately they share some with their junior partners, the landlords). But in the woollen production of the eighteenth-century English putting-out system, it was possible for cottage workers to embezzle at least some of the yarn or cloth and sell it on the side, thus cutting into capital's surplus-value. In order to discourage such practices, the British Parliament passed draconian Anti-embezzlement Acts that enabled merchants to search cottages at will, and if caught embezzling, cottage weavers could be hung. This example, illustrates a situation where, because of the incomplete commodification of labour-power, coupled with a specific configuration of production, a particular intervention of state power was required to insure that the putting-out merchants got their full profit.

Marx's theory of capital not only demonstrates the necessary conditions for a commodity-economic logic to operate, but also in doing so demonstrates the difficulties in achieving and maintaining that commodification. The theory makes it dramatically clear that for capital the greatest problem is maintaining the commodification of labour-power. There are two reasons for this. First, capital cannot produce labour-power, and this means that to manage its supply and maintain its commodification an industrial reserve army and periodic crises are required. Second, workers can organize to resist the commodification of labour-power, and to the extent that they succeed, labour-power may become partially decommodified (in fact, in history, it always is to some extent).[2] And while labour-power presents the most difficulties for commodification, land, money, fixed capital and capital itself also present problems. Furthermore, competitive light industry lends itself to commodification, while expensive infrastructural projects like road building or projects like space exploration or nuclear weaponry that do not yield short-term profits nor produce an indefinite number of commodities for an impersonal market are difficult for a commodity-economic logic to manage by itself.[3] For that reason government contracts in these

2. For example the law of surplus population is disrupted by workers organizing. "Every combination between employed and unemployed disturbs the 'pure' action of this law" (C I, 794). Indeed worker combination was so threatening to capital in its formative period that "Workers' combinations are treated as heinous crimes from the fourteenth century until 1825" (C I, 901).
3. On the issue of the commodity-economic management of use-values Marx writes: "One can see that all this involves a very complex movement in which, on the one hand, the market prices in each particular sphere, the relative cost-prices of the different commodities, the position with regard to demand and supply within each individual sphere, and, on the other

areas are often on a cost-plus basis in order to ensure private capital a profit.

Where a theory like Marx's *Capital* demonstrates that a large number of abstract economic variables have necessary logical connections, how can we utilize such a theory in more concrete contexts where the logic is weakened by partial dereification, translated into relatively autonomous institutional practices, or subject to alteration by collective agencies?[4] Or, in other words, how can we theorize situations where quantitative relations are disrupted by qualitative ones, or economic relations are mixed up with non-economic relations, or where capital's inner logic loses some of its logical force at more concrete levels of analysis?

Marx's lack of clarity on these questions, and lack of headway in dealing with them, has been the central aporia bedevilling all subsequent interpretations of his work. Sometimes Marx seems to think that capitalism in history will approach so close to pure capitalism that there will be no need for a theory of mediations. This view is bolstered by the fact that he continually moves back and forth from the theory of capital's inner logic to historical illustrations of it without clearly distinguishing between the logic and illustrations, giving the impression that the illustrations are simply a function of the logic. For example, from the point of view of capital's logic the length of the working day is simply given, and yet Marx wants to make the point that in history the legislation for the ten-hour day in England was the culmination of a lengthy class struggle. As long as these positions are understood at two different levels of abstraction there is no problem. From the point of view of capital in general or capital's logic, we cannot specify the length of the working day because it is specific to particular times and places, and yet the history of the struggle for the ten-hour day in England is an instructive illustration of the important role that class struggle is likely to play in determining the length of the working day in history. And yet

hand, competition among the capitalists in the different spheres, play a part, and, in addition, the speed of the equalization process, whether it is quicker or slower, depends on the particular organic composition of the different capitals (more fixed or circulating capital, for example) and on the particular nature of their commodities, that is, whether their nature as use-values facilitates rapid withdrawal from the market and the diminuation or increase of supply, in accordance with the level of market prices" (S III, 464).

4. As Marx puts it: "In reality the mobility of capital is impeded by obstacles which we cannot consider in the present context" (C I, 1013).

it is only late in the discussion that Marx (C I, 411) leaves a clear marker to distinguish the historical illustration from his theory of value when he writes: "So if our *historical sketch* [my emphasis] has shown the prominent part played by modern industry on the one hand, and the labour of those who are physically and legally minors on the other, the former is still for us only a particular department of the exploitation of labour, and the latter only a particularly striking example of it." In other words, at the level of historical analysis modern industry is only one arena where the exploitation of labour occurs and its relative predominance varies from country to country; and the exploitation of child labour is a particularly acute example that shows capital's resistance to having limits placed on exploitation. In contrast, at the level of the theory of capital's deep structures, industrial capital is clearly the core or paradigm case of exploitation, and the working class is theorized as a homogeneous class for which the age (or any other qualifier such as gender, abled and disabled, sexual orientation or race) make-up cannot be specified.

There has been enormous confusion in interpreting Marx's *Capital*, in part because he himself waivered between thinking that the laws of motion of capital were so close to history that there was no need for mediating theory and at other times thinking the opposite. A metaphor that Marx (C III, 241, 275) uses more than once to refer to the close relation between abstract economic theory and empirical circumstances is "friction". The laws of motion of capital are like the laws of motion of mechanics (for example, the law of gravity) that do not always work the way they are supposed to because of local frictions. In "The Results of the Immediate Process of Production", Marx (C I, 1014) writes:

Classical economics regards the versatility of labour-power and the *fluidity* of capital as axiomatic, and it is right to do so, since this is the tendency of capitalist production which ruthlessly enforces its will despite obstacles which are in any case largely of its own making. At all events, in order to portray the laws of political economy in their purity we are ignoring these sources of friction, as is the practice in mechanics where the frictions that arise have to be dealt with in every particular application of its general laws.

But the laws of motion of capital unlike the law of gravity are not just slightly and measurably altered by things like atmospheric pressure, for the laws of motion of capital assume at least the following conditions: private property in the means of production, no foreign trade, no state intervention or intervention by any sort of extra-economic force, no monopoly, no trade unions, equal exchange, competition, mobility of capital and labour, only capitalistic production of commodities, a surplus population of convenient size for the maintenance of the commodification of labour-power, money as gold and convertible paper, inputs and outputs of production secured in commodity form, and so forth. For Marx, these assumptions are essential in order to theorize capital as a self-expanding commodity-economic logic, or, what is the same thing, as self-valorizing value. Basically what is being assumed is total commodification or total reification such that capital's inner logic can be fully exposed. But we know that such assumptions place the theory of pure capitalism far from even the most capitalist moment in actual history. Surely, then, it is misleading to say that it is enough to simply look for local frictions when applying the laws of motion of capital. Rather we must develop some way of mediating between abstract theory and history that involves a controlled unpacking of the commodity form when it is less than fully secured and fully self-valorizing, as is always the case in history. Since the commodity form is the form that private property takes under capitalism and since private property is basically a power relation, we must develop ways of thinking about partially dereified commodity forms where economic power is supported or opposed by political and ideological power. In other words, quantitative economic categories need to be rethought in connection with structures of power in developing mediations connecting abstract economic theory with empirical history.

Another example from Marx will further illustrate the problems that I am concerned with. Writing about the tendency towards a single rate of surplus-value in society, Marx (C III, 275) argues:

This assumes competition among workers, and an equalization that takes place by their constant migration between one sphere of production and another. We assume a general rate of surplus-value of this kind, as a tendency, like all economic laws, and as a theoretical simplification; but in any case this is in practice an actual presupposition of the capitalist mode of production, even if inhibited to a greater or lesser extent by practical frictions that produce more or less significant local differences, such as the settlement laws for agricultural labourers in England, for example. In theory, we assume that the laws of the capitalist mode of production develop in their pure form. In reality, this is only an approximation; but the approximation is all the more exact, the more the capitalist mode of production is developed and the less it is adulterated by survivals of earlier economic conditions with which it is amalgamated.

In other words, Marx is assuming that labour will move freely from employer to employer until wages and working conditions are equalized.

Let us consider the term "approximation" in this case. Marx is using the term to suggest that the more capitalism develops, the more its laws will approach asymptotically close to historical reality. The above example may work for England conceived as a tight little island, in which by custom wages do not differ a great deal from parish to parish even though the settlement laws almost totally block the mobility of labour. But what happens in a world where the mobility of labour between nations is severely blocked by immigration laws? Only in this case, the wage differentials are very large. Surely it would be wrong to assume a general global rate of surplus-value. And yet without such assumption, how can we utilize the laws of motion of capital? Perhaps we can apply the law to a single country like the US. But this won't work, not only because the segmentation of the workforce within the US has resulted in significant wage differentials internally, but also because it is too tied in with the rest of the world economically to treat it as an isolated economic unit. It would seem, then, that the law of value is far from being a close approximation to historical reality.

BRINGING THE OUTSIDE IN

I shall argue that one can find in Marx's economic theories implications that levels of analysis of some sort are needed to mediate between the laws of the commodity form and actual history. Further I shall argue that because of the way in which he theorized capital's inner logic, Marx offers a particularly powerful cognitive groundwork for developing mediating levels of analysis even if he himself achieved little that could be considered systematic in this regard.

In general Marx is very clear about what can and cannot be addressed within the theory of capital's inner logic. For example, the vast array of wage-forms and wage differentials that may exist in a particular historical context cannot be addressed. Marx (S III, 312) writes: "The rise and fall in the rate of profit – insofar as it is determined by the rise of fall of wages resulting from conditions of supply and demand ... has as little to do with the general law of the rise or fall in the profit rate as the rise or fall in market prices of commodities has to do with the determination of value in general. This has to be addressed in the chapter on the real movement of wages." Elsewhere Marx (C I, 683, 1042) refers to "a special study of wage labour" and "a special treatise on wage labour", which would clearly be more concrete than the theory of capital as such.[5] Or Marx (C II, 415) writes: "...a partial or local rise in wages ... depends on many circumstances", circumstances that cannot be included in a general theory of capital's logic. Indeed, Marx often refers to more concrete levels of analysis as "competition". For example, when Marx (C III, 342) discusses the reduction of wages below their value as a counteracting tendency to a fall in the rate of profit, he writes: "We simply make an empirical reference to this point here, as, like many other things that might be brought in, it has nothing to do with the general analysis of capital, but has its place in an account of competition, which is not dealt with in this work." Here it is crystal clear that pushing wages below the value of labour-power in order to augment profit cannot be part of the general analysis of capital that assumes throughout that over time average wages will equal the value of labour-power even though they may rise above it just prior to a crisis and may fall below it in the trough of a depression. And while in the theory of capital's deep structures the size of the industrial reserve army may be the primary causal force affecting wage levels, at the level of historical analysis "The relative surplus population exists in all kinds of forms" (C I, 794). Thus, when Marx discusses the rise of wages in agricultural districts in England between 1849 and 1859, it is clear that this is not part of his general theory of capital, and indeed, in this particular case he discusses very particular causes such as "exodus of agricultural surplus population caused by wartime demand" (C I, 791).

Furthermore, Marx argues that the actual complexity of class phenomena in history are outside the theory of capital's logic. For example, he makes it clear that at the time he was writing there were far more female domestic servants than factory workers, and that, as a result, the uncommodified domestic service of servants would need to be taken into account in any historical account of the British economy in this period. Indeed there are many different kinds of service workers that would need to be accounted for. And as Marx (S II, 562; C I, 574) puts it, "...with the accumulation of capital ... those classes and subclasses who do not live directly from their labour

5. Lebowitz (2003) ignores the fact that Marx gave up on this project for good reasons. Contrary to Marx's theory, Lebowitz proposes to complete *Capital* by supplying the "missing book on wage-labour". Though misguided, Lebowitz's efforts are interesting.

become more numerous and live better than before, and the number of unproductive workers increases as well". The point is that the actual complexity of class phenomena in history are clearly outside the theory of pure capitalism and can only be addressed through the use of mediating levels of analysis.

As previously pointed out, Marx (S I, 407) argues that the production of independent craftsmen and peasants "does not fall under the capitalist mode of production". Similarly in spheres where there is a

transitional form to capitalist production ... in which the various scientific or artistic producers, handicraftsmen or experts work for the collective trading capital of the book trade – a relation that has nothing to do with the capitalist mode of production proper and even formally has not yet been brought under its sway ... the exploitation of labour is at its highest precisely in these transitional forms.... (S I, 410)

Clearly, then, transitional forms cannot be part of a theory that presents fully developed capitalist forms, even though such a theory is ultimately the best way to clarify these transitional forms. Indeed, in historical analysis "...the circuit of industrial capital ... cuts across the commodity circulation of the most varied modes of social production ... the capitalist mode of production is conditioned by modes of production lying outside its own stage of development" (C II, 189–90).

Just as self-employed production is outside the theory of value precisely so that it becomes possible to think clearly about how capital's logic impacts on them and vice versa, so must the historical variations of labour within the family be excluded. From the point of view of capital's logic some kind of family is required as a unit of expanded biological reproduction, but that logic by itself cannot determine who does what kind of labour within the family, who lives together for how long, or what kind of pooling and division of resources takes place within family settings. And there is no single family form that can be deduced as a necessary adjunct to capital accumulation. For while we might hypothesize that there would be an historical tendency for the commodity form to increasingly penetrate the family simply because of the reifying force of capital, we cannot deduce at what rate, in what form, and with what specific consequences this tendency may unfold. For example, Marx (C I, 518, FN 39) writes:

Since certain family functions, such as nursing and suckling children, cannot be entirely suppressed, the mothers who have been confiscated by capital must try substitutes of some sort. Domestic work, such as sewing and mending, must be replaced by the purchase of ready-made articles. Hence the diminished expenditure of labour in the house is accompanied by an increased expenditure of money outside. The cost of production of the working-class family therefore increases, and balances its greater income. In addition to this, economy and judgment in the consumption and preparation of the means of subsistence become impossible. Abundant material on these facts, which are concealed by official political economy, is to be found in the *Reports of the Inspectors of Factories*, the *Reports of the Children's Employment Commission*, and particularly in the *Reports on Public Health*.

Here Marx is suggesting that there is a general tendency for capitalistically produced commodities to replace family produced use-values, but he says nothing about the specific ways this might unfold in different class strata in different times and places. Similarly, while there must be some way of feeding infants, the logic of capital cannot by itself determine whether special arrangements (workplace crèche and so forth) might enable working mothers to do this, or whether it will be done by a "wet nurse", by someone with expressed mother's milk, or by someone with infant formula.

Also Marx (C I, 922–3) notes that in various industries in particular times and places, the low wages and docility of children make of them the perfect source of labour-power for capital. Indeed, it was not uncommon to find unemployed adults supported by their children. Marx (C I, 599) sarcastically points out that in the land of the "Christian" family "The wretched half-starved parents think of nothing but getting as much as possible out of their children." Thus, to give a full historical account of accumulation, it is necessary to consider how the logic of capital impacts on the family and on the basic provisioning of food and shelter.[6] The Victorian world was critical of child labour because the family was considered such an important basis for the development of moral values such as respect, deference, obedience and duty. Child labour made it all too apparent that an unrestrained commodity form which replaces human to human relations with a cash nexus could penetrate the family and undermine that morality required by the economy.

6. "But for a full elucidation of the law of accumulation, his condition outside the workshop must also be looked at, his condition as to food and accommodation" (C I, 807).

The forms of rent or vast array of credit phenomena that may exist concretely in history also cannot be addressed at the level of abstraction required to theorize capital's inner logic. At the start of *Capital* volume three, part six, entitled "The Transformation of Surplus Profit into Ground-Rent", there is a particularly clear statement about the scope of Marx's theory (C III, 751):

The analysis of landed property in its various historical forms lies outside the scope of the present work. We are concerned with it only in so far as a portion of the surplus-value that capital produces falls to the share of the landowner. We assume therefore that agriculture, just like manufacturing, is dominated by the capitalist mode of production, i.e. that rural production is pursued by capitalists, who are distinguished from other capitalists, first of all, simply by the element in which their capital and the wage-labour that it sets in motion are invested. As far as we are concerned, the farmer produces wheat, etc. just as the manufacturer produces yarn or machines. The assumption that the capitalist mode of production has taken control of agriculture implies also that it dominates all spheres of production and bourgeois society, so that its preconditions, such as the free competition of capitals, their transferability from one sphere of production to another, and equal level of average profit, etc. are also present in their full development.

Here the gap between abstract theory and history is particularly large, for Marx is fully aware that agricultural production only begins to approach this picture of "capitalist agriculture" in Victorian England. For "English conditions are the only ones in which *modern landownership*, i.e., landownership which has been *modified* by capitalist production, has been adequately developed" (S II, 238). In other words, no other country came at all close to having its agriculture dominated by the capitalist mode of production when Marx was writing. Here, the need for a mediating level of theory to connect abstract theory with historical analysis is obvious. The distance between the theoretical concern to situate capitalist rent within the laws of motion of capital in the abstract and in general, and the highly diverse and historically specific forms of agriculture and land management, suggest that any direct application of the theory of capital's logic to history would be an enormous folly.

As for credit, again Marx is only interested in showing how interest-bearing capital in general receives a portion of the surplus-value when capital itself becomes an automatic interest-bearing force, and how credit-granting institutions in general mobilize social savings to serve the needs of capital. It follows that the law of value cannot include within its motion the international flow of credit, state credit, or consumer credit, to mention a few of the larger excluded categories. If, as Marx (S II, 201) claims: "The levelling out of *values* by labour-time and even less the levelling out of *cost-prices* by a general rate of profit does not take place in this direct form between different countries", then not only would international credit be outside the law of value, there would also be no international law of value in general. Indeed, power relations significantly disrupt international value relations such that even in his time Marx comments on "A new and international division of labour ... [which] converts one part of the globe into a chiefly agricultural field of production for supplying the other part, which remains a pre-eminently industrial field" (C I, 580).

But at the level of value categories, the colonies are largely outside the capitalist mode of production. According to Marx (S II, 302–3):

There are the colonies proper, such as the United States, Australia, etc. Here the mass of the farming colonists, although they bring with them a larger or smaller amount of capital from the motherland, are not *capitalists*, nor do they carry on *capitalist* production. They are more or less peasants who work themselves and whose main object, in the first place, is to produce *their own livelihood*, their means of subsistence. ...

In the second type of colonies – plantations – where commercial speculations figure from the start and production is intended for the world market, the capitalist mode of production exists, although only in a formal sense, since slavery of Negroes precludes free wage-labour, which is the basis of capitalist production.

Marx frequently makes the point that self-employed persons are outside the capitalist mode of production. It may seem strange that he would then go on to include slave plantations within the capitalist mode of production. He can do this because of the distinction that he makes between formal and real subsumption. Real subsumption occurs when labour-power is commodified within what is primarily a factory system. Formal subsumption would include large profit-making units of capital oriented to the market, but where labour-power is not commodified as in putting-out production and slave production.

Self-valorizing value cannot be *self*-valorizing if it relies on extra-economic force. Whether it is the power of monopolies or of the state or of some other agency, all such power influences can only distort and confuse the commodity logic of capital. Thus it is not surprising that Marx (C III, 525) should write: "...state credit remains outside our discussion". Similarly insofar as banks become "semi-state" institutions, a status claimed by Marx for the Bank of England, they also institutionalize a degree of extra-economic force that places them outside the theory of pure capitalism.[7]

For Marx the theory of capital in the abstract and in general is essentially a theory of how surplus-value is created, circulated and distributed. This means that capital is essentially a commodity-economically organized profit-oriented force. And while its inner logic may in some cases be far removed from empirical reality, it is this logic that can give the best orientation to more concrete levels of analysis. Indeed, to repeat a quotation that began this chapter, capital, as self-valorizing value may display "...endless variations and gradations in its appearance, as the result of innumerable different circumstances, natural conditions, racial relations, historical relations acting from outside, etc., and these can only be understood by analysing these empirically given conditions" (C III, 927–8). And I would add that given the particular refinement of Marx's theory that I am arguing for, analyzing these conditions would be oriented by the theory of capital's deep structures and by a mid-range theory.

LEVELS OF ANALYSIS AND CRISES

In order to further develop a notion of levels of abstraction deriveable from Marx's *Capital*, I shall illustrate it in more depth with respect to some of Marx's theoretical formulations on the issue of crises. Marx's theory of crises is important for several reasons. First, it sharply differentiated his theory from bourgeois theories of political economy all of which denied that crises could be traced to causes endogenous to capitalist economics. Second, for Marx, crises illustrated most sharply the contradictions internal to capital's logic. Third, periodic crises indicate that the capitalist mode of production is historically limited. Fourth, Marx's theory of crises is in a sense his entire theory of capital, since as soon as money appears in the theory and with it the possibility of separating the sales effort and purchases, the abstract possibility of crises is first posed. Fifth, the contrast between

7. "Is there anything more crazy that that between 1797 and 1817, for example, the Bank of England, whose notes only had credit thanks to the state, then got paid by the state, i.e. by the public, in the form of interest on government loans, for the power that the state gave it to transform these very notes from paper into money and lend them to the state" (C III, 675–6).

the most likely causes of crises within capital's logic and the causes of actual historical crises that Marx discusses, sharply poses the need for some kind of relatively autonomous levels of analysis that can connect abstract theory with the analysis of history. While anything approaching even an initial theorization of levels of analysis is too large a project to be attempted here, some aspects of a levels of analysis problematic can be illustrated by outlining some of the ways in which the theory of capital in the abstract and in general can help us to better understand the economic crisis of 1847.

In *Capital* volume one, chapter three, Marx writes:

Circulation bursts through all the temporal, spatial and personal barriers imposed by the direct exchange of products [barter], and it does this by splitting up the direct identity present in this case between the exchange of one's own product and the acquisition of someone else's into the antithetical segments of sale and purchase. To say that these mutually independent and antithetical processes form an internal unity is to say also that their internal unity moves forward through external antithesis. ... .Hence, if the assertion of their external independence ... proceeds to a certain critical point, their unity violently makes itself felt by producing – a crisis. There is an antithesis, immanent in the commodity, between use-value and value, between private labour which must simultaneously manifest itself as directly social labour, and a particular concrete kind of labour which simultaneously counts as merely abstract universal labour, between the conversion of things into persons and the conversion of persons into things; the antithetical phases of the metamorphosis of the commodity are the developed forms of motion of this immanent contradiction. These forms therefore imply the possibility of crises, though no more than the possibility. For the development of this possibility into a reality a whole series of conditions is required, which do not yet even exist from the standpoint of the simple circulation of commodities.[8]

This dense passage requires some unpacking. First, there is the sharp distinction between the local, subjective and one-time-only nature of

8. C I, 209. In a footnote to this passage Marx writes: "There are two points here which are characteristic of the method of the bourgeoisie's economic apologists. The first is the identification of the circulation of commodities with the direct exchange of products, achieved simply by abstracting from their differences. The second is the attempt to explain away the contradictions of the capitalist process of production by dissolving the relations between persons engaged in the process of production into the simple relations arising out of the circulation of commodities." Both of these apologetic twists are common to this day as demonstrated in Milton Friedman's *Capitalism and Freedom*.

barter, and the society-wide, objective set of equivalences that result from the exchange of commodities facilitated by money as universal equivalent. Once the opposition between value and use-value inherent in the commodity form is externalized as an opposition between commodity and money, purchase and sale become "antithetical segments". This is because for the owner of a commodity (a capitalist in the process of becoming), the commodity is only a potential exchange-value, but if a purchaser does not soon appear offering to pay the commodity's price, the commodity may end up being sold for a loss or not at all. Now, if this should happen with many commodities of different types all at the same time, we have the making of a possible crisis. The result is an absurd situation where people need jobs and they need the things that capital produces, while factories lie idle due to a general paralysis. Typically a large quantity of value must be destroyed before value and use-value can be realigned, even though this may mean people living in the streets and going hungry. This is what Marx means by a crisis violently reasserting the unity between value and use-value.

For Marx, simple circulation is a "metamorphosis" because in the movement C-M or M-C the quantity of value does not change but only the form of value. Yet the phases of this metamorphosis, selling and buying, are antithetical in the sense that the seller wants the most value for the least use-value and the buyer wants the most and best use-value for the least value. Now, while relations between sellers and buyers may break down when sellers cannot sell for anything like the price offered, such a breakdown constitutes only an initial abstract possibility of crisis that Marx will develop more concretely as he unfolds the dialectic of capital.

In order to further illustrate the sense in which the dialectic of capital as a whole is an unfolding of a theory of crises, I will briefly consider the second abstract possibility of crisis that Marx theorizes, which has to do with money as means of purchase. Money as means of purchase refers to credit money or what is essentially the circulation of credit contracts as money. Thus if you contract to pay me $5,000 six months from now, for a slight discount I can use this contract as money. If, however, for some reason many debtors are unable to pay their debts, the whole system of credit money can collapse as part of a general crisis when everyone wants hard cash precisely when it is most unavailable.[9]

---

9. "In a crisis, the antithesis between commodities and their value-form, money, is raised to the level of an absolute contradiction" (C I, 236).

Any manifestation of the contradiction between value and use-value may be implicated in a crisis. The major contradictions usually referred to as the most centrally implicated are underconsumption, disproportionality, overproduction and profit squeeze, but in a sense they may all be implicated. Having said this, because capital cannot directly produce labour-power and because labour-power can resist capital, its continued commodification poses the greatest challenge to capital's commodity-economic management. And it follows as one would expect, that periodic crises are necessary in order to maintain the commodification of labour-power in a purely capitalist society. How does this work?

An industrial reserve army is necessary in order for capital to be able to hire new workers as is usually required when capital expands. In other words, increased demand for labour-power can be satisfied only by having a pool of unemployed at the ready. With any other commodity except land, increased demand can be satisfied by increased production. Since Marx assumes no shortage of land in pure capitalism, it is only when the demand for labour-power presses against the limits of the industrial reserve army that labour-shortages would force wages up. But this may occur precisely at the point when production has expanded beyond even the increased demand caused by higher wages. Thus profits will be levelling off because of higher wage costs and saturated markets. At the same time, there is increased demand for liquid funds to pay the weekly wage bill pushing higher an interest rate that was already high because of the rapid expansion of capital in its prosperity phase. A crisis would necessarily set in as the rate of interest approached the rate of profit as a result of declining profit rates and rising interest rates. The many resulting bankruptcies would rapidly expand the industrial reserve army, destroy capital value, centralize the remaining capital, and as capital reorganizes it would introduce new labour-saving technology (made economic by the general devaluation of capital, the depreciation of fixed capital that has occurred since the last depression, and the larger units of capital that can afford to invest in new technology). Eventually with wages pushed below the value of labour-power, a replenished industrial reserve army, and new larger and retooled units of capital, capital would enter a renewed phase of expansion.

And there are other important economic relations that may contribute to crises that can only be specified at the levels of mid-range theory or historical analysis. For example, anything that might significantly slow, disrupt or block the turnover of capital can contribute to a crisis. Too expensive or unavailable inputs in key industries would, of course, create problems. Generally such problems would be solved by the movement of capital except where that movement would be blocked or where the commodity involved is not capitalistically produced (only labour-power and land in a purely capitalist society). And while the unavailability of labour-power caused by a shrinkage of the industrial reserve army is a key cause of crises in the theory of capital's deep structures, at this abstract level of analysis we can theorize the commodity-economic management of land of different quality, but not the situation where there is an absolute limit to land-like resources as in the exhaustion of nonrenewable resources, since such considerations are historically specific. Also the disruption of the production process (by, for example, a general strike), or inability to sell the product in a timely fashion (because of boycotts or other historically specific reasons) would not be theorizable at the level of pure capitalism. Another historically specific factor would be problems posed by fixed capital becoming enormously expensive to replace, as in the steel industry. In such cases, the extreme "lumpiness" of fixed capital could disrupt the circuit of capital. Indeed very large fixed capital investments (such as the tunnel under the English channel) that can only pay for themselves over a long time, tend not to be well managed commodity-economically, and therefore nearly always involve some kind of state involvement (and this requires theorization at a more concrete level of analysis). Furthermore, as was common in the nineteenth century when transportation to distant foreign markets took a considerable amount of time, commercial capital may encourage over-production by immediately buying the entire product of industrial capital, thus encouraging it to expand, only to discover later that the expected foreign market for the product does not materialize. While Marx (G, 623) does not produce the concept "excess capacity", he does claim that at the level of history it is in "…the nature of capital to be never completely occupied…". It is also possible that financial capital may cause bubbles to form in any sort of futures market (where things are bought merely because a rapid appreciation of value is expected in the near future), but this is also an historically specific situation where numerous subjective and objective factors may influence the formation of a bubble.

At this point, with this extremely truncated sketch of some of Marx's thoughts on crisis in the context of capital's inner logic and the limits of that logic, I want to consider how such a theory can be used to help us understand a particular crisis. I have selected the crisis of 1847 because it is the one that Marx has the most to say about in *Capital*. First of all, it is fair to say that in sorting out the causes of this crisis, Marx would encourage us to consider all sorts of power relations (particularly class relations) that may be implicated: economic, political and ideological. For example, in the crisis of 1847 the profit rate fell as the interest rate rose, but behind these changing numbers are significant power relations that are not always totally economic, as, for example, the Opium War of 1839–42. No adequate understanding of any actual "economic" crisis can be achieved by simply looking at economic numbers because the numbers themselves are projections into commodified space of power relations. Also Marx would encourage thinking in terms of historical processes about both important immediate and less immediate causes. Some causes set the stage or create an atmosphere, whereas others are movements on the stage or within the atmosphere. For example, the introduction of opium into China by the British in order to balance the trade in tea was facilitated by an atmosphere of ideological racism. The British would not have dreamed of introducing opium into America in order to balance the trade in cotton. In summary, one might say that Marx would advocate thinking first in terms guided by capital's logic, but then at a level of historical analysis he would think broadly in spatial and temporal terms; in economic, partially economic and non-economic terms; in terms of both process and agency; in class terms; and in terms that were dynamic and historical.

Mathias (1983, 209) refers to the crisis of 1847 as the "last of the great harvest crises". And it is true that in 1845–6 there was a potato famine and grain shortage causing a significant outflow of bullion to pay for food imports, an outflow that set the stage for higher interest rates (C III, 535, 550). Further, there was a Liverpool corn merchant and banking panic in 1847 when corn prices fell. Thus while harvest failure in Britain and Ireland played a role, we get an extremely one-sided and simplistic picture of the crisis with Mathias' explanation that simply labels it "a harvest crisis". Indeed, guided in his analysis by his understanding of capitalism achieved by his theory of pure capitalism, without even trying to give anything like a complete explanation, Marx offers many important elements that would have to be part of such an explanation at the level of historical analysis.

I believe that a fully adequate account of the crisis of 1847 would need to be informed by a mid-range theory of phases of capitalist development. At this level of analysis, we would theorize the typical forms of capital accumulation, of the state, of law and of ideology characteristic of the relevant phase of capitalist development. We would consider such questions as what are the most characteristic ways in which capital accumulation is organized and how do these dominant modes operate both nationally and internationally? What are the major political, legal and ideological supports for this mode of accumulation in the light of the major challenges (particularly use-value obstacles including class struggle) that it faces? How commodified are the key economic categories, and how is this degree of commodification supported? What are the most likely causes of crises, and how does capital try to contain them?

The crisis of 1847 falls into what I (Albritton 1991, Ch.6) would refer to as the phase of liberalism, when the most dominant and developed mode of capital accumulation is centred in Britain. Both capital and labour are mobile and competitive as never before. And while this phase of capitalist development can be usefully referred to as "liberalism" because of its tendencies towards "laissez-faire" and "free trade", when we examine the important international dimensions of capital accumulation, we see liberalism articulating with a variety of economic forms that persist from earlier eras. For example, from the phase of mercantilism, we see the persistence of practices developed by monopolistic trading companies like the East India Company; we see the persistence of a powerful merchant class and landlord class; we see trade wars (the Opium War was a trade war); we see colonialism with colonies supplying agricultural and raw material inputs for British manufacturing; we see plantations with various types and degrees of forced labour; and we see the persistence of certain crucial import duties despite the general push towards free trade. Furthermore, while labour within Britain was more mobile in this phase, the law made it almost impossible to strike without committing a criminal offence, and the potential collective power of labour had yet to be organized into effective trade unions.[10] At the same time, the state is for the first time organizing an effective police force and prison system to better enforce the law. Thus while state policy is far less interventionist than in the previous phase of mercantilism, justifying the use of the term "laissez-faire", the state is still interventionist in important ways, as will become apparent when we examine the crisis of 1847 in more detail.

10. Intimidation, molestation, obstruction and threats by striking workers towards management or replacement workers were all potential criminal offences (Hunt 1981, 265).

Following the guidelines offered by Marx in *Capital*, one would first look at the realm of production and its two leading industries in Britain at the time, cotton manufacturing and railroads, in order to see how they might be implicated in the crisis. This emphasis follows from the view that to the extent capitalism predominates, all surplus-value and ultimately profit comes from the exploitation of workers in industry. In this period Britain produced about two-thirds of the world's cotton textiles (Beales 1969, 175), and typically two-thirds of the total cotton textile product was exported (Landes 1969, 238), constituting over 50 per cent of Britain's total exports (C I, 720). Further, 58 per cent of the factory employees in the cotton industry were women and 36 per cent were person's under 18 (Crouzet 1982, 203).[11] Victory in the Opium War, which essentially opened China to trade, raised images in the cotton industry of the fortunes to be made clothing 400 million Chinese.[12] These images were fortified by expected free-trade legislation that would remove the 350 per cent import duty on Chinese tea (Mintz 1985, 138). Such a boom was expected that there was no shortage of funds as bills of exchange were given to cotton producers for textiles not yet produced (C III, 533–4, 539, 550). Such a rapid expansion of cotton manufacturing put upward pressure on the price of cotton bales, 80 per cent of which came from the relatively inelastic slave production of cotton in the US (C III, 219). Such high profits were expected that cotton capitalists were prepared to pay more for this key input. When the free-trade laws were passed in 1846, it eventually became clear that though import duties on almost everything else were to be removed, the duties on tea were to remain (C III, 618). There were several reasons for this. First of all, there was a huge investment of British capital in the Indian tea industry, which did not want competition from cheaper Chinese tea. Second, the duty on tea brought by far the most money into state coffers. And third, the duty on tea was a way of shifting funds from the working class, the main consumers of tea, to the state, and was thus a way of keeping down the new income tax (a replacement for the removed import duties) which not only taxed the middle classes but angered them as well. As foreign and domestic markets became saturated with cotton textiles and the Chinese market failed to open, their price began to plunge, ultimately

11. Typically women would have been paid about 50 per cent of men's wages and children as little as 10 per cent.
12. C III, 534. Marx estimates 300 million and Hobsbawm (1975, 156) 400 million.

bankrupting many cotton manufacturers, who could not borrow money at increasingly higher interest rates and could not pay their debts (C III, 550). In the meantime, the expansion of railways led to a speculative bubble in railway stocks, such that as the market for textiles dried up, many cotton manufacturers tried to save themselves by investing their profits into the rapidly escalating railway stocks. Eventually the bubble in railway stocks burst and many industrialists and financiers went bankrupt.[13]

The Bank Act of 1844 tied the hands of the Bank of England as a lender of last resort, so that as the desperate demands for liquidity increased, resulting in an ever higher interest rate, it could do nothing.[14] Upward pressure on the interest rate was caused by the export of bullion to pay for food needed as a result of crop failures, the rapid expansion of cotton manufacturing, the bubble in railway stock, and finally by the depression which undermined the trust-based credit system leading everyone to demand liquidity. As the depression deepened, The Bank Act was suspended just in time to avert economic catastrophe (C III, 535). This is not to suggest that economic crises are simply a function of the rate of interest, or that giving the state a free hand to manipulate the rate of interest can permanently avoid crises. First of all, at most times and places in the history of capitalism, there are severe limits on the state's ability to manipulate the interest rate, and secondly, such manipulation may not avert crisis or stagnation. Indeed, in this case, by the time the Bank of England stepped in to moderate the rate of interest, most of the causes of its rise were already losing their effect as the economy had bottomed out.

To fully understand the crisis of 1847 there are a number of crucial background conditions that are of great significance. First is the extent to which the highly competitive cotton industry was dependent on the world market for both the purchase of raw cotton and the sale of cotton cloth (C I, 609). Nearly all of the cotton was grown on plantations in colonies or former colonies with forced or semi-forced labour, with 80 per cent coming from US slave plantations. And over half of the cotton produced was exported, often to distant markets difficult to gauge in advance. For this reason, according to Marx (C III, 164) "the two major foci of crisis between 1825 and 1857 [were] India

13. C III, 219, 534–5, 538, 541, 550.
14. C III, 535, 550, 561, 689.

and America", precisely because these were the two most important foreign markets for cotton textiles.

While in a purely capitalist society one would expect part of the cause of reduced profits and higher interest rates to stem from the shrinkage of the industrial reserve army that would place an upward pressure on wages, this was not a factor in the crisis of 1847, primarily because of the supply of workers from the countryside of Britain, Scotland and Ireland (C I, 720). Between 1801 and 1831 there were 3,511,770 acres of commons enclosed thus further impoverishing rural workers (C I, 889). This impoverishment was also propelled by the failure of small farms as is indicated by statistics showing that in just a ten-year period 1851–61 the number of farms of less than 100 acres decreased from 31,583 to 26,597 (C I, 804). The concentration of landownership was such that by the 1870s, 7,000 landlords controlled 80 per cent of the land (Anderson, 1987). The general impoverishment of rural workers[15] meant that there was nearly an inexhaustible industrial reserve army, for even as late as the census of 1861, there were 1,208,648 servants, 1,098,261 agricultural workers, and only 642,607 textile workers (C I, 574). And in a way this inexhaustibility was necessary since the life-expectancy in the new industrial towns was 15 for Liverpool and 17 for Manchester during this period (C I, 795). Because of the high mortality rate and because in many families it was primarily the children who could get jobs, marriages were early and productive of many children. Prior to the Factory Act of 1833, it was not unusual for families to force their 8-year-old children to work in factories in order to stave off starvation for the entire family (such situations persist in some parts of the world). And while the Chartists were preparing another petition in 1847, their power did not prevent manufacturers from lowering wages in anticipation of the Ten Hour Bill which was to take effect in 1848 (C I, 396, 747). This is because the trade union movement was still very weak in England, and because there was no upward pressure on wages due to an insufficient supply of workers. While the strength of the Chartists no doubt prevented the dominant classes from totally resolving the crisis at the expense of workers, it did not prevent a general lowering of wages even before the crisis really set in.

The examination of this crisis illustrates in concrete historical terms the consequences of capital's indifference to use-value. First of all, to

---

15. Agricultural wages were typically half of the very low wages in industry (Mathias 1983, 241).

the extent that value becomes disconnected from its earthly, material, human, use-value anchor, it can very easily be swept up in the mania of get-rich-quick bubbles. The use of opium to open China to trade is a classically dramatic example of value's indifference to use-value,[16] as is the maintenance of the high tea tariff in deference to the East Indian tea interests. The Irish potato famine was a natural disaster, but it was not natural to let 1,000,000 people die of starvation, nor was it natural for the majority of rural people in the United Kingdom to live in grinding poverty, nor for workers in the new industrial towns to have an incredibly short life-expectancy, nor for children to be forced to work long hours in terrible conditions (C I, 861, 923). It is with such historical examples that we come face to face with the callous indifference of capital's profit-mongering to human suffering in all forms, something that continues to this day where capital can get away with it.

CONCLUSIONS

In this chapter I have tried to demonstrate why I believe so strongly that a levels of analysis approach is necessary to Marx's economic theory, and why even as Marx wrote it, the theory can be interpreted as almost demanding three levels of analysis. Indeed, levels of analysis enable us to break out of most of the stultifying arguments that seem to turn in endless circles having to do with such binaries as: structure/agency, economism/voluntarism, essentialism/relativism, static/dynamic, structure/process and theory/history. Elsewhere I (Albritton, 1991) have mapped out a version of mid-range or mid-level theory, as a theory of phases or stages of capitalist development. In that book, my aim was to present a framework for theorizing the dominant mode of capital accumulation during distinct phases of capitalist development. Mid-range theory is basically an institutional analysis where economic practices that represent various degrees of commodification articulate with political and ideological practices to constitute patterns of capital accumulation that are typical and dominant during a phase of capitalist development. And because at this mid-range level commodification is not complete, the logic of capital is no longer an "inner logic", indeed it is less a logic in the sense that it is partially disrupted by the historically specific institutions that it must operate through. It is clear, for example,

16. Britain imported approximately 43,000 chests (chest = approx. 64 kg) annually into China between 1844 and 1849 (Hobsbawm 1975, 49).

that though competitive cotton manufacturing is the most characteristic mode of capital accumulation during the phase of liberalism in the mid nineteenth century, the effectiveness of state laissez-faire policies are constrained even from the point of view of capital by, among other things, the articulation of Britain's economy with the international economy.

It is not my aim here to present a developed theory of levels of analysis, instead it is to demonstrate why Marx would not only be open to such an innovation, but also would most likely embrace it as necessary to the consistency of his overall approach to his theory of capital and of capitalism. It is my firm belief that Marxian political economy has barely begun to think the more concrete levels and their interconnections with each other and with the theory of capital's deep structures that is essential to getting clear precisely how capital's inner logic and mid-range theory shape the specificities of different historical contexts.[17]

In the next chapter, I shall focus on the conception of class in political economy both because it is of key importance in itself and because it can serve as a means to expand upon my conception of levels of analysis. My basic aim will be to demonstrate that levels of analysis can enable us to keep the theoretical clarity of the capital/labour relation as it is put forth in the theory of surplus-value, while at the same time avoiding class reductionism when utilizing abstract theory to orient more concrete levels of analysis.

17. In my view it is "regulation theory" and "social structure of accumulation theory" that have made the most headway, though in both cases their theorization of the levels and their interconnection remains weak.

6
Class Analysis and Political Economy

Not ¼ of the English population provides everything that is consumed by all. (G, 398)

We do not examine the competition of capitals, nor the credit system, nor the actual composition of society, which by no means consists only of two classes. (S II, 493)

...they [workers] achieve a certain quantitative participation in the general growth of wealth. (S III, 312)

Will class please come to order! Class is not only a disorderly concept, in being hotly contested, it is also loved and hated. Those that love it, mostly Marxists, often cling to it too tightly hoping that it will bring succour (or socialism); and those who hate it, either deny its existence or charge it with excessive self-importance (as in "class reductionism" or trying to explain too much as a function of class). And even considering those who have closely read *Capital*, we find readers that place so much emphasis on reification (Lukács and the Frankfurt School) that class pretty much disappears, and in sharp contrast there are interpreters who place so much emphasis on class that *Capital* becomes primarily a political sociology of class struggle. I shall argue, in contrast to these alternatives, that utilized within a levels of abstraction approach, "class" can yield enormous cognitive rewards when it comes to understanding the history of capitalism, and hence, also in thinking about strategies of altering a future that grows out of that history.

At the level of the theory of capital's deep structures, the structural position of class is presented in terms that are clear, precise and objectively grounded. The theory of surplus-value demonstrates that all profits in a purely capitalist society stem ultimately from the exploitation of homogeneous labour-power by homogeneous capital, and it is this relationship that defines the basic class relation between capital and labour. The completion of commodification at this level of theory implies that all economic agency is ultimately subsumed to a commodity-economic logic aimed at maximizing profit. But at the level of mid-range theory where we study the dominant patterns of accumulation specific to particular phases of capitalist development, commodification is not complete, and patterns of agency that are not fully economic and may be relatively autonomous from the economic mix it up with capital's logic. As a result, the dominant patterns of class struggle specific to a particular phase of capitalist development may be complex and not directly derivable or fully understandable by a simple deduction from the two-class dynamic of pure capitalism. Finally, at the level of historical analysis, where we cannot assume that the dominant patterns of a phase are fully manifest, the processes of class struggle become even more complex and more articulated with relatively autonomous political and ideological practices.

CLASS AND THE THEORY OF CAPITAL'S DEEP STRUCTURES

Marx's *Capital* is a theory that understands the deep structures of capital as a combination of certain property relations (i.e. class relations) and the commodity form. His theory demonstrates how a commodity form is possible that, on the one hand, generates extreme individualism, and on the other hand, can reproduce and expand a class structure. He goes even further to demonstrate that the more extreme the individualism, the more effectively the class relation can be reproduced.[1] To put it a little differently, capital, as self-expanding value, can only operate smoothly if the otherness of labour is effectively incorporated.[2] For if capital continually has to deal with an autonomous and potentially uncooperative other, its expansion can no longer be a *self*-expansion operating solely through a commodity-economic logic. I believe that this point is of crucial importance precisely because in the history of Marxist theory, a false opposition has been created between those who emphasize reification and those who emphasize class. In the theory of capital's basic forms, there is no such opposition since it is precisely complete commodification (reification) that ensures the reproduction of the capitalist class,

1. "Being independent of each other, the workers are isolated. They enter into relations with the capitalist, but not with each other. Their cooperation only begins with the labour process, but by then they have ceased to belong to themselves. On entering the labour process they are incorporated into capital. As co-operators, as members of a working organism, they merely form a particular mode of existence of capital" (C I, 451).
2. "As capital, therefore, it is animated by the drive to reduce to a minimum the resistance offered by man, that obstinate yet elastic natural barrier" (C I, 527).

including the property relations that ensure its continued structural domination over the working class. The false opposition arises because each side applies their particular interpretation of the theory of capital's inner logic too directly to history, or, what is essentially the same thing, they over-generalize or over-reify their favoured category, be it reification or class, resulting in an overly functionalist, totalizing and reductionist account of history. In other words, the high degree of reification that occurs when commodification is complete is injected into history where commodification is far from complete, or, history is seen too much to be a function of the simple two-class relation of pure capitalism, when, at the level of history, class phenomena are often complex, overdetermined by non-class phenomena (that is, they are only relatively autonomous), and not always decisive in historical outcomes.

My general position is that Marx's theory of capital is primarily a theory of surplus-value, the aim of which is to very precisely theorize the relation between capital in general, labour in general, and profit maximization. When we assume complete commodification and that all production is the capitalistic production of commodities, then we get a crystal clear theory of the relation between capital and labour at their most homogeneous. The result is a theory of the deep structures of capitalism. At the same time, because we know that neither of these assumptions (deep structures) is completely realized in history, we are alert to the fact that in any concrete circumstances both capital and labour will be heterogeneous conglomerations of various sorts of relatively autonomous groupings.

The emphasis in the theory of capital's deep structure is on capital's absorption of the working class into its commodity logic of self-expanding value. And while labour-power is unlike any other commodity because it can resist, insofar as it is abstract, simple labour, capital is indifferent to its particular and distinctive humanness.[3] The

---

3. "But capital has one sole driving force, the drive to valorize itself, to create surplus-value, to make its constant part, the means of production, absorb the greatest possible amount of surplus-value. Capital is dead labour which, vampire-like, lives only by sucking living labour, and lives the more, the more it sucks" (C I, 342). "It usurps the time for growth, development and healthy maintenance of the body. It steals the time required for the consumption of fresh air and sunlight ... food is added to the worker ... as coal is supplied to the boiler. ... It reduces the sound sleep needed for the restoration of the vital forces. ... It attains this objective [maximum profits] by shortening the life of labour-power, in the same way as a greedy farmer snatches more produce from the soil by robbing it of its fertility" (C I, 376).

only use-value of the commodity labour-power that capital in general is interested in is that labour in general is the source of surplus-value in general.[4] Labour then is simply a particular kind of energy input that creates more value than it costs. It is only when the industrial reserve army of labour is depleted to the point where wages begin to steeply climb, that the commodification of labour-power itself is threatened until a crisis replenishes the industrial reserve army and re-establishes profitability for capital.

Marx's theory grasps capital's deep structures by letting competition work out its patterns through the commodity form without opposition. For workers this is achieved if we imagine that the typical capitalist commodity is produced by unskilled factory labour that is totally mobile. As a result, workers would move from capitalists with below average wages and working conditions to capitalists with above average, until wages and working conditions would become more or less equalized for the working class as a whole. This is what Marx means by homogeneous labour, and though he is completely aware of the fact that labour is never homogeneous in an actual society, it is a theoretical simplification that is justified by competition that pushes economic relations in this direction.[5] Thus from the beginning

4. Marx claims that in a sense labour-power is *the* use-value for capital (G, 295); "...the use-value of the labour is, for him [the capitalist], that he gets back a greater quantity of labour-time than he has paid out in the form of wages" (S I, 156); "...the workers themselves appear as that which they are in capitalist production – mere means of production, not an end in themselves and not the aim of production" (S II, 548).

5. "And even though the equalization of wages and working hours between one sphere of production and another ... comes up against all kinds of local obstacles, the advance of capitalist production and the progressive subordination of all economic relations to this mode of production tends nevertheless to bring this process to fruition. ... In a general analysis of the present kind, it is assumed throughout that actual conditions correspond to their concept..." (C III, 241–2). A common rate of surplus-value "assumes competition among the workers, and an equalization that takes place by their constant migration between one sphere of production and another. ... In theory, we assume the laws of the capitalist mode of production develop in their pure form" (C III, 275). "This constant equalization of ever-renewed inequalities is accomplished more quickly, (1) the more mobile capital is ... (2) the more rapidly labour-power can be moved from one sphere to another. ... The second condition presupposes the abolition of all laws that prevent workers from moving from one sphere of production to another or from one local seat of production to another. Indifference of the worker to the content of his work [abstract labour]. Greatest possible reduction of work in all spheres of production to simple labour. Finally and especially, the subjection of the worker to

to the end of his theory of capital Marx assumes that all labour is average (intensity), simple (unskilled), abstract labour (indifferent to use-value), and that wages and working conditions are equalized by competition amongst workers.

By way of contrast to the working class, capital is only assumed to be homogeneous up to volume two of *Capital*, when he divides capital into two sectors: the production of the means of consumption and the production of the means of production. Marx makes this division in order to show that it is possible for capital to maintain the right ratio between two types of use-value, means of consumption and means of production, through a commodity-economic logic whose motion provides the basic productive inputs required by capital and the basic consumption inputs required by workers. In other words, Marx illustrates with his "reproduction schema" how it is possible at the same time for capital to reproduce and expand through self-regulating markets, and reproduce the class relation by producing the provisions of each class in the right quantities.[6]

In volume three, prices which previously were simply the money expression of a commodity's value are for the first time made determinant, as it becomes clear that capital's of different organic composition but the same size will draw equal amounts of profit from the collective pool of surplus-value. As previously claimed, the resulting prices of production are simply values made more concrete and specific.

Next Marx shows how commercial capital can also get a portion of surplus-value in accord with the average rate of profit for a capital of its size. This is done essentially by saving on circulation costs, which frees up more capital to produce surplus-value. And while the basic form of capital is industrial capital, the profit of industrial capital is always divided between between profit of enterprise and interest-bearing capital. The percentage of this division is determined by the supply of and demand for credit, which in turn is influenced by business cycles and long-term movements in the general rate of profit.

---

the capitalist mode of production. Further details on this belong in the special study of competition" (C III, 298). "We therefore save ourselves a superfluous operation, and simplify our analysis, by the assumption that the labour of the worker employed by the capitalist is average simple labour" (C I, 306). "We assume throughout, not only that the value of an average labour-power is constant, but that the workers employed by a capitalist are reduced to average workers" (C I, 418).

6. This is clearly theorized by Sekine (1997, Vol. I).

For as the rate of interest approaches the rate of profit all further investment in industry would halt. The extent to which commercial capital or interest-bearing capital become relatively autonomous sub-classes of capital, become more or less tightly integrated into capital as a whole, or become relatively dominant fractions of capital, depends on historical context. For example, banking capital earns interest by mobilizing social savings and placing them at the service of capital, but in some historical contexts banking capital becomes so highly concentrated and powerful that it may help to organize and direct industrial capital (as in late nineteenth-century Germany).

As essentially a feudal remnant that has been reshaped to be managed by a commodity-economic logic, the landlord class is an alien class that has been domesticated by capital. Marx assumes the landlord class does not collect monopoly rents because that assumes the disruption of the law of value by extra-economic force, which would place monopoly rents clearly outside the theory of capital's deep structure.[7]

It follows from the above analysis that within capital's deep structure there are three and only three classes: capitalists, workers and landlords; and the capitalist class has three potential fractions: industrial capital, commercial capital and interest-bearing capital. The landlord class and working class remain homogeneous throughout the theory. Because Marx considered the commodification of labour-power and the class relation to be so central to his theory, he considered writing a separate volume on wage-labour. Eventually he dropped this plan, no doubt because he became clearer on the scope of his theory of capital's deep structures, and as a result, the general need for a mediating level of theory and not just one dealing with wage-labour.[8]

One could also make the case for a separate volume on money or one expanding upon any other fundamental category of capital's inner logic. Take money for example. Marx assumes throughout

7. "Apart from this, rent can derive only from a genuine monopoly price, which is determined neither by the price of production of the commodities nor by their value, but rather by the demand of the purchasers and their ability to pay [that is, 'effective demand'], consideration of which therefore belongs to the theory of competition, where the actual movement of market prices is investigated" (C III, 898).
8. C I, 944. See Lebowitz (2003) for an argument in favour of reviving Marx's initial intention of including a book on wage-labour in the text of *Capital*.

Capital that money is gold or convertible paper, and this is because it is only such money that can be managed commodity-economically.[9] In *Capital* there is no theory that comes close to analyzing types of international monetary system, types of fiat money, the range of interconnections between monetary and financial systems, inflation, runs on national currencies, types of local currencies, state debt and credit, types of banking systems, diverse dimensions of credit money, etc. This does not mean that we should write a missing book on money and add it on to *Capital*, because a more concrete theory of money would clearly disrupt, and possibly even reduce to rubble, the theoretical exposition of capital's inner laws if an attempt were made to simultaneously incorporate it into such an abstract and general discussion of necessary inner connections. It would make more sense to theorize money at more concrete levels of analysis where we can consider the development of monetary practices and social institutions in different times and places and where we can consider how monetary practices relate to other economic practices considered concretely (for Marx this would amount to "a special study of competition") and also to ideological and political practices. In this way the theory of capital's inner laws could be presented in the strongest possible way, and the clarity thus achieved could be used to inform our analysis of more concrete social practices.

CLASS AND MID-RANGE THEORY

While Marx did not propose three levels of analysis, I have argued that his theory does imply at least two levels, and that his emphasis on "mediation" supports my view opposing an immediacy that would directly connect the theory of capital's deep structures and historical analysis. "Mediation", of course, does not necessarily imply three levels of analysis, but without a middle level of theory that attempts to present phase-specific patterns of capital accumulation, mediations would tend to become haphazard. Mid-range theory requires us to think through the mutual supports amongst the most significant relatively autonomous economic, political and ideological practices

9.   "Throughout this work I assume that gold is the money commodity, for the sake of simplicity" (C I, 188). I believe it is not only for the sake of simplicity, since money must be commodified in order for it to be managed commodity-economically, and while the money commodity need not be gold, the international gold standard was established.

when capital accumulation is occurring in its most typical and successful modes relative to a phase of capitalist development.

Another Marxian concept essential to mid-level theory is commodification, for it is precisely the specificity of use-value obstacles that present themselves in history that may require political and ideological supports to even maintain a partial commodification. For example, labour-power is less commodified in the British putting-out industries of the early eighteenth century than in the German steel industry of the late nineteenth and early twentieth centuries. In both cases strong political and ideological measures were adopted to suppress class struggle, but the measures differed greatly because the patterns of capital accumulation did too.

The dominant patterns of capital accumulation in the early eighteenth century appear first in Britain and most typically in the putting-out production of woollens. It was difficult for cottage-based workers to organize because of their dispersion across the countryside during an historical period when the technologies of transportation and communication were still primitive. Furthermore, the Settlement Acts[10] and Anti-combination Acts[11] further blocked worker organization. For these and other reasons, arguably, the most typical outbursts of class struggle often took the form of "bread riots", and these hunger-driven riots occurred despite draconian Riot Acts that made rioting potentially a capital offence (though those found guilty were more often than not transported to penal colonies). There were, of course, many other forms of class struggle characteristic of the pattern of capital accumulation in this phase, such as the previously mentioned embezzlement on the part of cottage workers.

In my view Germany and the United States were the two most characteristic and successful capital accumulators during the golden age of imperialism between 1890 and 1914. In Germany, the existence of a large revolutionary socialist party (SPD) with strong ties to the worker's movement made strikes in the dominant steel industry unacceptable for the dominant bourgeois parties because of their potential for turning into a revolution. In this case, workers were pacified by large doses of paternalism (e.g. low-cost housing provided by the corporations and a safety net provided by the welfare state), and by the threat of calling out the army should a strike occur.

10. Workers could not move from the parish of their birth without special permission.
11. Any effort by workers to combine their forces to resist being exploited was a criminal offence.

Further, many workers came from depressed agricultural districts in Eastern Europe so that they were relatively desperate to keep their jobs, and, since they spoke many different languages, organizing would have been difficult. Finally, there would be less need to strike where a powerful socialist party in a multi-party system could pressure dominant parties to adopt at least some pro-worker policies. These two examples indicate how the typical forms of class struggle in the leading capital accumulators may be quite specific to a phase of capitalist development, and this specificity can be clearly analyzed in the context of mid-level theory.

CLASS ANALYSIS AND HISTORICAL ANALYSIS

In the theory of a purely capitalist society, homogeneous labour implies that all productive labour is productive of profit for capital. But when Marx refers to class at the level of historical analysis, the definition of the working class is broader and looser. He writes: "Ultimately, most members of the society are transformed into wage-labourers, people who live from hand to mouth, who receive their wages by the week and spend them by the day..." (C II, 221). Viewed from this point of view, the working class includes everyone who works for a wage, whether directly productive of profit for capital or not. This suggests that it is futile to argue about the precise defining of boundaries around classes at the level of history.

At the level of historical analysis class phenomena may become complex with a variety of non-capitalist or partially capitalist classes and with sub-groupings inside classes and groupings relatively autonomous from class that articulate with them in various ways. Marx argues clearly and consistently that the actual complexity of class phenomena in history are outside the theory of capital's logic. In order to state the law of value in the clearest possible terms, Marx assumes that all individuals are a member of one of three classes: capital, labour and landlords. But he is well aware that this situation is not closely approximated even in mid-nineteenth-century Victorian England. For example, in the *Grundrisse* he quotes Ravenstone: "Not ¼ of the English population provides everything that is consumed by all" (G, 398). And in *Capital* volume one he quotes from the 1861 census of England and Wales (C I, 574–5) that out of a total population of 20,066,224 the servant class consisted of 1,208,648, those employed in textile factories 642,607, in mines 565,835, in metal works 396,998, and in agricultural labour 1,098,261.[12] In 1855 according to the official count there were 851,369 paupers, a number significantly larger than the total employed in textile factories in 1861 (C I, 807). Servants, who are outside capital's inner logic, are the largest single class; and agricultural labour, the second largest grouping, would include a large number of petty commodity producers who are not a capitalist class. It follows that the industrial working class would constitute 8 per cent of the population if we leave out agricultural labourers, whose division between petty commodity producers and wage workers is unknown. In response to these numbers, Marx claims that "the extraordinary increase in the productivity of large-scale industry, permits a larger and larger part of the working class to be employed unproductively" (that is, as domestic servants) (C I, 574). Elsewhere, he (G, 853–4) notes that "pre-bourgeois forms of production" such as putting-out production, domestic industry, or petty commodity production are often reproduced "in subordinate spheres within the bourgeois economy itself" and are often characterized by "The most odious exploitation of labour".[13] Further, "Those classes and sub-classes who do not live directly from their labour become more numerous and live better than before, and the number of unproductive workers increases as well" (S II, 562; S III, 50–1). Here Marx is primarily referring to groups like landlords and the rentier class that do not live off their labour, and servant or service workers who are unproductive of surplus-value. Marx points out that Malthus places his hopes on a class of consumers who do not produce as a means of overcoming the under-consumption tendencies of capitalism. Landlords being insufficient, Malthus resorts to "a mass of sinecurists in State and Church, of large armies, pensions, tithes for the priests, an impressive national debt, and from time to time expensive wars" (S III, 51). Marx argues (S II, 573) that with the growth of capitalism, the middle classes will also constantly grow, and "The middle classes maintain themselves to an ever increasing extent directly out of revenue" (for example, rent, stocks or other forms of financial interest). As a result of the growth of the middle class, the proletariat will become "a constantly declining proportion ... of the total population".[14]

12. In 1861, 26,597 farms were less than 100 acres.
13. "...the shirt factory of Messrs Tillie and Londonderry, which employs 1,000 workers in the factory itself, and 9,000 out-workers spread over the country districts" (C I, 591).
14. S III, 63. Of course, this is not necessarily the case globally.

These examples of historical class analysis taken from Marx's own economic writings, suggest that his observations are informed by the theory of capital's deep structures without being deducible from them. And to further advance historical analysis we would need much more contextual information about the make-up of middle classes or of pre-bourgeois classes and the consequences of that make-up for capital accumulation and class struggle. For example, putting-out labour has reappeared in the current globalized capital accumulation as a way of avoiding unions, overhead costs and protective legislation. Similarly, various forms of forced labour (for example prison labour and "workfare") and slavery are being reproduced by current forms of capital accumulation (Bales 1999, 2005).

As long as workers confront capital as individuals, there is little that they can do to resist low wages unless there are labour shortages; even so, as they begin to organize, workers may "...achieve a certain quantitative participation in the general growth of wealth" (S III, 312), though never fully keeping pace with their growing productivity. And yet

as soon as they [workers] discover that the degree of intensity of the competition amongst themselves depends wholly on the pressure of the relative surplus population; as soon as, by setting up trade unions, etc., they try to organize planned co-operation between employed and the unemployed in order to obviate or to weaken the ruinous effects of this natural law of capitalist production on their class. ... Every combination between employed and unemployed disturbs the "pure" action of this law. (C I, 793–4)

While Marx is here specifically referring to the potentially disruptive effect of worker organization on the relation between wages and the relative surplus population, the same could be said for any of the necessary inner connections amongst economic categories. Potentially any of them could be disrupted by collective human agency. Further, as pointed out earlier, Marx (C I, 794) claims with regard to this specific case, "The relative surplus population exists in all kinds of forms", and it follows that in any historical analysis, the precise specification of its various forms and their interrelation would be crucial.

At the level of historical analysis there may be wage differentials for all sorts of reasons: skill, education, merit, shift work, seniority, danger pay, part-time, temporary, union, status, productivity, gender, age, race, ethnicity, sectoral, geographic, and so forth. And clearly these sorts of differentials need to be studied at levels of analysis more concrete than capital's deep structure. Further, Marx (C II, 415) explicitly argues that at the level of historical analysis: "Given a partial or local rise in wages – i.e. a rise in just a few branches of production – it is possible that a local rise in prices for the products of this branch may result. But even this depends on many circumstances." Once again, the results here cannot be deduced from general economic laws, though such laws may help sort out the relevant circumstances once they are sufficiently investigated in their historical specificity.

Another example presented by Marx is the rise of wages in English agricultural districts between 1849 and 1859. While he does not analyze this in depth, he (C I, 791) suggests two causes: exodus of agricultural surplus population due to wartime demands (The Crimean War), and increased demand for labour resulting from "the vast extension of railways, factories, mines etc". Of course real wages may rise for various reasons including in some circumstances increases due to worker organization and militancy. And if the increase in real wages continues, the working class would become an increasingly important consuming force, opening the possibility that consumer identity could become as strong or stronger than worker identity. For "A worker who buys a loaf of bread and a millionaire who does the same appear in this act as simple buyers", (G, 251) and hence as undifferentiated. "From the moment he buys from the capitalist, his specific quality as worker is extinguished ... in circulation he confronts the capitalist simply as M, and the capitalist confronts him as C..." (G, 425). At the time Marx was writing, the global uneven development of capitalism had not yet produced anything like the wage differentials that exist in today's world, and hence he would not have addressed how such differentials might give rise to divisions within the global working class, including a strong consumerist consciousness amongst the better-off workers in the better-off countries.

The servant class is not part of self-valorizing value, and yet at the time Marx was writing there were far more female domestic servants than textile factory workers. It follows that servants' uncommodified domestic service would need to be taken into consideration in any historical account of the British economy in this period. Indeed there are many different kinds of service workers that would need to be accounted for at the level of historical analysis. At this level, class phenomena become complex, and hence Marx (S II, 493) writes: "We do not examine the competition of capitals, nor the credit system, nor the actual composition of society, which by no means consists only of two classes, workers and industrial capitalists, and where therefore consumers and producers are not identical categories."

And not only may capitalist classes be complex, but also groupings that are strictly speaking outside the capitalist mode of production further complicate matters. As previously noted, "In the United States of America, every independent workers' movement was paralyzed as long as slavery disfigured a part of the republic" (C I, 414). The point is that the actual complexity of class phenomena in history can be importantly determined by the ways that forms of oppression overlap with class exploitation. This suggests the need to consider class in relation to forms of oppression associated with gender, disability, race, ethnicity, caste, status, and so forth.

A further consideration is the relation of class to other important social groupings such as military, familial, religious, immigrant, national, linguistic, regional and/or groups based on strong political, ideological or cultural identifications. For example, in his famous book *The Making of the English Working Class*, E.P. Thompson (1968) focuses on the impact of particular religious groupings (particularly Methodism) on the development of a working-class consciousness in nineteenth-century England. Today there is an increasingly important relation between class and political socialization through religion, education and the mass media.[15]

At the level of history, capital can indirectly exploit non-capitalist workers through the commodity form. According to Marx (C III, 321)

...(in India, for example, where the *ryot* operates as an independent peasant farmer, and his production is not yet subsumed under capital, although the money-lender may well extort from him in the form of interest not only his entire surplus labour, but even – to put it in capitalist terms – a part of his wages), it would be quite wrong to seek to measure the national rate of profit by the level of the national rate of interest.

Here is a clear example of how the circuit of capital can "exploit" pre-capitalist or transitional forms of petty commodity production. To repeat an earlier quotation when "the circuit of industrial capital ... cuts across the commodity circulation of the most varied modes of social production ... the capitalist mode of production is conditioned by modes of production lying outside its own stage of development"(C II, 189–90). For while the theory of capital's deep structures is not

15. See for example, Massing (2005a, 2005b), McChesney (2004), Soley (2002).

conditioned by such historical variations, at the level of historical analysis clearly capitalist and non-capitalist economic practices may condition each other.

Just as self-employed production is outside the theory of capital's inner logic precisely so that it becomes possible to think clearly about how capital's logic impacts on it, so must the historical variations of labour within the family be excluded. From the point of view of capital's logic, some kind of family is required as a unit of expanded biological reproduction, but that logic by itself cannot determine who does what kind of labour, who lives together for how long, rates of fertility, or what kind of pooling and division of resources takes place within family settings. And there is no single family form that can be deduced as a necessary adjunct to capital accumulation. For while we might hypothesize that there would be an historical tendency for the commodity form to increasingly penetrate the family simply because of the reifying force of capital, we cannot deduce at what rate, in what form, and with what specific consequences this tendency may unfold. To repeat an earlier quotation:

Since certain family functions, such as nursing and suckling children, cannot be entirely suppressed, the mothers who have been confiscated by capital must try substitutes of some sort. Domestic work, such as sewing and mending, must be replaced by the purchase of ready-made articles. Hence the diminished expenditure of labour in the house is accompanied by an increased expenditure of money outside. The cost of production of the working-class family therefore increases, and balances its greater income. (C I, 518)

Here Marx is suggesting that there is a general tendency for capitalistically produced commodities to replace family produced use-values, but he says nothing about the specific ways this might unfold in different class strata in different times and places.   From the point of view of capital, domestic labour is "unproductive labour" that capital does not organize or profit from (at least directly). The working class "can only cook meat for itself when it has produced a wage with which to pay for the meat", and "This unproductive labour never enables them to repeat the same unproductive labour a second time [cook meat] unless they have previously laboured productively" (S I, 166). While labour that is "unproductive" from the point of view of capital (i.e. not productive of surplus-value) falls outside the theory of deep structures which focuses on what is central to capital, profit-making, it is clear that at the level of historical analysis, it would be important to look at who's labour cooks the meat. In the world of

McDonalds it turns out that capitalist wage-labour often cooks the meat and that as a result such labour becomes productive of profit for capital.

Generally the family, which is considered to be based upon love, generosity, respect and mutuality; or, in other words, which is considered to manifest some of the deepest and most meaningfully direct person-to-person relations, would seem to be anathema to the pure self-interested calculating reason associated with the motion of value. Here, and in other groupings where a strong sense of togetherness is important, the qualitative of use-value would seem most at odds with the pure profit calculations of capital as self-valorizing value. Ultimately, in the sphere of the family, indifference to use-value is indifference to children. And that is why the penetration of the commodity form into family life has been so resisted, and why its seemingly ever deeper penetration today has spurred so much dangerous reaction, while exposing a whole generation of children to an increasingly meaningless and terrifying world (Grossberg 2005). Indeed, the reason why so much emphasis is placed upon "team work" whether in business schools, the military or politics is precisely to overcome the extreme competitiveness so typical of capitalism. Arguably the commodity form is currently penetrating and undermining all those groupings based upon mutuality and a strong sense of community whether the family, education, religion or the military. Arguably, the consequence is that global capitalism itself will fall more and more deeply into crises that it cannot respond to, for no society can survive if it is based purely on a cash nexus.

What I have attempted to demonstrate in this section is that Marx himself was aware of at least some of the complexities of class analysis when carried out at the level of historical analysis. First there are the relationships within capitalist classes to be considered, including fractions, stratifications and segmentations. Within the working classes, particularly important would be wage differentials within the employed working class as well as relations between the employed, semi-employed and unemployed, both within geographical units and globally. And these categories could be explored in relation to types of worker organization and worker resistance, and in relation to types and degrees of political and ideological repression. Then there is the consideration of how the circuits of capital relate to non-capitalist or semi-capitalist labour whether of peasants, the self-employed, domestic labour, forced labour or voluntary labour.

CLASS AND CLASS STRUGGLE

Even amongst Marxists the debates over class are legion. For example, some years ago, E.P. Thompson (1968), the distinguished Marxist historian, argued that classes exist only in so far as actual class struggle creates a group with class consciousness. To his historical/ empiricist way of thinking, the very existence of classes depended on the intensity of class struggle, because presumably the greater the struggle, the more class consciousness will tend to form. One problem with such a position is that it cannot explain why class struggles are so common and widespread within the capitalist mode of production, because it cannot entertain the possibility of there being a dynamic of deep structures that continually generate them. Another problem with Thompson's position is that by focusing on the historical where class phenomena are generally complex and messy, he cannot generate a theory of class other than through generalizations from the messy empirical or by sneaking a more structural theory in the back door. As a result, he can abstract from class phenomena across numerous historical contexts, but such abstractions may leave out important aspects of class and may not get at underlying causal mechanisms. A theoretical impoverishment is likely to result from an approach that cannot get much further than arguing that we need a "history from below".

Some interpreters of Marx's *Capital* seem to think that it is very important to place class struggle at the core of the theory. Perhaps the strongest support for such an interpretation would be Marx's view that subsistence is a historically relative standard of living, the establishment of which would in general involve class struggle, as would the historical establishment of a working day of a certain length. A careful reading of *Capital* demonstrates, however, that while Marx often utilizes historical phenomena to illustrate his theory, he never falls into the sort of functionalism that would make theory or history a function of each other. Indeed, his assumption of complete commodification rules out class struggle per se, but it does not rule out a structural theory that demonstrates a structurally antagonistic relationship between capital and labour. As Marx theorizes exploitation, it is clearly a relationship of opposition and antagonism, but in a theory of capital in general it is not possible to include anything specific about the forms and consequences of this antagonism. It follows that Marx simply assumes a subsistence of a given level and a working day of a certain length in order to clarify the necessary connections between basic economic categories. However, this does not mean that at more concrete levels of analysis, it would not be possible to study the power relations, including class struggle, that play a role in determining a working day of a certain length. And Marx does just this when he examines the struggles to limit the working day of children through the British Factory Acts. In order to convincingly illustrate the antagonistic structural power relations between capital and labour, Marx gives many historical illustrations of class struggle, but this does not mean that such illustrations are to be considered a part of the theory of capital's deep structures. In one sense it is a moot point as to whether class struggle is included in the theory of capital's inner logic, since a theory of structural antagonism (but not actual class struggle) clearly is included and this theory is the basis for explaining why class struggle always accompanies capitalism in history and helps to explain the various forms that this struggle actually takes. To put it a little differently, the theory of capital's deep structures demonstrates why, given their structural positioning, capital and labour must be at odds, even though the agency involved in actual class struggle cannot be theorized in a context where commodification is complete.

The dialectic of capital clearly and precisely theorizes the fundamental structural dynamics between capital and labour, between capital and landlords, and between various fractions of capital. Capital and labour are the only two primary classes and their relationship is one of capital accumulation through the exploitation of labour. Any effort to theorize class struggle within this theory is a serious mistake for the following reasons: one, it will undermine the clarity of the theory of what capital is in its innermost logic (that is, undermine the law of value); two, it will reify class struggle (thereby producing reductionism) by theorizing it at a level of abstraction where all the main variables are highly reified social relations; three, it will weaken our ability to theorize class struggle (by reifying the concept "class struggle") at more concrete levels where this sort of theorization is crucial; four, it will cloud our thinking about what belongs to capital and what belongs to us by seeing the outcomes of capital's laws of motion as a result of capital and labour "mixing it up"; five, it will cloud clear thinking about alternatives to capitalism. It follows that by excluding class struggle from the theory of capital's inner logic, we can produce a stronger theory of class struggle within Marxian political economy as a whole. For the theory of capital's deep structures forms an objective ground for thinking about dominant types of class struggle at the level of mid-range theory where those patterns of capital accumulation most characteristic of different phases of capitalist development are theorized, and these two more abstract levels can inform the study of actual processes of class struggle in history. It follows that a post-autistic Marxian political economy needs at least three levels of analysis, where the theory of capital's inner logic needs to be supplemented by extensive work at more concrete levels.

CLASS, ECONOMICS, POLITICS AND IDEOLOGY

As I have argued repeatedly, it only makes sense to have autonomous economic theory when we can assume complete commodification. For it is only when economic life can be completely managed by a commodity-economic logic that the political and ideological can be relegated to being passive background conditions of the economic. In other words, the theory of capital's deep structures is the only theory that can be purely economic. As we move to mid-range theory and historical analysis, capitalist economic imperatives must be thought in connection with political and ideological institutions and practices, which, in their relative autonomy, may disrupt, artificially support or redirect capital's inner logic. It follows that the two levels of political economy that are more concrete than pure capitalism must be multi- or transdisciplinary.

One of the reasons that "class" is such a clear and distinct category in Marx's theory of capital's inner logic is that it is a purely economic category with property relations operating entirely through a commodity-economic logic. Within this theoretical context, the state and ideology are simply passive background reflexes of the commodity form. The state and ideology passively reflect and confirm property relations and the commodity form. Once we move to more concrete levels of analysis, however, the state and ideology need to be theorized as relatively autonomous since they can intervene in connection with actors to maintain or transform economic relations. I believe that Marxian political economy needs a great deal of work to be done at the levels of mid-range theory and historical analysis, and here I only want to put forward some further examples that indicate a certain awareness in Marx of the problems of thinking out how the economic articulates with the political and ideological at more concrete levels of analysis. Some of the examples above, such as the impact of racism on the American workers movement would fit here as well.

Marx refers to laws that may perpetuate small-scale farming allotments, such as those put into effect by the French Revolution. He points out that despite these laws a certain concentration of ownership is returning (as he is writing in the 1860s), presumably because of the reifying forces of capitalism that would cause concentration and centralization in the absence of laws blocking such tendencies. But the rate and degree of concentration of farm ownership would depend primarily on the balance of forces between capitalist reification and political law, which cannot be theorized in general. Thus, according to Marx, "The influence of laws in stabilizing relations of distribution, and hence their effect on production, requires to be determined in each specific instance" (G, 98). And all sorts of laws may figure in capital accumulation in important ways, whether laws constraining the real-estate market, protecting workers or the environment, or laws against "price fixing", "insider trading", "tax evasion" or "fraud". When we compare pure capitalism without state intervention to actually existing capitalism, it is apparent that the system of law can have an important impact on capital accumulation in all phases of capitalist development.

Marx argues that because capital continually revolutionizes the means of production and passes through periodic crises, it "...does away with all repose, all fixity, and all security as far as the worker's life-situation is concerned..." (C I, 617–18). And while this may be the general tendency of capital, there are very significant variations amongst different groups of workers in different times and places depending upon political and ideological conditions. In some parts of the world workers have achieved some success in reducing the insecurity of their position, and in some industries in other parts of the world there are no trade union protections and little or no legislated safety nets. Even where there are protections they are not necessarily secure, as, for example, when a worker on the brink of retirement may suddenly find his or her pension significantly reduced through various machinations of capital or the state.

Marx (C II, 591) also notes that "...Mr. Capitalist, as well as his press, is frequently discontented with the way in which labour-power spends its money...". Quoting the British Ambassador to Washington:

The working-people have not kept up in culture ... and have had things showered on them which they do not know how to use. ... The problem remains, how to raise him as a consumer by rational and healthful processes, not an easy one, as his ambition does not go beyond a diminution of his hours of labour, the demagogues rather inciting him to this than to raising his condition by the improvement of his mental and moral powers. (C II, 591)

Alas, similar statements of capitalist ideology have been repeated ad nausaum from Marx's day to the present, continually reappearing in slightly different packaging. "Why don't they work harder?" "Why don't they improve themselves the way that I have?" "Why do they waste their money?" "Why don't they show some restraint and discipline?" The particular articulation of such discourse and how it influences ideology that belittles human beings and serves to promote classist attitudes and legislation needs to be studied in particular historical contexts.

Any ethical discussion about how total social labour should be distributed and rewarded would require among other things a discussion of social need. Such discussions are avoided in pure capitalism by simply letting supply and demand settle the matter. But Marx makes it clear that "social need" "...is basically conditioned by the relationship of the different classes and their respective economic positions; in the first place, therefore, particularly by the proportion between the total surplus-value and wages, and secondly, by the proportion between the various parts into which surplus-value itself is divided..." (C III, 282). I think what Marx is suggesting here by placing "social need" in quotation marks is that to get far in discussing social need, a prerequisite would be to get rid of class. In other words, an economy based on class exploitation militates against an ethically based economics. When individuals are desperately insecure, how can they even begin to objectively consider questions of need?

CONCLUSIONS

While it is beyond the scope of this book to elaborate on the three levels of analysis that I have discussed elsewhere, I have attempted to show in this chapter some of the ways that class analysis can be enhanced by such an approach and that it is not inconsistent with Marx's awareness of the need for theoretical mediations connecting theory and history. Grounding class concepts in a purely capitalist society gives us the strongest possible understanding of the most basic class dynamics of capitalism, which in turn can serve to guide theory at more concrete levels where class phenomena become complex processes of struggle.

At the level of mid-range theory, the aim is to theorize those class patterns that are most connected to the dominant phase-specific mode of capital accumulation. In other words, the focus would be on the most characteristic relations amongst classes and class fractions, and in close connection, the most typical patterns of class struggle and most typical ideological, political and legal forms that serve to contain that struggle.

Finally, at the level of historical analysis, the main aim is to explain the role of capitalism in historical change. Here the role of class and class struggle in historical change can be analyzed in connection with the complex process of history either globally or in some specified spatial/temporal configuration. This is arguably the most difficult and most important level of theory precisely because questions of causality in connection with historical change are so highly complex in most instances. Also it is only at this level that we find the detail necessary for well thought through strategies of transformation.

In the next chapter, I shall explore some possible fruitful connections between a levels of analysis approach to political economy and ethical thought. Approaches that would apply mathematical economics directly to historical analysis do not offer the sort of theoretical framework that invites either effective historical or ethical thought. After all, if historical outcomes can be considered the resultants of mathematical equations, then where is the space for human responsibility? Furthermore, such theorizing, by not considering economic variables to be completely commodified social relations, has no basis for the sort of unpacking of commodification that can support critical thinking. For example, the indifference to use-value, the single-minded focus on short-term profit, the continual speed up of the pace of life, the insecurity of livelihood, the reproduction of an industrial reserve army, the subsumption of labour to machines, class exploitation, the reification of economic life: these and other tendencies of capitalism are most clearly understood and grounded within a theory of capital's deep structures considered as commodified or reified social relations.

7
Ethics and Political Economy

In the predominantly capitalist world of our time, the study of ethics has been largely reduced to a minor sub-discipline of philosophy within the academy.[1] This is not surprising given the widespread assumption that the hidden-hand of the market maximizes the general welfare, and given the influences of empiricism and positivism that would separate ethics from the social sciences in order to make them more "scientific". Indeed, the only ethics required of pure capitalism would be norms securing private property and contract, and norms discouraging those forms of wrongdoing that would disrupt business. And as would be expected, the general exclusion of ethical considerations from the social sciences and their closeting within marginalized sub-disciplines cannot help but create an intellectual ethos friendly to formalistic ethics abstracted from considerations of advancing human flourishing in the real world of practical life. Because there is no strong tradition connecting a cognitive ethics either with social science or public debate, there is little solid ground upon which to build.

One way forward is that of Rawls, who emphasizes procedure in the face of the lack of traditions of debate that might establish areas of agreement on substantive issues.[2] Given the abstractness of his theory, however, it is not even clear whether or not his procedural formulations are consistent with capitalism.[3] As with a great deal of ethical philosophy, Rawls makes little effort to discuss the extent to which existing economic and social structures facilitate or hinder human flourishing, and if hindering, what kinds of changes are desirable and possible. For example, if existing socio-economic

1. Which is not to deny that truncated forms of ethical studies may exist in other disciplines, such as "business ethics". I say "truncated" because issues such as distributive justice are very unlikely to be addressed systematically.
2. MacIntyre (1984) argues forcefully for the difficulties facing ethical thought in the modern world precisely because of a lack of any strong traditions of discourse that might have built at least a common vocabulary if not some common areas of consensus.
3. A case could be made that some sort of democratic socialism would be a prerequisite for the workability of Rawl's theory of justice.

practices tend to undermine the health of humans and of the environment in particular ways, what sorts of changes can we make? Or if the human impulses towards generosity are constrained or discouraged by an economy that privileges those most successful in accumulating money, what sorts of changes might free up human capacities for generosity?[4]

While most writings by Marx and Engels are critical and hence have ethical implications,[5] here I want specifically to explore the ethical implications of Marx's economic writings with two aims in mind: first, to present reasons for connecting ethical considerations with economic theory (indeed all social science); and second, to indicate what such a connection might contribute to ethical theory. This line of argumentation breaks radically with mainstream social science and its assumptions that the scientificity of a theory depends upon an empiricism that builds high walls to prevent incursions of normative theory. In opposition, I claim that it is natural for humans to always be interested in how social arrangements (particularly power relations) might either advance or retard human flourishing. And since the answers to such questions are often uncertain and contestable, to a great extent politics should involve continual debate and experimentation on how best to advance human flourishing in the short- and long-run.

The fundamental problem with a great deal of ethical philosophy is that it is too abstract and secluded and therefore circles continuously around the most basic questions: should the self come first, or should the other; should reason or love; right or the good; the individual or society; utility or contract. Recently some more economically informed thinkers have focused on needs and quality of life,[6] and while this emphasis points us towards the concrete, it often does

4. "In bourgeois economics – and in the epoch of production to which it corresponds – this complete working-out of the human content appears as a complete emptying-out, this universal objectification as total alienation, and the tearing-down of all limited, one-sided aims as sacrifice of the human end-in-itself to an entirely external end. This is why the childish world of antiquity appears on one side as loftier. On the other side, it really is loftier in all matters where closed shapes, forms and given limits are sought for. It is satisfaction from a limited standpoint; while the modern gives no satisfaction; or, where is appears satisfied with itself, it is *vulgar*" (G, 488).
5. Probably Marx's concept of alienation has been most widely used as an "ethical" critique of capitalism.
6. See Nussbaum (2006), Sen (2000), Nussbaum and Sen (1993), Doyal and Gough (1991).

not actually get far, because of a lack of prioritization and political realism. What is needed is a perspective that would enable us to move ahead in particular contexts by focusing energies on achievable goals that would make the most immediate difference in people's quality of life and would mobilize them in ways that would enable them to sustain and expand the gains made. It is grand to propose the redistribution of wealth on a global scale, but just throwing money at problems does not necessarily make them go away unless it is utilized in ways that the populations concerned can agree to and can sustain. For this reason, I believe that questions of ethics are generally also questions of politics, such that abstract rights need ultimately to be connected with realistic proposals for human flourishing, the implementation of which must always involve a significant degree of democracy. Questions of justice, democracy, freedom, rights, duties and equality are not only interconnected, but are also connected to the fundamentally important arena of economic life. Indeed, it seems to me that no mode of thinking can potentially contribute more to the making of ethics a reality in concrete situations than economic ethics as a practical ethics.

I shall refer to the sort of ethics that I see emerging out of Marxian political economy as "Negative Ethics" in the sense that its aim is less to arrive at a universal theory of justice, the good or right than to alleviate those situations that are damaging to human flourishing in the here and now.[7] And in using the word "alleviate", I do not mean to suggest that alleviating the wrongs and damages to human flourishing may not sometimes require radical transformation. The more radical the transformation, however, the more massive the mobilization of human energy required to successfully carry it through, and this is because change that is deep and wide will only produce reaction and violence if it is not carried out democratically and non-violently. The basic premise of negative ethics is that it is in principle possible to achieve widespread agreement on what to do about at least some basic injustices without agreement on the nature of justice in the abstract and general. It follows that negative ethics is practical, and transformative: always aiming at improving the conditions for human flourishing from the level of the individual to the level of the entire earth. Over time, I believe

7. My conception of negative ethics has nothing to do with Berlin's "negative freedom". Also, debate over universal principles is by no means a waste of time. It only becomes an obstacle when it gets in the way of reaching high levels of agreement on dealing with immediate problems.

that a negative ethics would also produce more agreement on general or universal principles of a positive ethics.[8] In a sense, then, there are always universal norms in the background, but in many cases their implications in the here and now may be clarified and gain broader agreement by focusing less on them than on immediate practical situations that truly hinder or block the possibilities for human flourishing.

And as long as capitalism lasts, I believe that ethico-political struggles will either tend to be reactive holding actions responding to the fallout of capital's indifference to use-value, or they will be proactive and transformative. At the same time all apocalyptic and romantic visions of transformation need to be resisted. Transforming capitalism will not be achieved by a single generation because alternatives must be worked out through trial and error and through the difficult work of deepening democratic processes. Indeed, even making some significant headway in undoing the extremely dangerous militarization of capitalism that has occurred in the post Second World War period will be a long and difficult struggle. And the struggle is made even more difficult when insecurity, poverty and desperation generated largely by capitalism itself undermines the very effectiveness of human agency as it struggles against the continuous and crippling fallout of late capitalism.

My basic aim is to give some indication of the powerful contributions that Marxian political economy can make to a negative ethics. In developing my argument in this chapter, I shall follow the chapter sequence starting with the theory of the commodity form, then the theory of surplus-value, followed by the theory of dialectical reason, the theory of levels of analysis, and finally the theory of class. But to begin with, I want to make it clear that ethical theory is not internal to the dialectic of a purely capitalist society; however, once the structural dynamics of such a society are clearly theorized, those dynamics can be critically analyzed for the ethical problems their directionalities will create. In fact in some ways the dialectic of capital and ethics are diametrically opposed, since a dialectic depends upon a complete commodification that removes all human responsibility from economic outcomes. Were we truly responsible for our economic life, a dialectic of capital would be impossible.

8. There is perhaps already widespread agreement on certain universal norms such as the desirability that promises be kept or that lying is to be avoided; however, there is less agreement on exactly what the implications of these universal norms are in specific circumstances.

Before turning to the analysis of the ethical implications of the structural dynamics of pure capitalism, I need to develop the meaning of "human flourishing", given its vagueness and importance.

HUMAN FLOURISHING

We know a lot about what humans need to flourish materially (diet, shelter, exercise, healthy natural environment, absence of threat of physical violence, and so forth) and are gradually becoming much more knowledgeable about what sorts of social, political and psychological conditions (love, care, friendship, generosity, respect, purpose, freedom, democracy, social justice, and so forth) promote the richest possibilities of human development. If our enormous research capacities were directed away from the means of violence and means of profit, we could certainly learn a great deal more about creating healthy and sustainable material and social environments. For example, we only know the carcinogenic properties of a small proportion of the total number of chemicals that we have spread about our environment. We seem to be failing our youth as more and more fall into poverty and all the social ills that accompany it. At the same time, we know a great deal about what sorts of food intake and what sorts of exercise will advance bodily health. Also we know something about the sorts of caring and loving social environments that will advance mental health and sociality. And while we should know that violence breeds violence, we are doing an extremely poor job of reducing the level of violence in the world.

I use "human flourishing" to refer to what we know about how to make our lives more fulfilling while improving the health of the earth for future generations. I believe that we often know a great deal more about human flourishing than we think, and that there is also more agreement about basic conditions of human flourishing than we admit. Indeed, in some areas our beliefs are backed up with very strong evidence. And just as we can be clear about various injustices without agreement on a theory of justice in the abstract and in general, so we can know a great deal about obstacles to human flourishing without knowing fully what conditions would most advance it in general. We know with a great deal of certainty that malnutrition and starvation are obstacles to human flourishing. We know that people whose lives are brutalized (for example, by poverty and violence) are susceptible to the appeals of fundamentalisms that offer simplistic stories about the source of evil and that offer hope for a better life either on this earth or in an afterlife. And all sorts of fundamentalism, whether religious or political, are based on an in-group that is good and out-groups that are evil. When fundamentalism is powerful, it will be difficult to achieve much agreement on human flourishing, or to advance it through trial-and-error experiments that would, for example, democratize the economy. While there are no doubt many explanations that contain at least some truth for the sudden rise of fundamentalism from the 1980s to the present, it is my view that once the dust settles and we get a little distance from our immediate past, capitalist fundamentalism (i.e. neo-liberalism) will emerge as a major cause. Arguably it was Ronald Reagan's capitalist fundamentalism that first encouraged American religious fundamentalism to expand and become more political. And the hysterical anti-communism that was attached to this fundamentalism also led to an enormous boost to Islamic fundamentalism in the effort to drive the "Evil Empire" out of Afghanistan.[9]

I believe that the idea of human flourishing implies that social life should aim to maximize the human flourishing of each, consistent with the human flourishing of all. And while an organization of economic life that would equally enable all to explore and develop their potentials may seem highly utopian, it is a utopia worth working towards, by always working to remove those barriers that seem most damaging to human flourishing in the present.

THE COMMODITY FORM AND ETHICS

Hegel believed that private property, as the most basic materialization of the human will, was the basis of ethics. Clearly the paradigm case of private property for Hegel was the result of the individual mixing his life energy with nature in order to appropriate something, as in land.[10] Further, private property gives each family (with sufficient wealth) a home and sense of place as well as each individual a sense of social/political status or position.[11] Finally, private property assured

9. For a good account of some of this history see Mamdani (2005).
10. "A person has as his substantive end the right of putting his will into any and every thing and thereby making it his, because it has no such end in itself and derives its destiny and soul from his will. This is the absolute right of appropriation which man has over all 'things'" (Hegel 1971, 41).
11. "The family, as a person, has its real external existence in property; and it is only when this property takes the form of capital that it becomes the embodiment of the substantial personality of the family" (Hegel 1971, 116).

that each individual would be surrounded by things that to some extent reflected their or their family's application of life energies.[12] Living at a time and in a place where the hyper-mobility of the commodity form had not taken off and where the factory system with its private ownership of the means of production were yet to assume centre stage in economic life, it was easy for Hegel to think of private property primarily in terms of land (as in the family home) or in terms of the self-employed economic activity of the shopkeeper, small farmer, skilled craftsman, and so forth. And as Marx asserts, I think correctly, this way of conceptualizing private property, that is so completely at odds with the realities of capitalism, is characteristic of bourgeois economic theory, not only in Marx's day, but to this day![13] Presumably if all property accumulations are self-earned, they are deserved, and no degree of inequality should be challenged.

Marx's *Capital* is a totally devastating critique of the tendency of bourgeois economists to collapse capitalist ownership of the means of production into self-earned private property. He does this by demonstrating that even if capitalist private property were initially self-earned (rare indeed), it would in short order (that is, after passing a few times through the circuit of industrial capital) be reconstituted as the accumulated unpaid labour (surplus-value) of workers (C I, 715). And the commodity form, by subsuming the class relation embedded in private property in the means of production to a system of *quid pro quo* exchange, seemingly free contract, and a neutral system of prices – much like a magician – makes the class relation vanish into the thin air of "free and equal exchange."

Although Marx makes a mockery of this disappearing act, academic economics is still spellbound by it, cloaking such sleight of hand with the trappings of scientific theory. One reason economists can

12. "The infinitely complex, criss-cross, movements of reciprocal production and exchange ... become crystallized ... and distinguished into general groups ... in other words, into class-divisions" (Hegel 1971, 130–1).
13. Referring to bourgeois economists Marx writes: "Here the existence of capital is denied, in order to transform the capitalists into people who carry out the simple operation C-M-C and who produce for individual consumption and not *as* capitalists with the aim of enrichment..." (S II, 534). Also: "... in order to rescue production *based on capital* ... all its specific qualities are ignored and their specific character as forms omitted, and capital is conceived as its inverse, as simple production for *immediate use value*" (G, 411). And finally: "Hence, the general juridical notion from Locke to Ricardo is always that of *petty-bourgeois ownership*, while the relations of production they describe belong to the *capitalist mode of production*" (C I, 1083).

carry on so is that unlike Marx they never problematize commodification. Complete commodification is always simply assumed with
the result that quantification is complete and the numbers games
can spin on forever without ever a thought of the underlying power
relations. In antithesis, Marx shows how complete commodification, even when operating through "voluntary" equal exchange
and the system of "neutral" prices, reproduces class domination and
exploitation. And while eventually ethics needs to be concretized
through levels of analysis, just as the theory of capital does, the
starting point here is the theory of complete commodification, where
we explore purely economic and purely capitalist social forms. In the
context of a commodity-economic logic, it is the ethical implications
of the structural power relations and the general directionalities of
structural dynamics that are the focus of ethical theory. Far from
being internal to the dialectic of capital, ethical theory is required
precisely because the dialectic removes responsibility for economic
outcomes from human responsibility.

We start then with the assumption that insofar as social agents are
capitalists they are connected only by the commodity form, or, to
be more specific, by the value-form, since ultimately they are simply
agents of self-expanding value. Since the aim of each capitalist is
to maximize profits, they will compete and direct their behaviour
in accord with price signals that are the result of their aggregate
economic activity. To say that value is the basic social connection,
implies that capitalists direct their behaviour by the quantitative
information (price) expressed through the commodity form. If I am
making little or no profit and I see another capitalist making very
large profits, then, as a rational capitalist, I will shift production into
the large profit sector. What I produce, how I produce, and how much
I produce is ultimately shaped by price signals that I pick up from the
commodity form. Strictly, from the point of view of capital, all other
signals are noise. In other words, if not interfered with, capitalist
economic behaviour proceeds entirely on the basis of quantitative
calculation, even when the results of this are highly damaging to
the quality of social life. The first ethical problem of capital, then,
is the privileging of profit above all other human values. And the
solution that this problem suggests is an integration of quality into
quantity such that many different qualities of life can be weighed
against and possibly alter a course of behaviour flowing from pure
profit considerations.

Humans value many things other than profits, but in pure capitalism the value of these things will not register unless they are profitable. According to capitalistic rationality a beautiful factory will not be built unless it is profitable to do so, and since making workplaces beautiful would cut into profits, in a purely capitalist society considerations of beauty would not enter their design. Indeed, industrial workplaces are often noisy, dirty, dangerous and ugly. If testing the carcinogenic properties of a chemical might reduce profits by increasing costs, no test will be performed. Indeed social and environmental costs that do not register in the profit structure are clustered together as "externalities." Because of capital's indifference to use-value, it has no interest in costing "externalities", and even if we wanted such costing, it is often difficult to convert something primarily qualitative into a quantity. And yet this is precisely what we must do if we are to make the qualitative dimensions of human life count in our economic calculations. What is the cost of the malnutrition affecting 50 per cent of the world's population?[14] What is the cost of poverty, when half the world's youth live in poverty?[15] What is the cost of air pollution? What are the costs of slums, when one-third of the world's urban population lives in slums? (Davis 2006, 19). What is the cost of ill-health? Just because the motion of capital itself does not cost these things, we should greatly expand our efforts in this direction (of course some efforts in these directions already exist). It is only by systematically bringing the qualitative side of human life into our economic calculations that we can truly begin to improve the quality of human life.

In a purely capitalist society any use-value will be produced or procured if it is profitable to do so. And according to the prevailing doctrine of "consumer sovereignty", it is the spending decisions of consumers that determine profitability. Letting profits be the sole determinant of what is produced and how may work to some extent where natural resources are inexhaustible, where a high degree of economic equality exists, where work places are democratic, where the quality of products is transparent, where waste and pollution

14. According to UN studies, in 2000 approximately one half of the people in the world (3 billion) suffer malnutrition; and furthermore, "hunger, overeating, and micronutrient deficiencies ... account for an estimated half or more of the world's burden of disease" (Gardner and Halweil 2000, 6–8).
15. According to Oxfam, by the end of the 1990s 1.2 billion people were living on less than $1 per day (Seabrook 2002, 12, 131).

can be easily reabsorbed by nature, and where capital is competitive. But since none of these conditions presently exist, I believe that it follows that a strong case can be made for public debate on the production and distribution of use-values that have large social or environmental impacts. At present there are constraints on pollution, there are environmental assessments, and there is some regulation of use-values considered endangered (for example, exotic species or ivory), or use-values considered unhealthy (for example, cigarettes or opium), but we are entering a period of history when capital's basic indifference to use-value is becoming increasingly intolerable, and when we have much more knowledge than ever before about what is good for the health of humans and the environment. It follows that a strong case can be made that it is unethical to subsume use-value production to pure profit maximization. Two glaring examples of what can happen are represented by the international pharmaceutical industry and the international arms trade.[16] It is time that we redirected much of our research towards use-value as quality of life and quality of environment and get over our phobia about intervening in the economy at the level of use-value.

The reification associated with the commodity form makes it easy for both capitalists and politicians to avoid responsibility for "tough" decisions. Laying off workers, paying low wages, avoiding costly environmental regulations, avoiding taxes, skirting health and safety regulations, moving production to low-wage areas, can all be justified by the unavoidable imperatives of profit. Shifting income and wealth from the public sector to the private sector can also be justified by the necessity to keep the profits of the private sector high enough to encourage investment, as can massive hand-outs of public money to the private sector. It follows that the advance of ethics requires greater democratic controls and public responsibility at every level from the shop floor to the global economy.

The second ethical problem arising from the commodity form is its impact on the subjectivity of capitalists as the dominant figures of capitalism. As a personification of self-valorizing value, a capitalist can only establish status recognition on the basis of the size of his capital. Placing such weight on size as the basis for a

16. There is little research by big pharmaceutical companies on effective medicines for infectious diseases that effect millions of poor people, such as malaria and tuberculosis, for the obvious reason that this is not where the big profits are to be found. And the arms trade not only diverts money from humanitarian uses, but also radically destabilizes places like Africa.

sense of self adds a dimension of desperation that intensifies the competitive struggle amongst capitalists. In the absence of enforced legal constraints, this desperation must always tempt capitalists into cost savings (for example, the health and safety of workers) and profiteering that can be highly damaging to a society. Historically these destructive spin-offs have been so widespread that a large portion of total social life energy not spent in labour (always the largest portion) has been spent in mobilizing and fighting against this damage. And it includes everything from the exploitation of children, highly dangerous work places, desertification of land and polluted environments, to stock-market fraud, false advertising, tax avoidance and collusion in the restraint of trade. The enormous importance placed on sheer size of profit always tempts capitalists to push the legal and ethical boundaries, find areas without boundaries, find ways to cross boundaries without being caught, or to operate outside of boundaries.[17] The only other marker of subjectivity required in pure capitalism is that each capitalist must be accorded the minimal requirements of legal subjectivity associated with the ownership of private property. As legal subjects they have the exclusive ownership of means of production and the commodity outputs of those means, which also entails the exclusive right to buy, sell and contract with regard to that which they own. But a legal subject is a totally hollowed out, externalized subject, whose subjectivity consists of economic transactions aimed at increasing profits. And the sharp contrast between total control within the boundaries of a capitalist's private property and total lack of control outside, places a further imperative on expanding size as the only means of expanding control. But since no single capitalist can own everything, the impulse to expanding total control is always blocked by competing capitalists with the same aim. And given the generalized instability and insecurity generated by the hyper-mobility of the commodity form, capitalists must have a very great need for control. One might say that size is all that matters.

If capital is self-expanding value and if as values commodities are the same qualitatively, differing only quantitatively, then Levinas' (1969) "the same" that in his view has had such unfortunate effects in western metaphysics, reaches its maximum possible materialization in pure capitalism. According to Levinas (1969), western metaphysics

17. See Palan (2006) for an interesting discussion of the "offshore" in global capitalism.

has attempted to make the world more comfortable through a sort of imperialism of the self that views others as simply forms of the self, thus nearly removing the difficult task of being receptive to true otherness or alterity. In many respects, pure capitalism can be viewed as the most extreme materialization of the metaphysics of the same. For, in pure capitalism, the self makes its mark by subordinating otherness to a money-making self that is indifferent to qualitative difference except as it can be subsumed to money-making. In other words, the other, as difference, is either ignored or absorbed into a quantitatively expanding self, resulting in the imperialism of number manifested through the activity of a money-making self. In pure capitalism, the other is always related to as a means and never an end in itself, and hence there is no openness to or appreciation of its qualitative specificity in and of itself. Levinas' ethics of openness to radical alterity, then, must be diametrically opposed to this normative order of capital, which is not only indifferent to alterity, but also totally subsumes qualitative difference to the sameness of the quantitative as self-expanding value.

While Levinas' ethics may serve as a corrective to the extreme ethical bankruptcy of capitalism it is, in my view, too abstract and vague to provide guidance in concrete situations. Arguably, openness in itself cannot be an ethical goal, since too much openness of certain sorts is a basic characteristic of some mental illnesses. Instead what is needed is an ethics that can disrupt and ultimately radically transform self-expanding value precisely by bringing the fullest possible appreciation of use-value (the qualitative) right into the heart of value itself. In other words, to radically alter the domination of capitalistic value expansion is ultimately to deconstruct value itself, so that capitalist profits are themselves completely altered by the consideration of many predominantly qualitative human values. What would follow in my view is that in many cases the most capitalistic cost-effective way of doing something will be far removed from ways that most advance human flourishing. For example, would we rely so heavily on the automobile as our primary mode of transportation, if all of its impacts on long-term human flourishing were factored into its costs?

SURPLUS-VALUE AND ETHICS

Marx argues that historically class exploitation exists whenever property relations allow a particular group to control the surplus product defined as that product above and beyond what is required for the producers to reproduce themselves. Capitalism differs from other modes of production, because, in principle, the class relation can be reproduced without reliance on extra-economic force when commodification is complete. Ideologically this has enabled capitalism to hide economic domination behind what ideally should be free and equal market exchange. And it has placed the burden on each individual to be totally responsible for their own economic well-being.

In the first instance, surplus-value is the difference between the total value created by aggregate homogeneous labour employed by aggregate homogeneous capital and the value of the commodities required to reproduce such labour. In order to make this relationship crystal clear, Marx assumes that all units of capital have the same ratio of constant to variable capital and all units of labour are simple, average and abstract such that each unit of capital will always produce the same amount of surplus-value with the same quantity of labour.[18] As a result there will be a society-wide rate of exploitation. It is this theory that is at the centre of Marx's theory of capital and at the centre of his critique of bourgeois economics, which, in all its forms fails to directly and clearly conceptualize the class relation that is central to capital. For, if capital is fundamentally self-valorizing value, and if it is only by generating surplus-value that capital can valorize itself, then surplus-value must be the crucial variable. But since most critics of Marxian economics have focused on the labour theory of value, and since once they have dismissed this theory, the concept of surplus-value goes with it, I shall start by defending the labour theory of value as the best way to integrate economics with ethics.

A fundamental dimension of economic theory ought to be how best to organize life energy to advance the quality of life for society and for individuals. This requires a division of labour, an organization of labour processes, and a division of the total product. Unless issues of organization and division are handed over to some supposed automaton like the market, a computer or a lottery, they require ethico-political deliberation. Thus, if we assume complete commodification, the laws of motion of capital will determine that

18. "The same labour, therefore, performed for the same length of time, always yields the same amount of value, independently of any variations in productivity" (C I, 137). "But each individual capital forms only a fraction of the total social capital, a fraction that has acquired independence and been endowed with individual life, so to speak, just as each individual capitalist is no more than an element of the capitalist class" (C II, 427).

the working class on average will receive "subsistence" as defined by Marx. But even in a purely capitalist society, the labour theory of value, by implication, raises a number of ethical issues. First, capital will attempt to maintain subsistence and working conditions at as low a cost as possible in order to maximize surplus-value. Second, according to the labour theory of value, on average one person's hour of labour is worth no more and no less than another person's hour of labour. Third, as owner of means of production, capital in principle has complete control over life in factories such that the organization of that life is by definition authoritarian. Fourth, it is capital and capital alone that decides what to do with surplus-value (save, invest or spend on luxurious living). Fifth, the periodic crises of capital combined with the authoritarian control of capital in the workplace may create enormous job insecurity for workers.[19] Sixth, in order to maximize profit, capital will continually try to speed up the circuits of capital thus intensifying work and increasing the pace of life generally.[20] These states of affairs suggest the following issues of equity.

First, if we start from the position that an hour of unskilled labour on average creates the same value, then any deviation from an equal division of the product needs to be justified (dull, dirty, demanding or dangerous work might be paid more as might skilled work).[21] Second, there is the need to consider an equitable division of labour. How can we make labour as pleasurable as possible and how can we equitably share the labour that is not pleasurable? Third, since up to now in history most people devote most of their life energy to labour, good working conditions including democratic practices in the workplace would seem essential to human flourishing.[22] Fourth, given the importance to society of the surplus, it would seem to be irresponsible to leave decisions concerning its use to private individuals and this implies ethico-political debate on its use. Fifth, the radical insecurity of the job market implies the need for everyone to have access to the means of subsistence either through a job or community support. Sixth, the pace of economic activity should always be considered in relation to the human need for a balanced life containing sufficient

19. Capitalism "...does away with all repose, all fixity and all security as far as the worker's life-situation is concerned..." (C I, 618).
20. "He is fanatically intent on the valorization of value; consequently he ruthlessly forces the human race to produce for production's sake" (C I, 739).
21. See Baker (1987) for an excellent discussion of issues of equality.
22. Pateman (1970) is the classic on this. See also Albert and Hahnel (1991).

rest and relaxation and the need for the environment to "recover".[23] These considerations have to do with core human values such as freedom, equality, democracy and justice and they arise more or less naturally when the labour theory of value is posed as it is by Marx.

DIALECTICAL REASON AND ETHICS

It is the unique self-reifying ontology of capital that underlies the possibility of both dialectical reasoning and quantitative reasoning that is the focus of ethical thinking in this section. For it is the completion of commodification in theory that makes it possible to theorize the inner logic of capital as a logic that can reproduce capital without reliance on extra-economic force (the basis for bourgeois ideology). The ethically problematic result of this in pure capitalism is a private sector that totally swallows up the public sector except as a kind of mirror that passively confirms legal subjects and their dealings. In other words, politics is reduced to minimalist law limited to protecting private property as a "passive reflex" of economic relations,[24] and since bourgeois economists tend to worship something like pure capitalism minus class, they assume that the best of all possible worlds is a laissez-faire competitive capitalist economy. But Marx demonstrates convincingly that such an economy will simply reproduce and deepen inequality, will create massive insecurity, and will make freedom relatively meaningless to the majority whose lives consist mainly of getting a job and trying to make ends meet. In short it will create a dog-eat-dog mode of social life. At the same time, in the face of these problems, the state can throw up its hands helplessly pleading lack of resources precisely because all the resources are held by the private sector that cannot be interfered with.

The oft-repeated "consumer sovereignty" of mainstream economics is, of course, a farce.[25] The so-called casting of dollar ballots is hugely skewed in favour of the rich, and even they can only throw their dollars at what is offered in the market by capital. As consumers they have no control over the wages and working conditions of producers or over how capitalists choose to spend their profits. Thus,

23. For the recovery of nature see Teresa Brennan (2003).
24. "The juridical relation, whose form is the contract ... is a relation between two wills which mirrors the economic relation" (C I, 178).
25. "Let us note here ... that the 'social need' which governs the principle of demand is basically conditioned by the relationship of the different classes..." (C III, 282).

for example, pharmaceutical companies spend billions on researching life-style drugs while infectious diseases like tuberculosis and malaria run rampant amongst the poor of the world.[26] And American slaughter-houses speed up the lines, forcing unprotected illegal aliens to work at such a pace that this industry has the highest injury rate of any in the US with over 40,000 workers a year requiring medical treatment for work-related injuries (Schlosser 2001, 172). Typically consumers do not know the conditions under which commodities that they purchase are produced nor the environmental costs of producing them. When they shop, they see only commodities with price tags. They cannot vote against the use of pesticides that poison the environment or poison the workers who use them because they are largely unaware of the precise conditions of production of agricultural products.[27] They cannot vote against agricultural practices that are dangerously unsustainable, unless they are aware of them and are offered affordable alternatives. They cannot vote against carcinogens in the environment since the carcinogenic properties of most chemicals are not well known, and because most people are not well informed even where carcinogenic properties are known. Most people do not know that child slaves have been widely used on cocoa plantations in the Ivory Coast where 50 per cent of the world's cocoa is grown (Robbins 2001–4). And even if they ethically object to child slavery, they do not know which chocolate to withhold their dollar ballots from. They cannot vote against economic practices that have resulted in one-third of the global urban population living in slums. It is the supposed automaticity of self-governing markets to optimize welfare that disarms the public when faced with the crippling fallout of capitalism. We must not interfere with free enterprise we are told, when in fact most enterprise is highly exploitive, undemocratic and cost-cutting at the expense of all human values but profit. We must not interfere with free consumer choice, when for over a billion people choice means malnutrition and hunger, when fully half of the world's one billion young people between 15 and 24 are living in poverty (Worldwatch 2004, 153),

26. An estimated 1 million Africans die of malaria each year (*The Economist* 2003: 73). An estimated 3,000 children a day die of malaria, and 200 million people alive in 1998 will develop tuberculosis, and yet no major pharmaceutical firm has a research programme devoted to drugs that would deal with these diseases (*The New Internationalist* 2001, 24).
27. Globally an estimated 200,000 agricultural workers die from pesticides each year and over 5 million suffer pesticide poisoning (*The New Internationalist*, 2000, 10).

and when over 25 per cent of children born in the US are born into poverty (Grossberg 2005, 60). In order to work our way out of the ethical contradictions of capitalism, as a start, we need to have a totally instrumental view of the market in the sense that we intervene in it whenever and wherever it makes sense to in terms of ethical values that the short-term profit orientation of capitalism so often tramples on. Indeed, we would hopefully arrive at an economy that would make the automaticity and inner necessity of dialectical reason impossible precisely because we would take active responsibility for its outcomes. Dialectical reason is possible precisely because of the reification associated with complete commodification.

The self-reifying dynamics of capital mean that when commodification is complete so is capital complete (it constitutes a purely capitalist society). But such a society implies that socio-economic relations have been objectified by the commodity form in the sense that the commodity form is in charge. Thus we can say that capitalism represents a self-objectification when the "self" is society as a whole. And while capital manifests a particularly powerful reifying dynamic, wherever there are social structures there is reification to some extent, for reification implies that social relations may have enduring structures that are not easily changed in the short-run. Thus religions constitute reified structures of belief, families reified structures of child-rearing, and grammar the reified structure of language. Each of these is an example of social self-objectification. But whenever objectified social structures dominate us, we can ask whether or not these particular objectifications foster human flourishing, and when they do not, we can attempt to alter them by concerted action. A reconstitution of the social sciences around the analysis of structures of objectification and their impact on human flourishing is implied by the reconstitution of economics as advocated here.[28] For capital is a peculiarly dynamic and powerful reifying force that we can allow to run roughshod over us or we can resist and alter in line with ethical concerns.

LEVELS OF ANALYSIS AND ETHICS

So far I have been discussing the ethical implications of a purely capitalist society, or, in other words, of economic theory at the most abstract level. But in the academy, both economic theory and

28. See Albritton (forthcoming [a]).

ethics have a tendency to remain highly abstract, creating distinct difficulties making connections with history, with the present, and with possible futures. I have pointed out, for example, that in a purely capitalist society the public sphere is shrunk down to almost nothing, while the private sphere is expanded to include almost everything. But of course in any actually existing capitalism, the state always plays a significant role. And while Marx never explicitly advocated a mid-level theory to mediate between the theory of capital's logic and historical analysis, I find such a theory extremely important because there are distinct phases of capitalism, and in each one the dominant mode of capital accumulation manifests important qualitative differences making for phase-specific modes of accumulation. Since I have expanded on mid-range theory elsewhere, here I shall simply say that it tries to theorize the most characteristic and hegemonic patterns of capital accumulation at various phases or stages of capitalist development.[29] For the sake of contrast, I shall make a few comparisons between the golden age of liberalism in Britain in the mid nineteenth century and the golden age of consumerism in the US in the mid twentieth century (arguably each case represents the most developed and typical mode of capital accumulation for its particular phase). For capital's indifference to use-value may always result in an indifference to the quality of life, and quality of life issues differ between various stages.

In the phase of liberalism a few of the areas of indifference to use-value that people had to struggle against were the pollution, bad sanitation and bad living conditions in new industrial towns that resulted in average life-expectancies below 20 (C I, 795). The lack of the right to vote in parliamentary elections was an important issue for workers, because they felt they could influence the course of legislation through the ballot box. Also people struggled to limit the length of the working day, which in the first Factory Act of 1833, was set to start at 5 am and end at 8 pm (C I, 390). Another issue for workers was that although they had had the basic right to organize in the workplace since the 1820s, this right was in practice hedged in by various constraints that undermined its effectiveness, and this combined with a notion of freedom of contract that was a travesty in the face of deep inequalities between contracting parties.[30]

29. Albritton (1991). "Phases" or "stages" are not used here in Rostow's sense that implies a necessary sequence.
30. Intimidation, molestation, obstruction and threats were all potentially criminal offences making picket lines virtually illegal (Hunt 1981, 265).

Finally, this period witnessed the beginning (the bare beginning) of consumer protection legislation with, as an example, laws prohibiting the adulteration of bread, a widespread practice in Victorian England that increased profits at the cost of public health (C I, 359).

The particular use-value indifferences that people in the US found problematic in the phase of consumerism after the Second World War reflected the huge gains in productivity, the mass production of consumer durables, the significant state intervention in the economy, and the virulent anti-communist ideology characteristic of capitalism in this phase. One of the most important indifferences was indifference toward meaningful freedom of speech as dissent. The growth of a cold war, mass education and mass media conspired to terrorize Americans, utilizing the twin evils of communism and nuclear war to maintain a mind-numbing fear that made meaningful dissent dangerous (given the existence of loyalty oaths and the growth of security agencies like the FBI and CIA) and in most respects impossible (the vast majority were too indoctrinated to even hear dissent). At the same time, trade unions, the main working class organizations that might have become bases for dissent, were legislatively depoliticized by the Taft-Hartley Act and ideologically depoliticized by McCarthyism.

A second area of indifference was towards the specific problems for African-Americans and women created by racism and sexism. For example, the process of urbanization/suburbanization consigned African-Americans to life in ghettoized urban slums and women to lives of desperate boredom in the isolated boxes of suburban housing. And at the same time both lacked access to the better jobs and better education (particularly for African-Americans).

Third, working people tried to increase their well-being by expanding the welfare state, but despite a rapidly growing economy, this expansion was constrained by the fact that typically somewhere around 60 per cent of government spending went to national security (Webber and Wildavsky 1986, 508). The expansion of consumer credit made it possible for working people to expand their consumption of consumer durables, but at the same time the heavy debt load forced them to work hard without hazarding dissent in order to pay down their debts. Finally not so durable consumer durables raised the need for increased consumer protection.

The contrast between the types of use-value indifference characteristic of the leading accumulators in the stage of liberalism (UK) as opposed to the stage of consumerism (US) is meant to give the reader a sense of the type of ethical issues that can be addressed at the level of mid-range theory, where the main focus is on the characteristic patterns of the dominant accumulators. I turn next to the level of historical analysis where I will focus on just a few important global trends that manifest use-value indifference today.

During the so-called "golden age" of capital accumulation in the US (1946–70), struggles against the suppression of dissent registered significant gains with oppressed groups taking advantage of this to better their positions. Further, despite the continued expansion of the warfare state, welfare and consumer's credit also expanded, generally improving the quality of life of working people. However, with the onset of "stagflation" in the early 1970s, it gradually dawned on the ruling class that they had over-expanded the welfare state (national debt), and, given their unwillingness to make deep cuts in military spending, the survival of capitalism depended on a massive shift of wealth from the social wage (generally health, education and welfare) to the private sector (including the military-industrial complex). At the same time, the continual expansion of the petroleum-based mass production of consumer durables (most typically the automobile) began to push up against the limits of the environment and sustainability. The growing freedom of dissent was dampened by the growth of a prison-industrial complex, by the general militarization of capitalism, and by the growth of a reactionary fundamentalism and super-patriotism that increasingly shut down the possibilities of rational public debate (Massing 2005a, 2005b). Increasingly the American population has been bought-off by mindless consumerism and by the bread and circus spectacles of the mass media and commercialized sport, while the standard of living of the majority has declined (even with credit expansion) with one in four American children being born into poverty by the first decade of the twenty-first century.[31] Poverty grew in the US despite an increasingly globalized capitalism that sourced the world for cheap labour and cheap resources while generally ignoring the growing ecological crisis. The current trends of capitalist use-value indifference of greatest concern can be summarized as indifference to growing inequality, indifference to deepening ecological crisis, and indifference to increasing oppression, repression and violence. Existing state policy and international political policy, so influenced as it is by capital, is wholly inadequate in addressing these issues.

31. Since 1972 wages for men in the 25–34 age group have fallen 26 per cent (Anelauskas 1999, 71). See also Medrick (2006).

Negative ethics would wherever possible mobilize human energies into transformative movements aiming at altering these trends in ways that would produce real and immediate improvements in quality of life for this and future generations. The ethical question in this case is not what is right, just and good in the abstract, but what injustices or what use-value indifferences most immediately cry out for alleviation in the here and now, and how we can best alleviate them. Negative ethics is practical; and it leads to economic, political and ideological transformation. We do not need a universal theory of justice to know that the use of child slaves in cocoa production is unjust or to see the injustice in a situation where one hour of work for a CEO at Nestle's may be paid well over a thousand times one hour of agricultural labour (for example, cocoa producing labour) that provides the basic inputs of Nestle's food empire. It is not hard to see the injustice where capital's indifference to the environment enables a minority to live in extreme luxury while generating an environmental debt at the expense of all future generations.

CLASS

The class exploitation that is central to capitalism has always been a central ethico-political concern of Marxists. Indifference to its crippling effects on the human body and mind has always been a hallmark of capital, and has always been an important basis for mobilizing against capitalism. But a levels of analysis approach suggests the inappropriateness of applying the basic two-class social relations of pure capitalism directly to history. In his historical works such as *The 18th Brumaire*, Marx himself illustrates the complexity of class analysis at the level of history, where economic, political and ideological forces intersect to create contextually specific multidimensional class phenomena, where class and non-class groupings merge in ways that may defy efforts at drawing clear boundaries. And if this was the case in the French Revolution of 1848, it is even more the case today in light of the uneven development of capitalism globally. Indeed, at the level of history strict capitalism mixes with the pre-capitalist, non-capitalist, quasi-capitalist and post-capitalist; and strict economic class mixes with a host of relatively autonomous groupings that overdetermine class while being overdetermined by class. For example, the capitalist influenced International Monetary Fund imposes "Structural Adjustment" policies on the Ivory Coast, where 50 per cent of the world's cocoa is grown. Because they face monopolist buyers, the mainly petty commodity producers of cocoa receive little for their crops, and thus require government support. But because of the structural adjustment policies imposed on them, the Ivory Coast government withdrew such support. This forced impoverished farmers to resort to child slavery to harvest their crops, something they could get away with because of the extreme poverty of the region (Robbins 2001–4). This is an example of what can happen when capitalism intersects with petty commodity production.

The situation becomes even more complex when forms of oppression associated with race, gender or sexual orientation are articulated with relations that are primarily economic. These situations may necessitate many overlapping, but not necessarily coinciding, ethico-political struggles to operate cooperatively. Indeed, a major weakness and source of sectarianism in the Marxian tradition has been a narrow-minded focus on the working class as a kind of saviour, when much broader alliances will be necessary in order to produce effective, democratic and lasting transformations of capitalism. And as history has proven, seizing state power in the name of the working class does not ensure significant headway towards a more democratic and more socialist economy. And still less advance has resulted from violent reactions that lash out against capitalism, since their main effect is usually to cause a further militarization of capitalism and less toleration of dissent.

CONCLUSIONS

While Marx used concepts such as "alienation", "reification", and "exploitation" in ways that have ethico-political implications, there has been little effort to study how Marxian political economy might alter and strengthen ethical thinking in general or how a more systematic consideration of the ethical implications of Marx's theory of capital might strengthen that theory. Since little serious theorizing has been done in either of these directions, what I have attempted to do in this chapter is simply present some possibilities in light of the analysis of Marx's economic theories as presented in this book. To locate ethical theory close to economics tends to make it more political, more practical and more contextual. And to locate economics close to ethical theory is to demystify the market and to finally take more responsibility for moulding economic outcomes to advance human flourishing. This is a radical break with mainstream economics that has generally considered economics as the most scientific of the social sciences precisely because its positivist and quantitative methods would keep ethics out of social science. Indeed, for mainstream economists a principal criterion of scientificity has always been the exclusion of value judgements from scientific discourse. In contrast, I am suggesting that we continually explore and debate the ethical implications of our social scientific theories with the aim of reshaping social structures in ways that will advance human flourishing. Ultimately this approach would make politics more concerned with ethics and ethics more political. A case could be made for having a strong ethical orientation in all social sciences, which need to combine their expertise to address ethical issues in historically specific situations.

The last three chapters have not dialogued very much with orthodox economic theory, because it generally does not problematize the relations between abstract theory and history.[32] And while Marx does not recognize the need for a systematic approach to levels of analysis, by his actual writings the problem is exposed and left open for others to confront. In the next chapter I turn briefly to consider a few interpretations of Marx by influential thinkers who appear to be less aware than Marx himself concerning the issue of the nature of quantitative economic variables and the need to unpack them in relation to the broad range of social power relations active in history.

32. For an excellent account of this neglect in the history of economic theory see Hodgson (2001).

8
A Critique of Some Critics

What could be a very long chapter will instead be a short chapter. I only want to discuss a few thinkers to further illustrate the close connection between dialectical reason and levels of analysis in opposition to what I have called, following Marx, "crude empiricism", which in my view represents a sort of epistemological rush to judgement or a wish fulfillment that theory would achieve immediate relevance. One manifestation of this would be an impatience with all statics in favour of a dynamic economics that would make economics more immediately relevant to historical analysis. But if we really can theorize the "economic laws of motion of modern society" (Freeman and Carchedi 1996, x), it would imply a sort of economic determinism such that neither human agency nor relatively autonomous ideological and political practices could significantly affect historical outcomes. And while there may be those who would argue for such a determinism, neither Marx nor I would be one of them. Which is not to say that economic forces may not predominate in determining many historical outcomes, but rather the point is that rarely would historical outcomes be well understood without considering relatively autonomous economic and non-economic practices including the complex of power relations.

While no thorough discussion of the relations between Hegel's philosophy and the theory of capital's deep structure will be undertaken here, one of my emphases in this book has been to argue that dialectical reason takes theory much more seriously than empiricism. Empiricism tends to be beholden to the world of immediacy: immediate sense perception, the immediate conceptualizatons of everyday language, or the direct and immediate connections between theoretical models and empirical data. Whereas dialectical reasoning questions and problematizes, and in the process realizes the difficulties in making direct connections; hence the difficult task of developing theoretical mediations and levels of abstraction. Lukács is one of the better known thinkers who has pointed out the difficulty that empiricism has in studying history because immediacy tends to collapse historical time into the immediacy of sense perception on the one hand or into the immediacy of the eternal on the other.[1] Good theoretically informed history is no doubt difficult to write no matter what approach is used. But at least a dialectical approach with its potential for both intense sensitivity to the internal integrity of theory and the internal integrity of history (Hegel is obviously weak here) opens the possibility for developing the sorts of mediations that will not reduce history to being a function of theory or vice versa.

It is important here to repeat a point previously made. In a sense dialectical reasoning is "good" empiricism. That is, it is better than crude empiricism in determining what is the case because it produces better theory and better mediations between theory and historical reality. In the case of theorizing capital, it is important to start by considering exactly what kind of object of knowledge it is. Does it have a deep structure? Can this deep structure be theorized as some kind of totality? What sort of inner connections exist amongst the categories required to theorize this deep structure? In light of these inner connections how should the presentation of categories be sequenced? Once we have constructed the most rigorous possible theory of capital's deep structure, what sort of theoretical mediations are required to utilize it to best inform our analysis of history?

In this chapter I shall only deal with a few interpreters of *Capital*, and I will be less concerned with critiquing every detail of their interpretations than with failures that stem from an inadequate appreciation of the dimensions of Marx's thinking emphasized in this book. I will start with the left-Keynesian interpretation of Joan Robinson, both because it was and is influential and because it well illustrates the best of British empiricism. A brief analysis of the Neo-Sraffian position will enable me to expand on the issue of the place of quantitative analysis and mathematics in economic theory and the issue of levels of analysis. Finally, I will very briefly refer to some recent efforts to strengthen Marxian economics. My central concern in this chapter will be to illustrate the difficulties that empiricist approaches have connecting theory and history in ways that could effectively understand historical change. In the common language of economics, it is often the distinction between "statics" and "dynamics" that is used to theorize this problem, though, as I shall argue, this binary is often itself problematic.

---

1. "The greater the distance from pure immediacy ... the sooner change will cease to be impenetrable" (Lukács, 1968, 154).

JOAN ROBINSON

In her book *An Essay on Marxian Economics*, Joan Robinson (1966, vii) declares her intention to translate Marx from the unfortunate metaphysical (Hegelian) language of the nineteenth century to "language that an academic could understand". In other words, she will remove the rational kernel from the metaphysical shell, thus preserving the essential fruit of Marx's labours. For, in her view, there is much that economists have to learn from Marx. Robinson (1966, 92) faults static equilibrium analysis as the main cause that has prevented economic theory from connecting to the real world, and suggests that it is time for Marx's economic thinking to enter the field of vision of academic economics because he offers a more dynamic and historically oriented approach. Though there is much in Marx that she (1966, 2) criticizes, she is yet more critical of mainstream academic economics for its "elegant elaborations of minor problems, which distract the attention of pupils from the uncongenial realities of the modern world". In comparison, "Marx's intellectual tools are far cruder, but his sense of reality is far stronger, and his argument towers above their intricate constructions in rough and gloomy grandeur." Indeed, she (1966, 95) ends her book with the call for a new theory of the "laws of motion of capitalism".

I can wholeheartedly agree with her about the immense superiority of Marx's "sense of reality", and with some other important points that she makes. For example, she (1966, 52) recognizes that the most fundamental difference between Marx and orthodox economists like Smith and Ricardo is his conceptualization of surplus-value (but we are diametrically opposed in assessing the importance of the concept surplus-value). Also, along with Marx, she recognizes that to a very large extent mainstream economics has always projected petty-bourgeois individualism on to capitalism, thus fundamentally distorting its true character.[2] Further, she (1966, x) recognizes that "once the overall rate of exploitation is given, relative prices are not particularly interesting", and that if there is any transformation in *Capital*, it is from more quantitatively determined prices into less quantitatively determined values and not the other way around (1966, xi).[3] With these points, I strongly agree.

2. "...they were apt to project the economics of a community of small equal proprietors into the analysis of advanced capitalism" (1966, 2).
3. If the central goal of economics is a theory of price determination and such a theory can be formulated without any reference to value magnitude,

In order to make Marx accessible, Robinson (1966, 6–7) offers what she, and probably most of her readers, would consider a set of non-controversial definitions. For example, she writes: "Marx divides the net product of industry into two parts: *variable capital* and *surplus*. Variable capital (*v*) is the wages bill. Surplus (*s*), which covers net profit, interest, and rent, is the excess of net product over wages." Here, Robinson is essentially converting Marx's categories into the empiricist categories of national accounting, but in my view, such categories are totally incompatible with Marx's. In the context of Marx's value categories, "net product of industry" would have to refer to the value added to capitalistically produced commodities by homogeneous aggregate labour organized by aggregate competitive capitalist industry under equilibrium conditions prior to any consideration of differences in organic composition. Further, in the theory of capital's deep structure, it is not Marx who "divides the net product", rather it is capital itself that divides between the total value created by living labour and the value it receives back in order to subsist. If I am right, then it follows that Robinson's translation of Marx's "metaphysical" categories into more understandable "empirical" categories produces a radical misconception of what it is Marx is doing in *Capital* volume one.

Robinson argues that Marx's "value" is a metaphysical concept and that volume one is dogmatic, while she much prefers the more empirically-oriented volume three. But what apparently makes volume one dogmatic for her is her inability to appreciate the dialectical reasoning employed by Marx in which the sequence of categories unfold from the simplest and most abstract by gradually adding layers of complexity and concreteness. Thus what appears as a certain unreality is Marx's effort to show in the simplest possible terms how class exploitation can occur through the commodity-form without systematic reliance on extra-economic force. It is only after this relationship is clarified that he turns to address the heterogeneity of capital and forms of profit as well as dynamic con-

---

for those unable to appreciate the dialectical conception of distinct levels of specification (empiricists and analytic philosophers), it would follow that value is a useless category. Indeed, from Roemer to Steedman, a very crudely empirical reading of the labour theory of value serves as a basis for rejecting it. This leads Roemer to perform unnecessary (and generally unsuccessful) acrobatics separating the theory of exploitation from the theory of value, when it is precisely the great strength of Marx's theory to integrate them.

siderations concerning the historical limitedness of capital and its propensity towards periodic crises. Volumes one and two clarify the reified character of basic social relations as the basis for the more fully quantitatively determined economic variables of volume three.

In Marx's quasi-dialectical reasoning, it is crucial to present the theory of surplus-value prior to the theory of profit, which is a more concrete, complex and quantitatively specified category. Robinson (1966, 16) can't understand this at all, as is clear when she claims "...there is no reason why the *rate* of exploitation should be treated as either logically or historically prior to the rate of profit". And indeed, in accord with a strictly empiricist mode of analysis where our only concern is the relation between two purely quantitative ratios, Robinson is correct. But in Marx's dialectical mode of reasoning where the sequence of categories is crucial, the rate of exploitation must be theorized logically prior to the rate of profit. Why? Because the rate of profit is the rate of exploitation made more complex, concrete and quantitatively determinant.

Robinson fails to consider the equilibrium conditions assumed by Marx in volumes one and two, though she (1966, 40) does note that he assumes competition. In fact, based on the emphasis she places on volume three, she claims (1966, 11–12) that "There is no tendency to long-run equilibrium in Marx...". And this is no doubt true at the level of historical analysis given its partial commodification and concomitant resistance to use-values being completely managed by value, but she does not consider the possibility that a purely capitalist society would approach a short-term equilibrium in the phase of expansion prior to a crisis. Her failure to note the extent to which Marx's theory relies on tendencies towards equilibrium perhaps stems from her desire to emphasize the historical orientation of Marx's theory as opposed to the "unrealism" of static equilibrium theory. According to Robinson (1966, ix): "It is the great merit of Marx's method that it lends itself to historical interpretation, unlike the mechanical equilibrium theory of the academics...". It follows that her preference for volume three would seem to stem from its greater concreteness and its concern with cycles, which implies a more dynamic and historical orientation. Elsewhere, referring to Marx, she (1966, 9) writes: "he conducts his argument in dynamic terms...", but unfortunately she never focuses her analytic powers on exactly how the "dynamic terms" might relate to the analysis of history. She does, however, mention some of the foci that would be required of a "dynamic" theory, including: a theory of the "maldistribution of consuming power" (1966, 48) or "effective demand" (1966, xxiii, 42–3), a theory of the inducement to invest (1966, 50, 61), a theory of interest (1966, 8, 68), a theory of monopoly (1966, 78), a theory of the hierarchy of profits (1966, 58), and "a full theory of the trade cycle, or of the long-run movement of capitalism..."(1966, 48).

The problem with this list of foci is that it cannot be developed at the level of the theory of capital's deep structures, and it is not clear at precisely what level of analysis it can be developed.[4] First, there is no problem of "effective demand" because pure capitalism approaches a state of equilibrium during the "average phase" prior to a crisis. Second, subjective factors like "inducement to invest" cannot be explored in a context of complete commodification where capitalists are simply personifications of economic categories. Third, in the context of pure capitalism, the theory of interest is limited to considerations of the commodity-economic management of interest as a portion of surplus-value. Fourth, the economics of monopoly cannot be dealt with in a context where capital is assumed to be competitive. Fifth, as pure capitalism approaches a state of equilibrium, there is no hierarchy of profits since all profits approach the average rate of profit. Sixth, in a levels of analysis approach, a full theory of the trade cycle would need to be developed across all three levels, and it would not be possible either to deduce a specific historical crisis or "the long-run movement of capitalism" from the theory of capital's inner logic which can only present very general directionalities.

Robinson (1966, 95) ends her book with the claim that: "Marx, however imperfectly he worked out the details, set himself the task of discovering the law of motion of capitalism, and if there is any hope of progress in economics at all, it must be in using academic methods to solve the problems posed by Marx." It would seem to follow, then, that the central task of economics ought to be "discovering the law of motion of capitalism". And yet she (1966, 92) cautions us that "It has generally been the fate of economic theory to run a losing race against the course of history, and never to have completed the analysis of one phase of economic development before another takes its place."

I have argued throughout that for Marx there is a distinction between the theory of capital's deep structure and the theory of

---

4. This is a general problem with Keynesian approaches that often take their cue from Keynes' book, *The General Theory of Employment, Interest, and Money*, and that are far from actually being general theories (Hodgson 2001, 227).

capitalist history. This distinction can be marked by distinguishing between "capital" (referring to capital's inner logic) and "capitalism" (referring to the entire historical existence of capitalism). Where commodification is complete, as in pure capitalism, quantification poses no great problems, but at more concrete levels of analysis, quantities cannot constitute a system of inner connected variables, and hence need to be bracketed in order to be rethought in connection with power relations and human agency. From this it follows that there are no economic laws of motion of capitalism that can be theorized independently of the complex articulation of relatively autonomous practices that is history, and to assume that there are is to fall into extreme economic reductionism. The theory of capital's deep structures does not chase after history in order to establish its validity, which instead depends upon the accurate theorization of capital's expanded reproduction through a commodity-economic logic where commodification is assumed to be complete. Neither does mid-range theory chase after history. While accepting Robinson's assumption that there are distinct phases of capitalism, these phases can only be adequately theorized in retrospect, when it becomes possible to make informed judgements about the most characteristic mode of accumulation specific to a particular phase. And finally the analysis of capitalist history would require the skilful use of both the theory of deep structures and mid-range theory to think complex processes where the capitalist and non-capitalist interact as well as the economic and non-economic (it would necessarily be multidisciplinary). In the interpretation of Marxian political economy presented here, the only laws of motion are at the level of deep structure, and these laws are too abstract (indicating only a very general directionality) to connect directly with historical time. For example, at the level of pure capitalism, capital has an abstract tendency to centralize, but we cannot know from this tendency how fast centralization will occur, what its specific modalities will be, in what industries it will first occur, in what part of the world, and so forth. In short, it is not possible to deduce the concreteness of historical spatiality and temporality from the theory of capital's deep structures.

Further, as I conceive of mid-range theory its aim is to characterize the most typical patterns of capital accumulation specific to a phase of capitalism. But theorizing a pattern is quite different from theorizing historical change. It constitutes a set of mutually informing snapshots, grouped according to principles derived from the dialectic of capital. In the interpretation of Marx that I am advocating, there is a full recognition of the extreme difficulty in understanding the complexity of historical change. Indeed, in my view there is absolutely no point in theory chasing after history. There simply are no laws of motion of history, and to assume there are would deny the possibility of human agency altering history's course. If current history hurts, the best we can do is try to understand it and in the light of this understanding reduce the hurt. Hence, I would argue that in a sense, even historical analysis does not try to keep up with history, for we can only come to understand what has already happened, and the more recent the happening, the more we are likely to misunderstand it. Thought, and certainly abstract thought, cannot engage in what must always be a losing race against history. And I think there is a connection between Robinson's empiricism and her race against time since clearly sense-data will always be at least a step ahead of theory and a step behind history. Staying ahead of history is not possible, for knowing the future can at best be based on speculations themselves based on the projection of current trends. And since human agency can always alter trends, we can never get beyond well-informed speculation about what seems most likely to happen.

I have claimed that historical time tends to pose insuperable problems for empiricism. Here, I want to point out difficulties with Robinson's use of the static/dynamic binary that is so central to much current theorizing. While static general equilibrium theory is, for her, the main obstacle to making progress in economics, she (1966, 82) admits that the "concept of equilibrium, of course, is an indispensable tool of analysis", but "one has to keep it in its place … strictly in the preliminary stages of an analytical argument, not in the framing of hypotheses…". Here the static/dynamic binary is connected to the analytic/synthetic binary in which theorizing involves starting with an analytic framework and then filling it in with testable synthetic hypotheses. We are urged to utilize the concept "equilibrium" in our analytic framework, but "not in the framing of hypotheses". And this is because "The whole apparatus of equilibrium theory therefore seems to be without application to reality" (Robinson 1966, 61). But it remains unclear why Robinson would want a concept to play a central role in one's analytic framework, only to be completely left out of the testable hypotheses that it generates. As I have been arguing, dialectical reasoning solves this problem through distinct levels of concreteness within a theory and between abstract theory and history.

For mathematically oriented economists "dynamic" theory must always be a losing race with history, because the more their models approach the dynamic complexity of history, the more indeterminant and impossible the mathematics becomes. The choice is between mathematically solvable equations that turn history into a function of a few mathematical variables and being true to historical complexity resulting in eschewing explanations rooted in mathematical equations. It is my contention that levels of analysis provide a way of solving this difficult problem of mediating between the abstract and general directionalities of a structural dynamic and the processes of historical change, which may to varying degrees be shaped by both relatively persistent structures and human agency.

If there were no tendency at all towards equilibrium in economic practice, capitalism could not exist, nor could a theory of capital's deep structures. Just consider a situation in which there was no tendency at all for capital to move from less profitable to more profitable branches of production. Lacking such a tendency, the connection between the total social product and effective demand would be totally haphazard and arbitrary, and economic activity could not fulfil its provisioning role even poorly. The problem with the concept of equilibrium, then, is not its use, but its abuse. And, as I have suggested, Marx himself thinks very much in equilibrium terms in mapping out the fundamental class relation of capitalism, even though he is quite aware that no such equilibrium would ever exist in empirical reality. The concept of equilibrium helps Marx to clarify the relation between homogeneous capital and homogeneous labour, though even a purely capitalist society would never arrive at full equilibrium. Marx makes it clear that such a society would come closest to a state of equilibrium during a phase of prosperity prior to a crisis. And, at the level of history, tendencies towards equilibrium are always operative without ever coming close to either a national or global state of equilibrium.

THE NEO-SRAFFIANS

A growing animus against static equilibrium theory has not stopped the Neo-Sraffians from utilizing such a theory to solve the perennial problem of price determination. The influence of Sraffa's work can be traced to the enormously high value that economists give to a mathematically neat solution to the theory of price determination. Here we have a static equilibrium model of simple reproduction in which physical quantities of product (as in a three commodity economy) produce commodities in the same proportions. This model enables one to generate a rate of profit and prices according to which the three commodities can reproduce themselves as long as we assume that wages are equal and that we know the real wage rate. The mathematical correctness of this theory has been the cause for great confidence amongst its perpetrators. For example, the young and impressionable Mr. Steedman (1977, 25) writes with fervour as though he has just discovered the truth: "The Sraffa-based critique of Marx *cannot* [emphasis in original] be met head on and rationally rejected, for the simple reason that is it correct."[5]

In one way, he is quite right. Assuming that we accept all of his assumptions and premises, his conclusions do indeed follow by the very ancient rules of deductive logic. Despite this seeming incontrovertible theory, however, Sekine (1997, Vol. II, 23–5) has demonstrated that Steedman's theory of price determination arrives at prices that are wrong even in a purely capitalist society. Furthermore, when it comes to understanding capital's inner logic, does Sraffa or Steedman offer anything even slightly approaching the explanatory-power of Marx's *Capital*? If our aim is ultimately to understand how capitalism works in general and how it has worked specifically in modern history, then Sraffa and Steedman offer us almost nothing. Why, then, all the excitement? The excitement tells us more about the academic discipline of economics than about the realities of capitalism. If it is capitalism that we want to understand, then a highly formalistic, and seemingly mathematically correct theory of price determination is of little or no interest. Of much greater interest is, among other things, a fully developed theory of the commodity form and of the tenuous nature of commodification; the indifference of capital towards use-value and a robust theory of exploitation as it relates to profit-maximization;[6] the pressures towards concentration, centralization, expansion and towards speed-up of capital's circuits; the theory of surplus population; the theory of the division of surplus-value between profit, interest, commercial profit and rent; the necessary inner connections amongst all the basic economic categories as commodity forms; and finally some awareness of the need to think systematically about levels of analysis which

5. Note that what is criticized is a crude version of Marx's value theory.
6. In embracing Sraffa, Keen (2001, 286) argues that we should simply ignore the question about where surplus comes from. But the great strength of Marx's theory is precisely to connect the property relation with profit.

will facilitate the articulation of capitalist economic categories with non-capitalist economic categories and non-economic categories.

Steedman recognizes the need for more concrete levels of analysis, but proceeds from a highly simplified and formal model to take a leap towards history without any clarity about how this might best be done. According to him (1977, 207):

It has been shown that the proximate determinants of the rate of profit, the rate of accumulation, the prices of production, the social allocation of labour, etc. are the physical conditions of production, the real wage and the capitalist drive to accumulate. The next step is to investigate the social, economic, political, technical, etc. determinants of those proximate determinates. That immense task will perhaps involve the study of, *amongst other things*, the historical conditions under which specific capitalist social formations developed, class relations (both at the point of production and at the level of politics), the role of trades unions, the role of state, the development of scientific and technical knowledge ... and international relations.

He (1977, 207) ends with the claim that "Marx's value magnitude analysis ... is a major fetter on the development..." of historical materialism. But why should this be, when value magnitudes only hold in the context of the more abstract regions of Marx's *Capital* that assumes homogeneous capital?

What I find most disturbing about Steedman's position is his assumption that just because you cannot mathematically derive prices from values, values are useless, and indeed, more than useless, for they confuse the whole picture. When, in fact, it is value categories that make the class relation crystal clear and at the same time illustrate the dynamic of the class relation that stems from its being subsumed to the commodity form. To turn the table on Steedman, I would argue that his adaptation of Sraffa is worse than useless, because it fetishizes a universal theory of price determination without throwing any light at all on the basic deep socio-economic structures of capitalism. After all, if the dialectic of capital is fundamentally a dialectic between value and use-value, and it is the reconsideration of this contradiction in contexts where commodification is not complete that offers the best stepping stones towards more concrete levels of analysis, then abandoning value removes all inner necessity from the theory leaving us floating in space wondering how to get back to earth. By getting the social relations and economic dynamics basically correct, it is *Capital* that should be utilized as the matrix for utilizing mathematics. Sekine's (1997) work is particularly interesting in this regard because it strengthens the dialectical structure of the theory of capital's logic, because it demonstrates the necessity of the labour theory of value, and because it utilizes mathematics to provide an elegant solution to the relation between value and price.

The Sraffians first move is to give a simplistic and I would argue, wrong, interpretation of Marx's labour theory of value. Then they produce a highly formalistic theory of price determination that does not rely on value magnitudes, and proceed to dismiss value as an antiquarian mystification. But even if value were to play no quantitative role in the theory of price determination, it is a crucial and indispensable category in setting the stage for an embedded theory of capitalist prices to emerge. It is the combination of facile deductivism and the fetishization of mathematics that disables a thinker like Steedman from appreciating that value is the most fundamental and important category in theorizing capital's deep structures. Indeed, stated most simply, capital is self-valorizing value.

VARIETIES OF EMPIRICISM

In recent years, voices from many points of view have been raised against "static equilibrium" as *the* concept most guilty of cutting off neo-classical economics from contact with the real world. Of course, every social scientist would like to produce a theory more in contact with reality, but this is easier said than done, as I shall evidence by numerous not so successful recipes. Connecting economic theory to the unevenness of historical development and the complexity of historical change is extremely difficult.

Freeman and Carchedi (1996, viii) argue quite simply that because the world is out of balance, no equilibrium theory can be relevant to understanding it, and that what we need to discover is the "economic law of motion of modern society" (1996, x). Sounds familiar! According to Freeman and Carchedi (1996, 19), "the real world is excised" from neo-classical general equilibrium theory, that by relying on simultaneous equations removes "time" from economic theory. But what constitutes the reality of the real world, and how are we to cozy up to it theoretically? Can we significantly advance economic theory by simply turning our backs on the concept "equilibrium". Freeman and Carchedi (1996, 13) give money a value in labour time (for example $1 = 5 minutes of labour) so that the actual price that a commodity sells for is its value. This reduces Marx's theory of capital's deep structures to accounting identities. This is empiricism with a vengeance, an empiricism that sweeps away all of the great achievements of Marx with a few flicks of the pen or of computer keys. According to Freeman and Carchedi (1996, 235), "Demand and supply are concretely and separately determined differently for every society at every stage." But, then, why not go further and say that demand and supply are determined differently in each spatial location at each moment of time? This may well be true, but why bother making the point? Knowledge is not gained by simply immersing ourselves in the sea of particulars. And if we want economic theory to help explain historical change, it will not do to simply make the counting easy. Instead the economic counting has to be thought in connection with different types of power structure, requiring that economics become transdisciplinary.[7] Making economic counting easy at the level of sense-data may have the effect of simply covering over or ignoring the power relations that must be accounted for at the level of historical analysis, thereby reproducing the tyranny of capitalism's quantifying mania. It may also result in another case of economic reductionism.

Farjoun and Machover (1983, 39) take another tack in trying to make mathematical economics directly relevant to the study of historical change. They point out that "Each investment of capital, each transaction in the market, is affected by a great variety of social, technical and economic causes, influenced by innumerable individual motives and volitions and subject to countless imponderable accidental circumstances." To deal with such complexity and unpredictability they propose utilizing the mathematics of probability such that economic variables oscillate within a probability distribution. They (1983, 32) reject equilibrium on the grounds that the "real economy is *always* so very far from it". But does probability mathematics enable us reduce the "real economy" to mathematical equations, or does it make the real economy largely indeterminate by having economic variables moving randomly within rather large probabilities of dispersion? It would seem that we have another fruitless attempt to explain historical specificity using mathematical equations. The general problem is either too many variables or variables dispersed in ways that give them a probable value somewhere between limits

7. Unfortunately the intense individualistic competition of the academic world militates against the sort of cross discipline collective research efforts required to develop truly effective historical analysis.

that may be wide apart, such that their probable value loses all explanatory power.

Farjoun and Machover want to bring economic theory more closely into contact with history by introducing probabilistic mathematics into economic theory. Thus instead of a uniform rate of profit, the rate of profit would move randomly within a probability distribution or dispersion. But what does this really contribute to understanding the history of capitalism? How would probabilistic mathematics contribute to our understanding of the 1847 crisis discussed in Chapter 5? And it is not a matter of separating economics from political sociology, for Marx's strength is precisely his theory of how the class relation can be reproduced through the commodity form.[8]

CONCLUSIONS

While some of the theories discussed in this chapter may be an improvement on general equilibrium theory, where they try to produce "dynamic" theory in order to connect with historical reality, they do not succeed. Indeed, I have indicated that the static/dynamic binary is a trap to be avoided, particularly when attached to crude empiricism. For the effort to make immediate contact with historical change tends either to produce economic reductionism or to dissolve theory into a sea of particulars. The Sraffa approach, the only one that accepts static equilibrium, revels in its mathematical solution to price determination. Its theory of price determination, however, is not embedded in a theory of capital's inner logic, and hence it lacks the wherewithal to develop the sort of mediations that would connect with historical analysis. It is a theory of price determination floating somewhere in outer space.

The levels of analysis approach, which I claim makes the most sense out of Marx, attempts to take the internal integrity of both theory and history seriously. But once such a position is taken, no empiricist rush to relevancy or rush to catch up with history is acceptable. Developing adequate mediating levels of analysis between the theory of capital's deep structures and the analysis of capitalist history is hard work. Foley (1986, viii), for example, claims that by making the value of money equal to a particular amount of labour time, Marx's value theory can become immediately empirical, and

8. Roemer (1988, 2) claims that Marx's theory is interesting as sociology and ethics and not as economics.

that this neat move "...avoids the pitfall of imposing a very complex discussion of levels of abstraction on the student...". But if levels of abstraction are ultimately necessary in order to move from abstract theory to the analysis of history, students should not be taught that something complex is in fact simple with the resulting distortions to both theory and history. For, as I have already indicated, solutions to the labour theory of value like Foley's can never come to grips with the theory of capital's deep structures. As a result the rigorous grounding of Marxian economics in reified social relations is lost as is the possibility of unpacking the power relations behind the maintenance of quasi-commodified social relations that is required to make sense of economic variables at more concrete levels of analysis. Thus I would argue that the discussion of levels of abstraction is indeed difficult, but it is a difficulty that should be fully embraced. To dissolve Marx's theory of value into empirical prices is also to dissolve the clarity and grounding that it can give us on the deep structural dynamic of social relations that pure capitalism reproduces and expands. And with this dissolution, the critical distance from the immediate present required of ethical political economy is lost. A theory of capital's deep structures gives us firm grounds upon which to criticize the social structures that capital tends to reproduce and expand when left to its own logic. Shallow economic theory cannot support anything but shallow and uncritical ethical theory and ultimately shallow political practice.

9
Conclusions

There are many who think that the downfall of the former Soviet Union must discredit Marx's writings. But the fact is that Marx wrote very little about socialism or communism, and what he did write indicates that any regime deserving the name "socialism" much less "communism" would have to be qualitatively more democratic than any capitalist regime. Of course, the long deceased Marx would have control neither over the use of his name nor of the words "socialism" or "communism" to label this or that regime, but it seems likely that he would not have applied these labels to the former USSR, lacking, as it did, the radically participatory democracy that in Marx's mind would have been a necessary condition for any regime to deserve a name so praiseworthy as "communism". And, of course, the association of "communism" with "evil" in American discourse may make it difficult for many to read Marx with an open mind, even though he wrote very little on the topic of communism precisely because he felt that a blueprint would suggest social engineering from above, and he believed that communism would need to take shape according to the democratic will of the vast majority of people from below. I want to appeal for open mindedness, for it is becoming increasingly crucial to our survival in a world deformed by close minded fundamentalisms be they religious or political.

While Marx had little to say about communism, he did, however, write a great deal about capitalism, and he himself considered *Capital* (even though unfinished) to be his greatest theoretical contribution. Indeed, Marx spent years of his life in the British Museum reading every significant piece of economic theory ever written. If his passion was for democratic socialism, why such focus on economic theory? First, he believed that modern society was first and foremost a certain kind of economic society: a capitalist society. Second, though in his view this society had certain positive features, such as advancing productivity and technology, in the long term, its negative features would inspire and galvanize human agency to transform it. But, efforts to transform capitalism are likely to succeed only to the extent that we have a clear understanding of what it is we are trying to transform, and, because of what it is, how to transform it in order to get the desired results. For a blind lashing out at capitalism's negative features could only have positive results by luck, and would in most cases be destructive by simply feeding into cycles of reaction and violence. It follows that for Marx, being very clear about precisely how capital operates in its deep structure must be crucial to making transformations that would significantly advance human flourishing. Third, an accurate theory of capital's deep structures is also important because capital itself will always promote theories that whitewash capitalism and fail to trace its real impacts on social life.

I have argued that Marx did indeed at least lay the foundations for a successful theory of capital's deep structures, and that his advances at this level of theory place him head and shoulders above all other economists. Few economists have even understood the crucial importance of a theory of the commodity form, much less enlarging and refining Marx's brilliant contributions. The amazing theoretical achievement of synthesizing a theory of class structure with the quantitative variables of the commodity form is also little understood or appreciated. These two advances in the theory of capital's deep structures alone would be enough to set his theory apart, making it the basis for a political economy appropriate to a present searching for a post-autistic economics.

While Marx did not fully realize the potential to theorize capital's inner logic as a rigorous dialectical logic, his conception of this logic as a set of necessary inner connections makes significant headway in this direction. The enormous significance of having such a strong theory to serve as a touchstone in the social sciences has been recognized by only a precious few. The theory of pure capitalism is essentially an objective theory, and further it is a theory of social self-objectification, suggesting a research programme for the social sciences that would examine types and degrees of self-objectification as they contribute or fail to contribute to human flourishing.

Marx made even less headway in theorizing the nature of the mediations required to connect a dialectical logic of capital to historical analysis. Because capitalism in history was becoming more and more capitalist during most of his life, he often seemed to suggest that little in the way of mediations would be necessary. He did not think, for example, that monopoly capitalism, the first signs of which he observed, could be more than a brief transitional phase towards socialism. This was no doubt wishful thinking, and in fact capitalism has persisted in history without ever approaching very close to pure capitalism.

But Marx also indicated in many places an awareness of the need for a relatively autonomous analysis of history with mediations connecting the theory of capital's deep structures with the analysis of historical specificity. I have advocated three levels of theory in order to achieve this, with both mid-range theory and historical analysis being relatively autonomous and multidisciplinary forms of institutional analysis. As a result, a theory of capital's deep structures serves as a touchstone to orient theory at the two more concrete levels. In particular, this approach preserves the powerful orienting structural dynamics of the theory of capital's inner logic, while remaining sensitive to the complexity of causal analysis at the level of historical specificity. In other words, it provides a way of utilizing abstract economic theory while avoiding economic reductionism in historical explanation.

Finally, Marx was aware that revealing what is the case with regard to capital's deep structures would generate ethical critique. Indeed, it would be hard not to conclude that profit based upon the exploitation of workers violates Kant's categorical imperative that humans should be treated as ends in themselves and not as means to other ends. Of course, there are other ethics than Kant's, and the point is that knowing what is the case with regard to capital's deep structures enables us to assess what changes might be made to advance human flourishing. The theory of capital's deep structures is a paradigm case of a theory that is at the same time both objective and critical, suggesting that the social sciences in general might open themselves more to ethical critique.

The argument in this book suggests a radical reshaping of the academic discipline of economics. First, mathematical economics belong primarily at the level of the theory of capital's deep structures where power relations are swallowed up by the commodity form. Second, most of the work required is at the much neglected levels of mid-range theory and historical analysis. Third, this theoretical work would be necessarily transdisciplinary or multidisciplinary since it primarily requires the study of economic power relations as they articulate with political and ideological power relations. In other words, the economy needs to be understood as it is embedded in social life. Fourth, socio-economic knowledge needs to be critical in the sense that it should be used to continually inform thinking about transformations that will advance human flourishing.

We live in a world where an academic economics divorced from the real world is no longer a luxury that we can afford. For the enormity of the socio-economic problems that we face suggests the need for radical transformations directed by the united power of the people and all the power of reason that we have. And I am suggesting that this means an economic discipline rooted in the theory of capital's deep structures so brilliantly set forth by Marx.

This book has presented an interpretation of Marxian political economy that places particular emphasis on the centrality of the theory of the commodity form, both for understanding Marx's radical break with mainstream economic theory and as a basis for understanding capitalism. My focus has been primarily upon explicating the theory and not utilizing it to understand the course of modern history. Yet, from time to time in the exposition, it is clear that I could not resist suggesting particular interpretations of history based on this theory. And I cannot resist ending on such a note, for it points towards areas of pressing thought and action as we move through the early years of the twenty-first century.

I have argued that the basic contradiction of the dialectic of capital's deep structure is that between value and use-value, taking "use-value" to mean the qualitative dimension of life and matter. It seems to me vitally important to develop a version of Marxian political economy like the one I have recommended, precisely for its strength in understanding this contradiction. Although capital is indifferent to use-values except as they affect profits, arguably capitalist society has always been dependent upon qualitative and ethical human relations developed by predominantly non-capitalist institutions such as the family, education, religion, the state and the military. To a greater or lesser extent all of these institutions work best where direct human-to-human relations, based upon love, friendship, trust, respect and a sense of duty are strong. Or, in other words, where various types of a sense of togetherness are prevalent. It seems to me that each of these institutions has been increasingly penetrated by the atomizing effect of the commodity form, thus undermining the sense of togetherness to varying degrees. For example, as the competition for good jobs has increased in advanced capitalist countries, getting married and having children has been put off. More and more sons and daughters stay at home hoping with time to get a good job and accumulate the kind of money required to get married and start a family. Here the capitalist commodity form tends to turn the home into a kind of rooming house for aging children.

The cut back in public sector spending required to maintain the capitalist private sector has meant that schools have had to commercialize to some extent in order to access badly needed funds from the private sector. They have in many cases received funding and even books from the fast-food sector in exchange for that sector's access to education's young and impressionable students. And this is only one example of the many ways that the capitalist commodity form is penetrating the educational system. For example, the intense competition for the grades required to get those well-paid professional jobs alienates many students, thus pushing up the drop-out and failure rate.

The atomizing effect of the commodity form on the family and education is pushing many towards religion as a kind of salvation, and the greater the need for an intense sense of togetherness to counteract the effects of the commodity form, the greater the tendency to embrace fundamentalist religion with its intense binding of "good people" in opposition to "evil people". Similarly the military can offer intense togetherness, but usually only in opposition to an enemy that threatens our very being. But the American military is increasingly a mercenary military, where recruits need the money or in some case the citizenship offered to illegal alien recruits. Further, more and more supports for the military are being contracted out to the private sector, where very often big profits and high salaries are the result.

Finally, no doubt it is the state sector that has traditionally had the most penetration by the capitalist commodity form. But in the US today this penetration has increased to dramatic proportions, given the enormous power of big money to fund campaigns and create indebted politicians. Indeed, money has to such an extent become the lubricant of politics, that the United States' claim to be a democracy is farcical.

The problems created by the commodity form's penetration of non-economic and at least partially non-capitalist institutions have occurred in the world's leading capitalist power with a long history of popular struggles to constrain capital's indifference to use-value. Popular struggles over at least two hundred years in the US have created a web of institutions to curb capitalism's excesses. And yet enormous problems are occurring despite this history. In countries or parts of the world where such institutional networks are weak, the excesses of a pure profit-oriented economy will in all cases be greatly multiplied. And this is precisely what has happened in much of the

Third World and in the former Soviet Union creating a seed bed for every kind of fundamentalism whether familial, economic, religious or political. Perhaps the first step in clearing our heads is to break with the neo-liberal economic fundamentalism that has made it so difficult for policy makers to hear criticisms of capitalism. We need to fearlessly approach capitalism with a will to make radical changes if such changes are to advance human flourishing.

Bibliography

"A Survey of Agriculture and Technology" 2000, *The Economist*, March 25.

Aglietta, Michel 1979, *A Theory of Capitalist Regulation*, London: New Left Books.

Albert, Michael and Hahnel, Robin 1991, *The Political Economy of Participatory Economics*, Princeton, N.J.: Princeton University Press.

Albritton, Robert 1991, *A Japanese Approach to Stages of Capitalist Development*, London: Macmillan.

—— 1995a, "Theorising the Realm of Consumption in Marxian Political Economy" in Robert Albritton and Thomas Sekine (eds), *A Japanese Approach to Political Economy: Unoist Variations*, Basingstoke: Macmillan.

—— 1995b, "Regulation Theory: A Critique" in Robert Albritton and Thomas Sekine (eds), *A Japanese Approach to Political Economy: Unoist Variations*, Basingstoke: Macmillan.

—— 1998, "The Unique Ontology of Capital" in Panasiuk R. and Nowak. L. (eds), *Marx's Theories Today*, Amsterdam: Rodopi.

—— 1999, *Dialectics and Deconstruction in Political Economy*, Basingstoke: Palgrave Macmillan.

—— et. al. 2001, *Phases of Capitalist Development*, Basingstoke: Palgrave Macmillan.

—— 2003a, "Superseding Lukács: A Contribution to the Theory of Subjectivity", in Robert Albritton and John Simoulidis (eds), *New Dialectics and Political Economy*, Basingstoke: Palgrave Macmillan.

—— 2003b, "Returning to Marx's *Capital*: A Critique of Lebowitz's *Beyond Capital*" in *History of Economic Ideas*, XI, No. 3.

—— 2003d, "Marx's Value Theory and Subjectivity" in Westra and Zuege (eds), *Value and The World Economy Today*, Basingstoke: Palgrave Macmillan.

—— 2004a, "Socialism and Individual Freedom" in Albritton et. al. (eds), *New Socialisms: Futures Beyond Globalisation*, London: Routledge.

—— et. al. (eds) 2004b, *New Socialisms: Futures Beyond Globalisation*, London: Routledge.

—— 2004c "Theorising Capital's Deep Structure and the Transformation of Capitalism", *Historical Materialism*, 12.3.

—— 2005, "How Dialectics Runs Aground: The Antinomies of Arthur's Dialectic of Capital", *Historical Materialism*, 13.3.

—— forthcoming [a], "Objectivity and Marxian Political Economy" in Jon Frauley and Frank Pearce (eds), *Critical Realism and the Social Sciences: Heterodox Elaborations*, Toronto: University of Toronto Press.

—— forthcoming [b], "Marxian Crisis Theory and Causality" in Ruth Groff ed., *Revitalizing Causality: Realism About Causality in Philosophy and Social Science*, London: Routledge.

Albritton, Robert and Simoulidis, John (eds) 2003, *New Dialectics and Political Economy*, Basingstoke: Palgrave Macmillan.

Althusser, Louis 1969, *For Marx*, New York: Vintage.

—— 1970, *Reading Capital*, London: New Left Books.

—— 1971, *Lenin and Philosophy and Other Essays*, London: New Left Books.

—— 1992, *The Future Lasts Forever*, New York: The New Press.

Anderson, Perry 1987, "Figures of Descent", *New Left Review*, No. 161.

Anelauskas, Valdas 1999, *Discovering America as It Is*, Atlanta, Ga.: Clarity Press.

Arthur, Christopher 2002, *The New Dialectic and Marx's Capital*, Leiden: Brill.

Ayer, A.J. 1952, *Language,Truth and Logic*, New York: Dover.

Backhouse, Roger and Creedy, John (eds) 1999, *From Classical Economics to the Theory of the Firm*, Cheltenham: Edward Elgar.

Baker, John 1987, *Arguing for Equality*, London: Verso.

Bales, Kevin 1999, *Disposable People: New Slavery in the Global Economy*, Berkeley: University of California Press.

—— 2005, *Understanding Global Slavery*, Berkeley: University of California Press.

Beales, D. 1969, *From Castlereagh to Gladstone: 1815–1885*, New York: Norton.

Bell, John 1995, "Dialectics and Economic Theory" in Robert Albritton and Thomas Sekine (eds), *A Japanese Approach to Political Economy: Unoist Variations*, Basingstoke: Macmillan.

—— 2003, "From Hegel to Marx to the Dialectic of Capital" in Robert Albritton and John Simoulidis (eds), *New Dialectics and Political Economy*, Basingstoke: Palgrave Macmillan.

Bhaskar, Roy 1989, *Reclaiming Reality*, London: Verso.

Blaug, Mark 1999, "The Formalist Revolution or What Happened to Orthodox Economics After World War II" in Backhouse and Creedy (eds), 1999.

Brennan, Teresa 2003, *Globalization and Its Terrors*, London: Routledge.

Brook, Timothy and Wakabayashi, Robert 2000, *Opium Regimes: China, Britain, and Japan, 1839–1952*, Berkeley: University of California Press.

Cohen, G.A. 1988, *History, Labour and Freedom: Themes from Marx*, Oxford: Clarendon Press.

Crouzet, F. 1982, *The Victorian Economy*, New York: Columbia University Press.

Davis, Mike 2006, *Planet of Slums*, London: Verso.

Doyal, Len and Gough, Ian 1991, *The Theory of Human Need*, London: Macmillan.

Ellwood, Wayne 2001, *The No-Nonsense Guide to Globalization*, Toronto: New Internationalist Publications.

Farjoun, Emmanuel and Machover, Moshe 1983, *The Laws of Chaos*, London: Verso.

Foley, Duncan 1986, *Understanding Capital*, Cambridge, Mass.: Harvard University Press.

Freeman, Alan and Carchedi, Guglielmo (eds) 1996, *Marx and Non-Equilibrium Economics*, Cheltenham: Edward Elgar.

Friedman, Milton 1982, *Capitalism and Freedom*, Chicago: University of Chicago Press.

Fullbrook, Edward 2003, *The Crisis in Economics*, London: Routledge.

Gardner, Gary and Halweil, Brian 2000, "Overfed and Underfed: The Global Epidemic of Malnutrition", *Worldwatch Institute*, Paper #150, March.

Grossberg, Lawrence 2005, *Caught in the Crossfire: Kids, Politics, and America's Future*, Boulder Co.: Paradigm Press.

Hacker, Andrew 2004, "The Underworld of Work", *New York Review of Books*, February 12.

Hegel, G.W.F. 1971, *Philosophy of Right*, trans. T.M. Knox, Oxford: Oxford University Press.

Hobbes, Thomas 1969, *Leviathan*, London: Collier.

Hobsbawm, Eric 1975, *The Age of Capital*, London: Abacus.

Hodgson, Geoffrey 2001, *How Economics Forgot History: The Problem of Historical Specificity in Social Science*, London: Routledge.

Hollis, Martin and Nell, Edward 1975, *Rational Economic Man: A Philosophical Critique of Neo-Classical Economics*, Cambridge: Cambridge University Press.

Hunt, E.H. 1981, *British Labour History: 1815–1914*, Atlantic Highlands, New Jersey: Humanities Press.

Jameson, Frederic 1990, *Late Marxism*, London: Verso.

Keen, Stephen 2001, *Debunking Economics*, London: Pluto Press.

Keynes, John M. 1973, *The General Theory of Employment, Interest and Money*, London: Macmillan.

Kourkoulakos, Stefanos (2003) "The Specificity of Dialectical Reason" in Albritton and Simoulidis (eds), *Dialectics and Political Economy*, Basingstoke: Palgrave Macmillan.

Lacan, Jacques 1977, *Ecrits: A Selection*, New York: Norton.

Landes, David 1969, *The Unbound Prometheus*, Cambridge: Cambridge University Press.

Lawson, Tony 1997, *Economics and Reality*, London: Routledge.

Lebowitz, Michael 2003, *Beyond Capital: Marx's Political Economy of the Working Class* (second edition), Basingstoke: Palgrave Macmillan.

Levinas, Emmanuel 1969, *Totality and Infinity: An Essay on Exteriority*, trans. A. Lingis, The Hague: Nijhoff.

Lewis, Paul (ed.) 2004, *Transforming Economics: Perspectives on the Critical Realist Project*, London: Routledge.

Lukács, Georg 1968, *History and Class Consciousness*, London: Merlin.

MacIntyre, Alasdair 1984, *After Virtue*, Notre Dame, Indiana: University of Notre Dame Press.

Mamdani, Mahmood 2005, *Good Muslim, Bad Muslim: America, the Cold War and the Roots of Terror*, New York: Doublday.

Mandel, Ernest 1975, *Late Capitalism*, New York: Monthly Review.

Marx, Karl 1963, *Theories of Surplus Value*, Vol. I, Moscow: Progess. (Abbreviated as S I.)

—— 1968, *Theories of Surplus Value*, Vol. II, Moscow: Progress. (Abbreviated as S II.)

—— 1971, *Theories of Surplus Value,* Vol. III, Moscow: Progress. (Abbreviated as S III.)

—— 1973, *Grundrisse*, London: Penguin. (Abbreviated as G.)

—— 1976, *Capital*, Vol. I. New York: Penguin. (Abbreviated as C I.)

—— 1978, *Capital*, Vol. II, New York: Penguin. (Abbreviated as C II.)

—— 1979, *The Letters of Karl Marx*, trans. Saul Padover, Englewood Cliffs, New Jersey: Prentice Hall.

—— 1981, *Capital*, Vol. III, New York: Penguin. (Abbreviated as C III.)

Massing, Michael 2005a, "The End of News?", *New York Review of Books*, Dec. 1.

—— 2005b, "The Press: The Enemy Within", *New York Review of Books*, Dec. 15.

Mathias, Peter 1983, *The First Industrial Nation*, London: Methuen.

McChesney, Robert 2004, *The Problem of the Media: U.S. Communication Politics in the 21st Century*, New York: Monthly Review.

Medrick, Jeff, 2006, "The Way to a Fair Deal", *New York Review of Books*, Jan. 12.

Mintz, Sidney 1985, *Sweetness and Power*, New York: Penguin.

Nussbaum, Martha 2000, *Women and Human Development*, Cambridge: Cambridge University Press.

—— 2006, *Frontiers of Justice*, Cambridge, Mass.: Harvard University Press.

Nussbaum, Martha and Amartya, Sen 1993 (eds), *The Quality of Life*, Oxford: Oxford University Press.

Pack, Spencer 1985, *Reconstructing Marxian Economics*, New York: Praeger.

Palan, Ronen 2006, *The Offshore World: Sovereign Markets, Virtual Places, and Nomad Millionaires*, Ithaca: Cornell University Press.

Pashukanis, Evgeny 1978, *Law and Marxism*, London: Ink Links.

Pateman, Carole 1970, *Participation and Democratic Theory*, Cambridge: Cambridge University Press.

Polyani, Karl 1944, *The Great Transformation*, Boston: Beacon Press.

Postone, Moishe 1996, *Time, Labor, and Social Domination*, Cambridge: Cambridge University Press.

Ricardo, David 1971, *On the Principles of Political Economy*, London: Penguin.

Robbins, John 2001–4, "Is There Slavery in Your Chocolate?", www.foodrevolution.org/slavery_chocolate.htm

Robinson, Joan 1964, *Economic Philosophy*, Garden City, New York: Anchor.

—— 1966, *An Essay on Marxian Economics*, London: Macmillan.

Roemer, John 1988, *Free to Lose*, Cambridge, Mass.: Harvard University Press.

Ross, Dorothy 1991, *The Origins of American Social Science*, Cambridge: Cambridge University Press.

Russell, Bertrand 1963, *Mysticism and Logic*. London: Allen and Unwin.

Saad-Filho, Alfredo 2002, *The Value of Marx*, London: Routledge.

Sahlins, Marshall 1972, *Stone Age Economics*, New York: Aldine.

Sayer, Andrew 1995, *Radical Political Economy: A Critique*, Oxford: Blackwell.

Schlosser, Eric 2001, *Fast Food Nation*, New York: Harper Collins.

Seabrook, Jeremy 2002, *The No-Nonsense Guide to Class, Caste, and Hierarchies*, Toronto: New Internationalist Publications.

Sekine, Thomas 1986, *The Dialectic of Capital*, Two Volumes, Tokyo: Toshindo Press.

—— 1997, *An Outline of* The Dialectic of Capital, Two Volumes, London: Macmillan.

—— 2003, "The Dialectic, or Logic that Coincides with Economics" in Albritton and Simoulidis, 2003.

Sen, Amartya 2000, *Development as Freedom*, New York: Anchor.

Sohn-Rethel, Alfred 1978, *Intellectual and Manual Labour*, London: Macmillan.

Soley, Lawrence 2002, *Censorship Inc.: The Corporate Threat to Free Speech in the United States*, New York: Monthly Review.

Smith, Adam 1993, *An Inquiry into the Nature and Causes of the Wealth of Nations*, Oxford: Oxford University Press.

Sraffa, Piero 1960, *Production of Commodities by Means of Commodities*, Cambridge: Cambridge University Press.

Steedman, Ian 1977, *Marx After Sraffa*, London: New Left Books.

The Economist 2003, May 3.

The Economist 2006, July 15.

The New Internationalist 2000, May #323.

The New Internationalist 2001, Jan./Feb. #331.

Thompson, E.P. 1968, *The Making of the English Working Class*, Harmondworth: Penguin.

Tucker, Robert 1978, *The Marx-Engels Reader*, New York: Norton.

Uno, Kozo 1980, *Principles of Political Economy*, Sussex: Harvester Press.

Waring, Marilyn 1999, *Counting for Nothing*, Toronto: University of Toronto Press.

Webber, Carolyn and Wildavsky, Aaron 1986, *A History of Taxation and Expenditure in the Western World*, New York: Simon and Schuster.

Weber, Max 1978, *Economy and Society*, Two Volumes, Berkeley: University of California Press.

Westra, R. and Zuege, A. (eds) 2003, *Value and the World Economy Today*, Basingstoke: Palgrave Macmillan.

Wiese, Heike 2003, *Numbers, Language, and the Human Mind*, Cambridge: Cambridge University Press.

Williams, Colin 2005, *A Commodified World? Mapping the Limits of Capitalism*, London: Zed Press.

Worldwatch Institute 2004, *State of the World*.

Index